Identity in
Algerian Politics

IDENTITY IN
ALGERIAN POLITICS

The Legacy of Colonial Rule

J. N. C. Hill

LYNNE
RIENNER
PUBLISHERS

BOULDER
LONDON

Published in the United States of America in 2009 by
Lynne Rienner Publishers, Inc.
1800 30th Street, Boulder, Colorado 80301
www.rienner.com

and in the United Kingdom by
Lynne Rienner Publishers, Inc.
3 Henrietta Street, Covent Garden, London WC2E 8LU

Library of Congress Cataloging-in-Publication Data
Hill, J. N. C., 1978–
    Identity in Algerian politics: the legacy of colonial rule / J. N. C. Hill.
    Includes bibliographical references and index.
    ISBN 978-1-58826-608-8 (hardcover : alk. paper)
    1. Algeria—Politics and government—1962–1990. 2. Algeria—
Politics and government—1990– 3. Postcolonialism—Algeria. 4. Nation-
building—Algeria. 5. Group identity—Algeria. 6. Algeria—Colonial
influence. I. Title.
JQ3231.H55 2009
320.965—dc22   2009002521

British Cataloguing in Publication Data
A Cataloguing in Publication record for this book
is available from the British Library.

Printed and bound in the United States of America

The paper used in this publication meets the requirements
∞   of the American National Standard for Permanence of
Paper for Printed Library Materials Z39.48-1992.

5   4   3   2   1

Contents

Acknowledgments

THE TINGE OF SADNESS I FEEL at completing this book (for it has been a labor of love) is more than made up for by the pleasure I gain from finally being able to thank everyone who has helped me finish it. Indeed, without the continued support of friends, colleagues, and well-wishers alike, it is doubtful that it would ever have seen the light of day.

To begin, I am extremely grateful to Matt Uttley, Stuart Griffin, Helen McCartney, Andrew Dorman, Wyn Bowen, and Sarah Somers for the opportunities they have afforded me to write and complete the book, and to Elisabetta Linton, Steve Barr, and the team at Lynne Rienner Publishers for making the publication process so painless. I would also like to thank Geraint Hughes for reading and commenting on Chapter 5, and Huw Davies, Patrick Porter, Ashley Jackson, Andrew Stewart, and Alex Marshall for patiently listening to me when they had their own work to be getting on with.

I also owe a debt of gratitude to Mike Osman in Reading for his hospitality during the flood; to Duncan Low, Kate Airey, Gavin Duck, Sheena Zain, Reid Cooper, and Grace Yohana and her sisters in Abuja for looking after me these past few months; and to my family in Derbyshire, Edinburgh, and elsewhere for their unstinting encouragement.

Finally, I must single out Sophie Hague for special praise. Her patience has been as inexhaustible as her support has been unwavering, and it has taken countless forms. From numerous cups of tea to endless proofreading, she has improved this book beyond measure. It is to her, therefore, that it is dedicated with both love and gratitude.

1

Introduction

"THE COLONISED MAN," FRANTZ FANON famously declared, "finds his freedom in and through violence."[1] Perhaps nowhere were his words more applicable than in colonial Algeria, the country whose struggle for independence he embraced as his own. On 1 November 1954, small bands of poorly armed men, members of a newly created rebel group called the National Liberation Front (Front de Libération Nationale, FLN), crouched and huddled in the freezing night in anticipation of the attacks they were about to make. Their targets—a gendarmerie barracks, a police station, some stores of tobacco and grain, and various telephone wires—were concentrated mainly in the *département* (administrative division) of Algiers in the far north of the country. But events did not go according to plan. Panic gripped some, and they abandoned their missions. Excitement got the better of others, and they launched their attacks prematurely, enabling the security forces to raise the alarm and make sufficient noise to deter their more patient comrades waiting elsewhere.

Yet, from this inauspicious start, the FLN sustained and expanded its uprising, recruiting, arming, organizing, and directing tens of thousands of men and women. Its armed rebellion formed the central strand, the immutable core, of its campaign to drive France from Algeria, to bring an end to over a century of French rule. Through violence the FLN aimed to convince France—its politicians, generals, and civilian population—that it could not afford the blood-price for staying in the country. By ambushing army units, attacking police stations, blowing up railway lines, cutting telephone wires, demolishing buildings, assassinating government officials, and terrorizing the European community, by killing, maiming, wounding, and destroying, the FLN strove to make Algeria unendurable for France.

The violence unleashed by the FLN was itself a response to that visited on the Muslim population by the colonial regime and European settlers. No quarter was ever given to those, such as the members of the Mukrani tribe,

1

who took up arms against the colonial state, or who, like the rioters at Sétif and Guelma, attacked and killed Europeans. Yet the real violence perpetrated by colonial rule took the form of a thousand petty abuses inflicted daily on ordinary Muslim men and women by the agents of the colonial state—policemen, gendarmes, soldiers, and bureaucrats. The source of this violence was a political, economic, social, and cultural order that labeled Muslims inferior and, because of that, afforded them only negligible rights and liberties.

In seeming contradiction to the doctrines of assimilation and *Mission Civilisatrice* (civilizing mission) that came increasingly to guide and shape French policy in and for Algeria, France steadfastly refused to grant the Muslim populace the same political and civil rights enjoyed by its own citizens. The marginalization and abuse of the Muslim population this gave rise to was encouraged and, on many occasions, demanded by the European settler community that developed during the course of the nineteenth and twentieth centuries. Numbering just under one million men, women, and children by 1954, it exerted a political influence both in Algeria and France far beyond its small size. Finding natural allies among the ranks of French conservatives, the settlers were well organized and financed, and able to block or emasculate most legislation they did not agree with.

The violence unleashed by colonial rule has remained an ever-present blight on Algeria. During the first few months of independence, the country was riven by division and discord as various factions fought for control of the new state. Eventually Ahmed Ben Bella emerged victorious, but he continued to be confronted by numerous armed challenges and was eventually overthrown in a military-led coup d'état. Under his successor, Houari Boumedienne, Algeria enjoyed its greatest period of stability, social harmony, and economic prosperity. But even then, it had to endure several rebellions and was rocked by at least two attempts on Boumedienne's life. Following his death in 1979, armed uprisings against the government became more frequent as the country was gripped by growing political, economic, and social instability. President Chadli Benjedid's government responded by introducing sweeping democratic reforms that brought the Islamic Salvation Front (Front Islamique du Salut, FIS) to the cusp of power. Determined to stop its impending victory, the army intervened in January 1992, sparking a bitter and bloody civil war that lasted for the remainder of the decade. And even when, in the late 1990s, the military gained a decisive edge over the insurgents, several terror groups have continued to attack the government and ordinary Algerians.

The centrality of violence to Algeria's ongoing development demands that every effort is made to understand its character—why it occurs, whom it involves, for what reasons, and with what consequences. And the importance of this task is raised still further by the appalling human cost it has exacted. Since the fighting began in the early 1990s, between 120,000 and 180,000 people, many of them civilians, have lost their lives. And that is to make no mention of the thousands more who have been imprisoned, tortured, raped, abused, disappeared, and forced to leave their homes. The primary goal of this book, therefore, is to assist in these efforts. And it seeks to do so by looking at how disagreements over national identity have given rise to and helped sustain the fighting and bloodshed.

At times this violence has placed the very integrity of Algeria in jeopardy. The late 1960s, in particular, were full of danger as the fledgling republic threatened to tear itself apart. On other occasions, the government's ability to rule effectively in certain parts of the country has been severely impaired. Indeed, for much of the early 1990s, vast tracts of the country's interior lay beyond Algiers' control. But consistently, it has been ordinary men and women who have paid most dearly. The prolonged, and at times chronic, instability and insecurity this violence has given rise to has prompted successive governments to try to unite the country behind their leadership and bind its various regions, communities, and ethnic groups more closely together. And like the governments of many other African countries that were once colonized by a foreign power, they have attempted to achieve all this through a process of nation building.

Integral to this process is the development of a national identity. Such an identity, along with the very act of its construction and promotion, is intended to distinguish and help bind the nation's members together. But as well as rendering Algerians distinct from their Moroccan and Tunisian neighbors, yet inextricably bound to the unknown individuals who are their fellow citizens, this identity also attempts to remove and obscure all differences between the governed and their governors. It seeks to do so in order to legitimize and normalize the governors' political authority. And it tries to do so by asserting the shared past and common future of the Algerian people. Both this history and this outlook are built around key historical events and figures and cultural traits.

Yet the incorporation of selected characteristics brings with it an assortment of unavoidable dangers. In particular, these risks spring from the very balance Algeria's political leaders strike between these characteristics, and overlay and compound the many other tensions that result from their inclusion of certain events, figures, and traits, and deliberate exclusion of others. In fact, it is these hazards, or rather the skill with which Algeria's leaders deal with them, that will determine the future direction of the nation-building process. For all these threats have political implications because they shape how individuals, communities, and ethnic groups relate to one another, to the government, and to the state. More precisely, they help determine how politically, economically, socially, and culturally incorporated and respected certain people and groups feel.

Algeria's first three presidents—Ahmed Ben Bella, Houari Boumedienne, and Chadli Benjedid—developed national identities built around three main characteristics—Islam, Arabism, and socialism. In an effort to ensure that their definitions achieved hegemony, each regime attempted to control public discourse on Algeria's national identity by systematically extending its authority over the country's media, political system, and social space. But such measures could not prevent the existence of opposition. Islamic groups for one were frustrated by the regimes' commitment to socialism, while many members of the Berber community were angered by the emphasis placed on Arabism. It has been frustrations such as these that have helped give rise to and sustain the violence that has gripped the country since independence.

But as well as casting new light on the violence that has gripped Algeria since the early 1990s, the book's examination of the postindependence nation-building process also exposes colonialism's lasting impact on the country. And it does so by tracing the origins and development of Algerian nationalism and anticolonialism. The ideology of nationalism made the journey from Europe to Africa on board the ships of the invading French, who used it to condemn the local inhabitants as barbarous and unworthy of the lands they occupied. Yet despite its origins, Algerians came to draw on nationalism, its concepts and vocabulary, to express their grievances against colonial rule and demand their independence. Somewhat ironically, therefore, it was at the very moment that French rule was most in jeopardy that it achieved one of its most remarkable successes as Algerians embraced a "framework of knowledge whose representational structure" corresponded to what they were seeking to repudiate.[2]

*   *   *

This book is broadly chronological in its organization, with Chapters 2 and 3 focusing on the period before independence, and Chapters 4, 5, and 6 concentrating on the period after independence. Chapter 2 begins by setting the conquest and colonization of Algeria in its broader historical context, looking at France's efforts to reestablish its overseas empire. In so doing, it highlights the development of its imperial policy throughout the nineteenth and early twentieth centuries. The chapter then continues by looking at the birth of Algérie française. Its creation was not without difficulties, as France had to overcome sustained, albeit fragmented, local resistance. Yet, once it had done so, and in accordance with the doctrines of assimilation and Mission Civilisatrice, it set about transforming Algeria and Algerians. It was during this time that the logic of the nation-state was firmly implanted in Algeria.

Chapter 3 charts the rise of Algerian nationalism by focusing on the fortunes of the main nationalist groups. As the twentieth century progressed, the popularity of the more moderate organizations waned as they were repeatedly thwarted in their efforts to secure greater political and civil rights for Muslim Algerians. Their place in the affections of this population was gradually taken by groups demanding independence from France, and who were willing to use extralegal and even violent means to get it. The chapter concludes by charting the main contours of the war of liberation.

Chapter 4 focuses on the aftermath of the war and life in Algeria under its first three presidents. It begins by detailing the various armed challenges to confront these leaders and how they responded to them. Part of their responses included pursuing programs of nation building, which entailed developing and then promoting a definition of the nation. The chapter contends that the definitions these leaders developed were heavily influenced by colonial rule. Then the chapter looks at how these definitions were promoted, the methods used by Ben Bella, Boumedienne, and Benjedid to control the media and extend their authority over the country's political system and social space.

Chapter 5 investigates the increasing economic and sociopolitical instability in Algeria from the mid-1980s onward and the steady rise in the number of armed challenges to confront President Benjedid. The chapter begins by examining the economic policies pursued by successive governments since independence. While these policies enabled rapid industrialization, they also created serious macro- and microeconomic weaknesses. Perhaps the most damaging of these was the country's overreliance on the hydrocarbon sector for its export and foreign currency earnings. This dependence rendered the economy extremely vulnerable to even the slightest downturns in the global oil and gas markets. It was just such a slump that threw Benjedid's nation-building program into chaos, causing him to abandon the socialist characteristic of his definition of the nation and to introduce political reforms that eventually led to the onset of civil war.

The chapter continues by charting the first few years of this conflict before looking at President Liamine Zéroual's reinitiation of the nation-building process. Chapter 6 then extends this analysis by looking at the nation-building process undertaken by Zéroual's successor, Abdelaziz Bouteflika. While both men introduced measures that eventually enabled the security forces to gain a decisive edge over the insurgents, they also promoted definitions of the nation that remained unacceptable to sections of the Islamic and Berber communities. And even though the threat posed to the state and Algerian population by the insurgents has receded (although significantly, it has not disappeared altogether), the definition of the nation outlined and advanced by the Bouteflika regime remains a serious source of grievance to these groups.

Notes

1. Frantz Fanon, *The Wretched of the Earth* (London: Penguin, 1963), p. 68.
2. Partha Chatterjee, *Nationalist Thought and the Colonial World: A Derivative Discourse* (London: Zed Books, 1986), p. 38.

2

French Colonial Rule and Its Enduring Legacies

PERCHED ON A HILLTOP A short distance north of Algiers sits the basilica of Notre Dame d'Afrique. Designed by Jean-Eugène Fromageau, it was built between 1858 and 1872 at the behest of the minister of Marine and the Colonies. Incorporating both Byzantine and Roman styles, la Madame was designed to embody in stone, timber, and glass the links between the Roman and French empires. Yet asserting France's claim to be Rome's rightful heir was only part of her purpose. For, unlike Rome, France intended never to leave that corner of Africa. La Madame, therefore, was also a display of imperial power and majesty, a warning to those who lived in her shadow to accept and respect France's authority. And her pairing with Notre Dame de la Garde in Marseilles emphasized Algeria's union with France, for now and for always.

The construction of Notre Dame d'Afrique also formed part of a much broader program that undertook to assimilate Algeria to France. But for that to happen, both Algeria and its inhabitants first had to be changed, to be refashioned into something that France was willing to embrace. The key to it all was the transformation of Algerian society, the complete overhaul of its political, economic, social, and cultural institutions, practices, and traditions. Their alteration would make Algeria look and function far more like France. And by making Algerians live, work, think, and exist in such an environment, they, too, would become, over time, more like the French. Such a transformation would not only make Algeria of some use to France, but it would raise Algerians up to become a civilized people. And France—in accordance with the doctrine of the Mission Civilisatrice—had a duty to make that happen.

The fundamental transformation of Algeria and re-creation of Algerians' identities were to have a profound impact on how Algerians expressed their opposition to French rule and the definition of the nation developed by Algeria's postindependence leaders. By drawing on nationalism to articulate and express their grievances, Algerians drew on an ideology that had been introduced by the French to justify colonial rule. And the postindependence leaders' choice of Islam, Arabism, and socialism as the central themes of the definition of the nation they developed and promoted was intimately bound to the changes wrought on Algeria by that rule.

This chapter charts how French rule affected Algeria's political, economic, social, and cultural structures, practices, and traditions, and Algerians' identities. To sustain this analysis, the chapter is divided into four main sections. The first takes a theoretical look at the introduction of nationalism into Africa and the challenges confronting postindependence nation builders. The second then focuses on French colonial doctrine, its enduring principles and objectives, and how it developed during the nineteenth and twentieth centuries. This leads, in section three, to an analysis of the invasion and conquest of Algeria, and the resistance offered by the local population. The final section explores the ways and extent to which French rule altered Algerians' identities. It concludes by outlining the political, economic, social, and cultural status and experiences of the Algerian population in the early 1950s, immediately before the outbreak of the war of liberation.

Nationalism and Nation Building in Africa

The twentieth century witnessed the final triumph of the nation-state.[1] It is now largely beyond question that among the various units of political, economic, social, and cultural organization and governance that exist worldwide, the nation-state is first among equals. So much so, that in popular discourse—and on occasion among academics too—the terms "nation" and "state" are often used interchangeably without any acknowledgment of the differences in meaning between them. Political leaders also are not averse—sometimes deliberately, sometimes not—to conflating these expressions. Intergovernment and interstate interactions are frequently labeled as being international, while the phrase "international relations" has become the catch-all description for all political activity outside the domestic sphere. And within that sphere, state governments legitimize their policies as being in the "national interest," of furthering the nation's aims and enhancing its well-being.

Of course, the nation-state has its challengers and is under constant pressure from both above and below. The European Union is a political and economic entity that does not claim to represent a single, identifiable nation. And one of its core aims is to break down boundaries between the various nation-states that are its members. Elsewhere in the world, states exist that clearly do not represent nations, while some widely recognized nations do not constitute states. Yet, far from debunking it, such exceptions actually help prove the rule. That some state governments claim that the diverse populations they represent constitute nations, when few people either at home or abroad recognize them as such, highlights the pervasiveness of the ideology of the nation-state. As do expectations that such acknowledged nations as the Kurds, Tamils, Scots, and Basques should form independent sovereign states. In each case, the breakdown of the supposed harmony between the nation and the state is seen as improper and even—so nationalists argue—unnatural, as nations should be states, and states should be nations.

The hegemony the nation-state now enjoys has come about through two distinct yet interrelated historical processes—the development of the ideology of nationalism and its dissemination around the world. At the heart of these processes lies Western Europe, for it was there that the earliest nationalists and nation-states emerged. The channels along which nationalism was first exported abroad were those established between London, Paris, Brussels, and Berlin, and the vast overseas territories they each governed. And from the very beginning, nationalism provided a justification for the creation of these empires. As well as being vital to the colonizing powers' national interests, the conquest and occupation of foreign lands was acceptable because the people who lived there did not constitute nations themselves. In this way, nationalism helped indicate the degree of civilization attained by a particular people or community.

So, in the beginning there were European nationalists. And what marked them out as such was their fervent belief that "the political and national unit should be congruent."[2] This, more than any other, was their most sacred truth, and it was something they all held in common regardless of which nation they thought they belonged to. And it is also what separates them from those who study nationalism. More specifically, it is nationalists' absolute conviction in the preexistence of the nation (for how else can it become congruent with the political unit?). Historians of nationalism are obligated to trace the emergence and development of nations, to identify and evaluate the plethora of political, economic, social, cultural, and technological factors that have led to their creation. To them, nations are historical phenomena, and, above all else, they are man-made, fashioned by people over time. While nationalists also trace the origins of their nations, they actively ascribe meaning and value to people, places, and events, and they do so for political purposes. They want to see meaning, and they incorporate and assign enormous national significance to seemingly unconnected historical occurrences. Indeed, to paraphrase Ernest Renan, getting history wrong is part of what it means to be a nationalist.[3]

Nationalists are touched with the gift of foresight; they can see things that other people cannot. They are able to identify the existence of a nation even while its members remain oblivious to it. One of their early tasks, therefore, is to help enlighten this population, make them aware of their nationality. In this regard, nationalists are conduits through whom the spirit of national consciousness flows. They put people in touch with their nationality and awaken them to the common bonds they share with the other members of their nation. Indeed, their goal is to make people trust these bonds, to accept that they are connected to individuals they have never met, and who perhaps live a great distance from them. It is to make them imagine that they are all members of the same nation.

Historians on the other hand view nationalists very differently. To them, nationalists are not conduits or soothsayers or spirit guides, but political and cultural activists. They are catalysts who, through their actions, help conjure nations and nation-states into existence. Indeed, their stories, or at least the parts relating to their nationalist activities, are inseparable from those of the nations they think they belong to. Yet again, the differences between how nationalists perceive themselves and how they are perceived by historians are tied to the preexistence (or not) of the nation. Nationalists see the nation as already existing and their beliefs as grounded in fact. Historians do not necessarily agree, as they question the evidence marshaled by nationalists.

Perhaps the most serious point of disagreement between nationalists and historians is the alleged antiquity of many nations. A nation is "a named human population sharing an historic territory, common myths and historical memories, a mass, public culture, a common economy and common legal rights and duties for all members."[4] The importance of history requires nationalists to, on occasion, retrospectively attribute meaning to people, places, and events in order to create the myths, memories, and traditions that they need. In this way, historical figures, for instance, are claimed as fathers and mothers of the nation, even though at the time they were alive they had no knowledge or concept of the nation by which they have subsequently been appropriated. And their actions were not necessarily motivated by a desire to safeguard or help their compatriots; nationalists have added that intention later.

The selective interpretation and presentation of history is vital to the stimulation and maintenance of national consciousness. It is through history (or some version of it) that the members of an imagined national community are made aware of—or persuaded to believe in—the immutable bonds binding them to one another. National myths, legends, and traditions tell of the ancestors they share and affirm and reaffirm the blood, kinship, cultural, and other ties that exist between them. And the process of preserving these myths helps bind the nation together regardless of whether anyone actually believes them or not. Indeed, they act as a sort of national password, knowledge of which automatically links that individual to anybody else who knows it. Both in their content and through the very process of remembering them, these myths emphasize the interconnectedness of the nation's members.

Yet stimulating and generating national consciousness is not the only function performed by history; it also helps build national pride. The instances and events remembered in myths and legends frequently, if not always, recount glorious episodes from the nation's past or celebrate the actions of heroic forebears. In these episodes, either the national community or some of its members do something of which the nation can still be proud. And even if the eventual outcome was not what was hoped for at the time, the nation's protagonists inevitably demonstrated an array of virtues, such as courage, resilience, intelligence, physical prowess, cunning, kindness, or generosity, which the national community can continue to celebrate. And through these acts of commemoration, such virtues are appropriated as key attributes of the national character, as demonstrated by the forebears who displayed them.

Yet the establishment of Europe's nation-states required more than just the belief and willpower of committed groups of nationalists. They were a product of a distinct set of political, economic, social, cultural, and technological conditions. Crucially the imagining of these nations was only made possible after three long-standing truths had lost their dominance. The first was the belief that Latin—the language of the Catholic Church—offered the best, if not only, access to "ontological truth." The second was the idea that the monarchs who ruled the continent's kingdoms and empires were divinely appointed. And the third was the explicitly Christian understanding of history in which the "origins of the world and of men [were] essentially identical."[5]

The steady decline of these beliefs—which happened at different rates across the continent—marked the end of the old, Christian-based certainties that had for centuries helped explain and legitimize Europe's ancien régimes. And as they slowly lost their dominance, the less the old order was able to resist the social and political changes demanded by nationalists. The demise of these ancient certainties, which took place from the seventeenth century onward, was triggered by various political, economic, social, cultural, and technological developments, the most important of which included the growth of capitalism, industrialization, advances in the means of communication, the spread of mass education, and war.

Most of these developments did not occur either in succession or isolation, but simultaneously over a prolonged period. Indeed, new technologies led to the creation of printing presses that were able, for the first time in human history, to mass-produce tracts and publications for popular consumption. Such materials were disseminated along trade networks and through markets developed and expanded by capitalism. The emergence of such print languages facilitated the creation and stimulation of national consciousnesses in a variety of ways. For a start, they helped establish common mediums, which were less formal than Latin but not as local as dialects, that allowed members of a bounded population to communicate with one another. And in so doing, these individuals became increasingly aware that they belonged to a broader group or body of people.

Second, processes of printing helped standardize these languages and make them more accessible to future generations. The printing blocks that were made for the presses constituted more permanent records of how words were spelled, the contexts in which they were used, and the grammatical structure of the sentences they were placed in. And obviously by extension, so too did the texts that were printed, while their mass production helped disseminate this vocabulary, spelling, grammar, and syntax to a broad audience whose members then incorporated it into their own speech and writing. The increase in volume of the tracts that were produced has created a wealth of documentary evidence that continues to offer valuable insights into what life used to be like. And perhaps more importantly, the consistency the presses helped impose on these print languages have given subsequent generations a far stronger linguistic connection to their forefathers of the seventeenth and eighteenth centuries than they had with theirs. Such connections continue to stimulate the sense of history and antiquity that is so central to national consciousness.

Finally, this process of standardization gave rise to certain dominant languages. Inevitably, some dialects and vernaculars were closer than others to the languages produced and established by the printing presses. By virtue of this proximity, this similarity to the emergent print languages, such dialects achieved new levels of political, economic, and cultural significance as they became the mediums through which government and big business was conducted. And in the process, members of the ruling and commercial elite were drawn into the new linguistic community that was being established. Whereas before language had sometimes separated and distinguished the rulers from the ruled, it increasingly bound them together.[6]

The eventual triumph of the nation-state in Europe was to have profound consequences for the rest of the world. Especially from the seventeenth century onward, when Britain and France, Germany and Italy, Belgium and the Netherlands, and Portugal and Spain set about building overseas empires. This new age of empire reached its peak in the years leading up to World War II. By 1939 there was hardly any part of Africa or Asia that was not claimed by one or another of Europe's imperial powers. And wherever European imperialists went, so too did the ideology of nationalism.

For a start, nationalism was used to justify and legitimize colonization. The local inhabitants of East and Central Africa, for instance, were not organized into nation-states. And the fact that they were not was seen as a demonstration of their backwardness and barbarity. Some of these inhabitants—albeit only a small minority in each territory—were introduced to nationalism and its ideas through the schools and universities set up by the colonizers. And so too were others, slightly more this time, through direct and sustained exposure to the colonizers' values. Mindful of the differences between British, French, German, Belgian, and Italian colonial rule, in most of the African territories they governed, no matter how loosely, there emerged small groups of local nationalists and nation-statists. In each case, part of such groups consisted of members of the indigenous intellectual elite, the men (and sometimes women) who had received a British or French or Belgian education and perhaps even spent some time in the metropole. Other members of these groups invariably included former or serving soldiers.

The prominence of intellectuals and members of the native intelligentsia in these groups came about as a result of the economic and education policies pursued by the imperial powers. From the beginning, the colonial territories were developed only insofar as it strengthened the metropoles' economies. Indeed, their development was entirely subservient to that of the European power that ruled them. Their primary purpose was to provide this power with essential products (usually raw materials or unrefined agricultural goods), new markets for its industries, and manpower for its armies at times of war. All the colonizing powers required of their colonial subjects, therefore, was that they hew wood, carry water, and lay down their lives when asked, tasks for which little or no formal education was required.

And as well as being economically unnecessary, the education of the local population was deemed both a needless expense and a potential threat to the territory's social and political stability. From the outset, the imperial powers were determined to turn their colonies into economic assets. This meant that, at an absolute minimum, these lands had to generate sufficient income to cover the cost of their own administration, policing, and general upkeep. And, ideally, there would be enough left over to pay the colonizing power a dividend. It was not enough for these territories to simply supply the metropole's industries with cheap materials, labor, and new markets. They also had to pay the imperial government for the privilege of doing so. Spending money on schools and teachers, therefore, constituted an unnecessary outlay that reduced a territory's profitability.

By extension, it was in the imperial powers' best interests to keep social unrest in their colonies to an absolute minimum. Any disturbances served only to disrupt economic activity and make the government of these territories more expensive and difficult to carry out. What the imperial powers wanted above all else were docile, compliant populations who did as they were told and refrained from questioning or challenging the sociopolitical status quo. It was thought that educating them, therefore, was something best avoided. For a start, there was no predicting what effect exposing these peoples to new ideas and concepts might have. It was quite possible that it might stimulate a desire for change, or give rise to expectations the imperial powers simply were not prepared to fulfill. More definitely, but no less worryingly, it would strengthen their critical faculties, making them better able to challenge colonial rule.

Yet quite aside from the exploitative intentions that informed this decision, such reasoning was hypocritical and, in part, self-deluding. Oftentimes, far from containing opposition to colonial rule, the denial of access to primary, secondary, and tertiary education actually stimulated it. And the justification put forward by the imperial powers for their conquest and occupation of African lands was that they would enlighten and civilize the peoples living there. Somewhat ironically, the ideas the imperial powers wanted to shield their colonial subjects from were those held most dear by their own citizens. Indeed, these ideas included notions of personal freedom, the inalienability of an individual's rights to life and property, and of nation-ness and nation-statehood.

Members of the native intelligentsias were, by virtue of the educations they received, some of the few indigenes to gain access to these ideas.[7] They, in fact, were taught to cherish these values and the supposedly superior civilizations that gave rise to them. Yet through this contact, they were also exposed to the inherent contradictions of colonial rule. Invariably, the imperial powers failed to put into practice the high-minded ideals they purportedly held so dear. And time and again, the path to becoming members of the colonizing nation was barred to local peoples on the grounds of race, ethnicity, and culture. And so, drawing on the ideology of nationalism and the concept of nation-ness they had been taught, some members of these intelligentsias came to view the colonized peoples as nations. Or even if they did not go that far, they recognized that only by achieving independence and sovereign statehood would they gain the political and civil rights continually denied them by the imperial powers.

The other significant group of indigenes to develop nationalist and nation-statist tendencies were the men who served in the imperial armies. And two experiences more than anything helped them to become so, namely, World Wars I and II. These conflicts led to the deployment of tens of thousands of African soldiers in Europe. And fighting side by side with white comrades on behalf of an imperial power that proclaimed its deep gratitude generated within these soldiers' breasts a far greater sense of equality with Europeans than many of them had ever had before.[8] They had proved their worth and made their contributions, so let no one say they were inferior in any way. And among those who survived, there developed great expectations that they would be rewarded for what they had done. When the political rights and economic benefits were either not forthcoming or as bountiful as they would have liked, some of these servicemen embraced nationalism in the belief that they would never get their just deserts or achieve genuine equality with Europeans so long as colonial rule persisted.

African nationalisms were intrinsically and instinctively anticolonial. And the men and women who propounded them drew on the ideas and ideals put forth by the imperialists "with the object of making the [colonial] state accountable and later transferring it to the population on whose behalf it ostensibly existed."[9] Some African nationalists genuinely considered the local populations to constitute nations. Others were more circumspect. Their anticolonialism was expressed as nation-statism. What drove them was not a belief in the necessity of aligning the political and national units, but rather that the "coming of the nation-state would strike away the chains of foreign rule and all that these had meant in social and moral deprivation."[10] In such instances, the formation of the nation-state was not the culmination of the nation's quest for independence and self-actualization. On the contrary, it was a first step toward generating a national consciousness among the territory's inhabitants.

Arguably, nation-statism was the prevalent tendency among Africa's nationalists, partly because of the arbitrariness of the borders of most colonial territories. In their negotiations with the imperial powers (if indeed any such talks took place) the nationalists were forced to accept the boundaries that were already in place regardless of their cultural, ethnic, or historical irrationality. And these borders persisted even after the imperial powers departed. Article III of the 1963 Charter of the Organisation of African Unity (OAU) committed its signatories "to respect . . . the sovereignty and territorial integrity of each State and . . . its inalienable right to independent existence."[11] The end result was that African nationalists came to represent and speak for populations whose creation was both random and somewhat accidental. In such circumstances, few nationalists actually viewed these assorted (and on occasion ill-matched) populations as nations.

Their difficulties were often compounded by how the imperial powers had governed their territories. Frequently, by accident or (more often) design, they favored one ethnic group over another. So it was with the Fulani-Hausa in Nigeria, the Tutsi in Rwanda, and, to a lesser extent, the Berbers in Algeria. In so doing, these powers fueled tensions between the various communities in their territories. Indeed, that was partly the aim so as to keep them competing among themselves rather than challenging the colonial government. And on occasion, these tensions were exacerbated or created afresh through the imperial powers' invention of traditions, privileges, titles, and hierarchies when none had existed before.[12] Partly through a misguided understanding of what their colonial subjects should be doing, and partly through a desire to create and foster divisions among them, the imperial powers established new rituals and myths that did little to unite the various regions and communities within their territories.

But despite such efforts, African nationalists were still able to find one issue on which the various peoples of the territory could largely agree—the need to bring an end to colonial rule. Of course not everyone concurred, especially those individuals and groups who had been favored by the imperial powers. To counter such reluctance and persuade the others of the need to overthrow the imperial power, African nationalists had to convince these peoples of the benefits of doing so. To do that, they emphasized the inequities of the colonial system and the advantages, including political rights, civil liberties, and economic prosperity, that would be accrued once independence was achieved. In fact, their aim was to polarize colonial society, to turn the local population against the imperial power and its representatives in the territory.[13]

Yet within such policies lay the seeds of later sociopolitical difficulties. For a start, the achievement of independence removed the very force that had bound the nationalist movements together—the imperial powers. Without the unifying force of these common enemies, the fragility of many nationalist movements and coalitions was cruelly exposed. Furthermore, once the early euphoria of independence had passed, the populations of these new states began demanding all the rights and riches promised to them by the nationalist leaders. And often, instead of managing popular expectations, postcolonial governments actually exacerbated them by using state resources to placate people. While this undoubtedly provided a short-term fix, in so doing these governments exaggerated, often greatly, how wealthy and affluent the state actually was.[14]

With the achievement of independence, the primary task of nationalism ceased to be that of orchestrating colonialism's demise and, instead, became one of trying to reintegrate the state with society. And this challenge was made all the more difficult by the legacies of colonial rule: the polyethnicity of the new states' populations;[15] the tensions and rivalries that existed among the various communities that comprised them; and the inauspicious economic circumstances that usually prevailed. To bring about this reintegration, most postcolonial African leaders have had to build and fortify "internal connections" between themselves and the people they govern "to create an experiential 'we' from whose will the activities of government seem to spontaneously flow."[16]

Perhaps unsurprisingly, given their earlier embrace of the ideology of nationalism and the emergence of the nation-state as the dominant unit of organization and governance, these leaders often set about trying to turn the peoples they ruled into nations. Through processes that were resolutely top-down, many of Africa's postindependence governments have attempted to construct and strengthen the national consciousnesses of their citizens. They have appropriated and fabricated myths and traditions in an effort to build national histories. And they have conjured up visions of glorious futures to highlight what the nation can accomplish if it remains united. Such labors form part of broader projects intended to develop and promote national identities that not only highlight who the members of these nations are and the ties that bind them to one another, but that also stress the immutable bonds between them and their governments.

French Colonial Policy and Doctrine

On 30 May 1814, France's defeat in the War of the Sixth Coalition was made absolute with the signing of the Treaty of Paris. Designed to restore equilibrium to the European order, the settlement set about limiting France's power, but not so much as to cause excessive resentment among the French or create a power vacuum for another country to exploit. One of the ways the members of the victorious coalition attempted to achieve this was by stripping France of some, but not all, of the territory it had gained under Napoleon I. It was, therefore, allowed to retain the captured city of Avignon and the surrounding area of Venaissin, and some of its overseas possessions. But it lost its territories in Italy and the Low Countries, and the strategically important colonies of Malta, the Île de France (Mauritius), Seychelles, Tobago, and St. Lucia.

The settlement imposed by the Treaty of Paris ushered in a new low in French imperial history. Not since the early seventeenth century, when France had first set about establishing its empire, had it possessed less territory overseas. The decline to which the treaty contributed had begun midway through the previous century with France's expulsion from India and North America. In both instances, it had been outmaneuvered, outgunned, and outspent by its old rival Britain. And just as Britian's empire went on to flourish, so that belonging to France grew ever smaller and more insignificant. So much so, that with the conclusion of the Treaty of Paris, it was left with only a handful of trading posts or entrepôts scattered around the globe.

The decline in France's imperial fortunes did not signal the end of its colonial ambitions. On the contrary, that particular fire continued to burn brightly in the hearts of a cadre of committed imperialists known from the mid-1800s onward as the Parti Colonial. The Parti was a loose confederation of different interest groups including conservative politicians determined to safeguard and enhance France's international standing; industrialists, capitalists, and chambers of commerce eager to gain access to new raw materials and markets; churches and religious organizations keen to spread the Catholic faith throughout heathen lands; military men impatient to win honor and glory on some foreign battlefield; adventurers desperate to chart new rivers, jungles, and mountain ranges; and settlers hopeful for the chance of a new and better life somewhere else.

As the nineteenth century wore on, the Parti gradually got the better of its anticolonial rivals by winning political and popular support for its cause. In fact, one of its greatest triumphs was pricking the interest of ordinary

French men and women who, for the most part, cared little for empire. But the true measure of its success was the steady expansion in the number and size of France's overseas possessions, which, by the end of the 1920s, covered nearly 4 million square miles (10 million square kilometers) of the earth's surface. And the more the empire grew in size and popularity, the more groups the Parti incorporated. In 1925, the French Section of the Workers' International (Section Française de l'Internationale Ouvrière, SFIO) completely reversed its position and declared its support for the imperial cause. Rather than decry the empire, its leaders pledged themselves to securing greater political and civil rights for its nonwhite members.

The SFIO's defection to the Parti's banner formed part of a broader trend that saw socialists, radicals, and other leftists reconsider their opposition to the empire. The main factor driving their about-face was their fear of fascism, which was on the rise throughout the 1920s and 1930s. The far right governments of Italy and Germany seemed to be coping far better than their democratic counterparts with the economic problems unleashed by the Wall Street crash. So much so that sympathetic groups and politicians in France implored their countrymen to follow suit. The growing popularity of these organizations and the increasingly bellicose noises emanating from Berlin and Rome persuaded many on the left that France would need all its strength to resist the threats it faced from both within and without. For the time being, therefore, Paris should retain the empire and use the resources and manpower it provided to overcome this present danger.

As a result of these developments, the Parti Colonial was able to achieve ascendancy over its chief protagonist, the anticolonial lobby. Yet, in some ways, the two groups were not so very different. Indeed, like the Parti, the anticolonial lobby was a loose association of individuals and groups of sharply contrasting political hues. It included conservative politicians who opposed colonial expansion on the grounds that it was an unnecessary and avoidable drain on French resources, not to mention a dangerous distraction from the country's primary goal of safeguarding its territory and influence in Europe. This position was greatly strengthened following the loss of Alsace and Lorraine in the wake of the Franco-Prussian war of 1870. France lost these provinces because it had failed to pay adequate attention to the European arena. And the only way it would retrieve them was by putting all its energies into doing so, not diverting them into other colonial adventures.

Some on the left, such as Jean Jaurès,[17] opposed colonial expansion because of the violence it often unleashed on the inhabitants of the territory being colonized. Jaurès and his fellow travelers in the socialist movement were also highly suspicious of the links between French industrialists and the Parti Colonial. As the champions of the working classes, they saw colonialism as a prop supporting the capitalist system in France. Others on the left, including radicals like Georges Clemenceau, emphasized the very real social problems that existed within France and declared that Frenchmen had a duty to address them first before colonizing other parts of the globe. Others still argued that empire ran counter to the revolutionary principles of 1789. Colonial rule, with its requirement that the colonies be politically and economically subjugated to the metropole, was simply incompatible with the values of liberty, equality, and fraternity.

Yet as the race between the imperial powers to acquire new territories grew ever more frantic from the late nineteenth century onward, the higher the level of popular concern in France that she might soon be left behind climbed. In such a context, the anticolonialists found it increasingly difficult to make themselves heard. The Parti, in contrast, encountered no such problems. Its message—that empire was good for France and good for the territories it ruled—was simple and seemingly without any downside. The Parti measured these benefits against an array of economic, political, cultural, social, and military criteria. Economically, the empire provided France with essential raw materials and exclusive markets for its industries. Politically, it increased France's influence and standing abroad. Socially, it offered far-flung destinations to which the country's excess population could be sent, while, militarily, it provided fighting men for France's armies. And finally, the very experience of gaining, expanding, and developing the empire gave the nation a vital outlet for its energies and, in so doing, prevented it from slipping into decadence and indolence.

From the 1860s onward, the Parti became increasingly adept at promoting its message. Bankrolled by businesses and industries keen to expand their colonial markets, the Parti shaped both political and public opinion through extensive lobbying and sustained information campaigns. Countless committees sprang up to represent colonies, protectorates, and regions within the empire. Bodies such as the Committee for Madagascar, the Committee for French Africa, and the Committee for French Asia set about generating popular interest in the colony or region they represented by publishing journals and organizing lectures cataloguing the work undertaken by French administrators, soldiers, businesses, engineers, missionaries, and doctors working there.[18] The main purpose of these efforts was to increase the level of private and public funding in the empire, to cajole businessmen and ordinary people to invest in it, and to pressure the National Assembly to vote ever-larger sums for its development.

In 1892, pro-empire deputies founded the Colonial Group (Groupe Colonial, GC). The greater coordination they hoped this body would impose on their actions would enhance their ability to force France to be more active in its expansion and development of the empire. The following year the French Colonial Union (Union Coloniale Française, UCF) was established. It brought together representatives from nearly five hundred businesses, companies, and industries operating throughout the empire. Then in

1898 a Colonial Group was founded in the Senate to perform the same functions as its sister body in the Chamber of Deputies. Such committees and groups gave the Parti Colonial the organizational and financial edge over the anticolonial lobby and underlined the steady shift that had occurred within French political and public opinion since the early decades of the nineteenth century.[19]

The construction of the post-1814 empire was carried out in piecemeal fashion. Some territories were added after years of vigorous domestic debate and careful international negotiation. Others were seized upon the initiative of a local administrator or military commander determined to stake France's claim. At no time was expansion carried out in accordance with a single overriding theory or master plan. Yet even so, and despite the constant fluctuations in the international arena and changes of government in Paris, the expansion of the empire was guided by a series of largely unchanging objectives.

Perhaps the most important of these aims was that every territory should be of economic benefit to France. Each colony's value to France was based on an assessment of various factors. For a start, the conquest, administration, and, where it occurred, settlement of the colonies must cost France as little as possible. And those expenses that were incurred must be recoupable, as far as possible, from the territories themselves. As well as being self-financing, each colony also had to provide France with essential raw materials and a market for its industries. If a colony was unable to pay its own way or was proving to be too much of a drain on the French treasury's coffers, then it should be cut adrift, either sold to another imperial power or exchanged for one of its territories, or simply discarded.

The actual process of colonial expansion took place in three distinct phases—1814 to 1855, 1856 to 1880, and 1881 to 1930. During the first phase, a strategy of restricted occupation was adopted in which France refrained from establishing vast new colonies "at great distance" from its shores. Such territories were expensive, in both blood and treasure, to conquer and administer, and of little value to France. Instead, it concentrated on acquiring "points on the globe . . . destined to become great centres of commerce . . . [and] where the fleet [could] obtain provisions and find a safe harbour."[20] Outposts such as these, located on key sea lanes, would not only act as trade hubs but enable the navy to resupply its ships and project French power over a much broader area.

As part of this initiative, France seized several territories throughout Africa and Asia. In 1840 and 1841 it took the islands of Mayotte and Nossey-Bé in the Indian Ocean. In 1842 it captured Tahiti and the Marquesas Islands in the South Pacific and Grand-Bassam off the Côte d'Ivoire. These were followed by the seizure of Ouidah in Dahomey in 1851, New Caledonia and the island of Basilan in the Philippine archipelago in 1853. The establishment and maintenance of French authority over these outposts cost France little in men, money, or resources. And even though some of these possessions proved to be of little commercial or military value, their seizure made a statement of France's intent to rehabilitate its empire and protect its status as a global power.

Throughout the 1850s and 1860s, the policy of restricted occupation gradually gave way to one of more extensive conquest. Much of the impetus for this development came from the colonies themselves as administrators and military commanders on the ground steadily increased the size of the areas under their control. Often they did so without the consent of the government in Paris. In North Africa, Governor-General Thomas Bugeaud systematically pushed back the frontiers of Algérie française as part of his campaign against the Algerian resistance leader, Abd el-Kader. In Senegal, Governors Auguste Protet and Louis Faidherbe both extended their control over the territory surrounding the port of Saint-Louis. And in Southeast Asia, the colony of Cochin China was added to the empire following the seizure of Saigon and the provinces of Da Nang, Bien Hoa, Gia Dinh, and Dinh Tuong.

In 1874, France expanded its possessions in Southeast Asia by seizing the territory of Annam, lying on the northern borders of the French colonies of Cochin China and Cambodia. And in so doing, it paved the way for a new expedition against Tonkin. In 1882 two companies of soldiers, made up of French officers and locally raised troops, set out north from Cochin China to capture the Tonkinese capital Hanoi. Led by Captain Henri Rivière, they succeeded in doing so but were later driven back by Emperor Tu Duc's forces. His death in 1883 returned the initiative to the French, who retook Hanoi and forced Tu Duc's successor, Duc Duc, to sign the Treaty of Hué on 25 August 1883, recognizing the establishment of a French protectorate over Tonkin and Annam.

Alarmed by the rapid growth of French influence throughout the Red River region, China mobilized its troops. During the course of 1884 and 1885, numerous clashes took place between French and Chinese land and naval units. In one such encounter on 28 March 1885, the commanding officer of a French brigade ordered a hasty retreat from the settlement of Lang Son, provoking fears among his superiors that the whole Red River Delta area was in danger of being overrun. When these concerns were relayed to Paris by the commander of the French expeditionary force, Henri Briere de l'Isle, it provoked what became known as the Tonkin Affair and led to the collapse of the second Ferry government.[21]

Despite the retreat from Lang Son, China recognized France's possessions. A little over two years later, in October 1887, the territories of Tonkin, Annam, Cochin China, and Cambodia were combined to form the colony of French Indochina, to which Laos was added after the Franco-

Siamese war of 1893. Yet Southeast Asia was not the only corner of the globe in which France was aggressively expanding its empire. Indeed, the 1880s marked the start of the third phase of expansion with the commencement of the so-called scramble for Africa during which France asserted its control over vast parts of the continent. From their bases in North Africa, Senegal, and the Gulf of Guinea, French soldiers and explorers cut a swath across West and Central Africa. Between 1880 and 1922, Chad, Côte d'Ivoire, Dahomey, Gabon, Guinea, Mauritania, the Middle Congo, Niger, Oubangui-Chari, Upper Senegal, and Upper Volta were all added to the empire as colonies. And Cameroon, Madagascar, Togo, and Tunisia were incorporated as protectorates.

Then in 1895, Côte d'Ivoire, Dahomey, Guinea, Mauritania, Niger, Senegal, Sudan, and Upper Volta were organized as the federation of French West Africa (Afrique Occidentale Française, AOF). This was followed by the creation of French Equatorial Africa (Afrique Équatorial Française, AEO) in 1910. It was made up of the colonies of Chad, Gabon, Middle Congo, and Oubangui-Chari. Although often collectively referred to as French North Africa, Morocco, Algeria, and Tunisia were never placed under a similar structure, primarily because Algeria was legally part of France,[22] and Morocco and Tunisia, as protectorates, remained under the nominal authority of their own governments.

Both the expansion and government of the empire were underpinned by an unshakable belief in the racial superiority of the French over other, non-European peoples. This belief found expression in the doctrines of assimilation and Mission Civilisatrice. Assimilation combined two distinct sets of impulses. The first was a desire to induct selected colonial subjects into the French nation. This took the form of granting citizenship to certain individuals or communities living in various colonial territories. This impulse manifested itself, among other ways, in the Royal Decree of 1642, the Crémieux Decree of October 1870,[23] and the Sénatus-Consulte of June 1889,[24] all of which offered citizenship to a new group of colonial subjects. In many cases, however, this offer was dependent upon the would-be recipient meeting certain cultural criteria. The 1642 decree, for example, promised citizenship to any colonial subject as long as they embraced Catholicism. And the naturalization law of 14 July 1865 pledged to grant citizenship to any Algerian Muslim or Jew on condition that they renounce their religious status.

The second impulse driving assimilation was a determination to standardize the units of political organization and governance across the empire. The earliest legislation introduced attempting to achieve this was passed by the Executive Directory in January 1797. It ruled that all French colonies should adopt the same administrative units as existed in France. During the nineteenth century, other such laws were passed, which, along with the new constitution of 1848, created a network of départements and *communes* throughout Algeria. The introduction of these units in Algeria was driven in part by a long-held belief in Paris that they constituted the most effective and civilized administrative and political structures. Their imposition was thought to not only strengthen the links between France and its overseas possessions, and make their government more efficient, but also to advance the civilizing process.

Although its origins stretched back to the early seventeenth century, assimilation only emerged as a clearly defined doctrine in the wake of the 1789 revolution. Key to its development was the Declaration of the Rights of Man and of the Citizen with its solemn commitment that "men are born and live free and in equal rights." Armed with such lofty values and a steely resolve to see them adopted in the colonies, the Executive Directory was the first regime to set about extending the rights of French citizens to colonial subjects and transporting French sociopolitical structures to the overseas territories.

Throughout the course of the nineteenth century, France's commitment to assimilation fluctuated as the Directory's early efforts were later reversed by Emperor Napoleon I. Anxious to ensure that the colonies continued to serve France's interests, he introduced a new constitution on 24 December 1799 making them subject to a separate set of laws. The legal and political wedge this drove between France and its overseas possessions remained in place following the restoration of the monarchy. The charters of 1814 and 1830, which marked the establishment of the Restoration and July Monarchies, respectively, both maintained separate legal codes for the colonies. It was not until 1833 and the promulgation of new legislation granting citizenship to all free persons in the colonial territories that France renewed its commitment to assimilation.

Yet it was the revolution of 1848 that placed assimilation more squarely at the heart of French colonial policy. Ushering in the Second Republic, the revolution was a reassertion of republican values that found expression in the new constitution of November 1848. Of particular significance were articles 21 and 109, which together declared Algeria and the colonies to be French territory and granted them representation in the National Assembly in Paris. The overthrow of the Second Republic and return of the Bonaparte dynasty under Napoleon III did little to divert the direction of this new colonial policy, although the constitution of January 1852 once again imposed a separate legal framework on the colonies.[25] But even this condition was gradually undermined by subsequent legislation. Furthermore, Emperor Napoleon III remained personally committed to strengthening the bonds between France and its overseas territories, going so far as to declare, in Algeria's case, that France was pursuing the "patient and continuous work of assimilation."[26]

The final triumph of assimilation, including its movement to the center of French colonial policy, came about following the creation of the Third Republic in September 1870. Throughout the 1870s and 1880s, numerous laws were enacted extending citizenship to an ever-increasing number of colonial subjects and imposing French administrative units on the overseas territories. The colonies were once again given the right to elect delegates to the National Assembly in Paris; the French penal code became law throughout the empire; the commune became the basic unit of administration and government in every colony; and citizenship was granted to Algerian Jews and the children of non-French Europeans living in Algeria.

It was at around the same time that French colonial policy became increasingly influenced by the doctrine of the Mission Civilisatrice. With its emphasis of France's duty to civilize its colonial subjects, the Mission supported the assimilationist aim of transporting French political, economic, and cultural structures and practices to the overseas territories. For both doctrines, such measures were integral to the advancement of their goals. Central to the Mission Civilisatrice was an assumption that a universal standard of human civilization existed that was achieved by nations and peoples through a linear process of advancement. Some peoples had progressed farther along this path than others. French culture, for instance, lay at the very pinnacle of human endeavor and achievement. Non-European peoples, by contrast, had barely progressed at all and remained mired in barbarism and savagery. As a consequence, they were ill equipped to govern themselves but could, given sufficient time and the right tutelage, be made ready to assume this responsibility. For this to happen, and to save them from themselves in the meantime, non-Europeans needed to be ruled by a civilized power. Only by submitting in this way could they learn to become civilized themselves.

Based on this logic, the establishment of colonies and protectorates was the best means by which France could perform this role. With the development of this doctrine, French imperial expansion and colonial rule was reevaluated and rebranded. The expansion of the empire was elevated from being a selfish quest for land, resources, and influence to being a noble mission aimed at helping the wretched peoples of the world escape from their barbarism. And colonial governance took on a sacred air. The destruction of indigenous political, economic, social, and cultural structures and practices and their replacement with French equivalents was all part of the painful process of dragging barbarian peoples out of savagery.

Belief in the racial and cultural superiority of the French nation had always been present in France's colonial policy. But it was not until the 1880s that such sentiments were developed into a coherent doctrine and routinely presented as a core reason why France should preserve and expand its empire. Like the doctrine of assimilation, the Mission Civilisatrice had a transformative agenda as it set out to develop and change the identities of the peoples whose lands France had colonized. And it aimed to do so, again in keeping with the doctrine of assimilation, by altering the political, economic, social, and cultural structures and practices of the colonial subjects.

Invasion, Conquest, and Resistance: The Battle for Algeria

The conquest of Algeria began on 14 June 1830 with the landing of nearly forty thousand troops on the beach at Sidi Ferruch. Although the chain of events leading up to the invasion stretched back to Napoleon's Egyptian Campaign of 1798, the expedition itself was a hastily organized and singular initiative. Charles X's government justified it as essential to the improvement of maritime security in the Western Mediterranean and as the only means by which French honor could be restored after the Dey of Algiers' shameful treatment of the French consul a few years earlier. While these considerations undoubtedly strengthened the case for war, they were of secondary importance. For Charles, the invasion was a final, desperate attempt to unite the country behind his leadership by presenting it with a glorious military adventure. Not for the last time, events in Algeria were to play a prominent role in shaping political outcomes on the other side of the Mediterranean.

Early efforts to repulse the invaders were slow and badly organized, giving the French expeditionary force time to secure a beachhead and prepare its defenses. When Dey Hussein Ben Hassan's army finally did attack on 19 June it was unable to dislodge the invaders as they were too well dug in. After repelling this assault, the French counterattacked and drove the Dey's forces toward Algiers. In disarray, they made for the relative safety of the Emperor Fort on the western outskirts of the city. Ten days later, the expeditionary force attacked the fort and, after a five-hour artillery bombardment, forced its garrison to withdraw. As it did so, it destroyed what remained of the stronghold and, with it, Algiers' last line of defense. With the city at the mercy of the approaching French army, a delegation of its leading citizens approached the French commander, Count Louis de Bourmont, and sued for peace. In exchange for his promises that the inhabitants' property, personal safety, and right to worship would be respected, Count Bourmont demanded the unconditional surrender of the defending forces and that the Dey enter voluntary exile. This he did, along with his family, on 10 July 1830.

In less than two months, the French expeditionary force had decapitated the Algerian regime and brought to an end over two centuries of Ottoman rule. Yet the ease with which the invading army had brushed aside the Dey's forces was misleading. Occupation of Algiers did not automatically give the French control over the rest of the province's territory or its population.

Neither did it herald popular acceptance of the invaders' victory. Rather it saw the torch of resistance gradually pass from the Ottoman authorities in the country to the Algerians themselves.

Two of the most significant and influential resistance leaders to emerge at this time were Hajj Ahmed, the Bey of Constantine, and Abd el-Kader.[27] In the years immediately following the fall of Algiers, the French set about expanding their influence eastward along the coast by occupying the cities of Bône and Constantine. To avoid having to expend men, money, and materiel achieving this, successive governors-general of the French Algerian territories attempted to negotiate a settlement with Ahmed whereby, in return for an annual tribute and acknowledgment of French suzerainty, he would be allowed to remain as Bey. When Ahmed refused, Governor-General Bertrand Clauzel dispatched a column of around eight thousand men to achieve by force what he had been unable to accomplish through diplomacy.[28] With the support of the Mukrani, Achour, and Ben Ghana tribes, Ahmed successfully repelled the invaders and drove them from his territory. This victory marked the apogee of his power.

In October 1837, nearly a year after Clauzel's humiliating defeat, a second French force was sent to capture Constantine. After a week-long siege that included a prolonged artillery bombardment the city finally fell and Ahmed was forced to flee. Despite the loss of his capital and Governor-General Valée's offer to restore his political powers in return for an annual tribute of one hundred thousand francs, Ahmed refused to surrender or acknowledge French sovereignty. For the next decade he and his small band of followers waged a guerrilla campaign against French forces in the east of the country. He finally gave himself up in 1848.

Hajj Ahmed's resistance to French rule was driven by his loyalty to the Ottoman Empire. Even though he made Arabic rather than Turkish the language of his court and replaced the Janissaries with locally raised troops, he never renounced the Grand Porte's authority or ceased trying to reestablish it. In stark contrast, Abd el-Kader opposed Ottoman rule. So much so that, on 12 July 1834, he fought and defeated the remaining forces of one of the Grand Porte's other Algerian vassals, the Bey of Oran. As a consequence of his struggle with the Bey of Oran and his attempts to extend the territory of his patron, the Sultan of Morocco, Abd el-Kader was brought into direct conflict with the French as they pushed westward and southward through the Oran region.

To take advantage of the instability generated by Dey Hussein Ben Hassan's defeat, the Moroccan Sultan Moulay Abderrahmane charged Abd el-Kader's father, Muhi al-Din, with the task of seizing the Algerian city of Tlemcen and its environs. Although Muhi al-Din failed to defeat the French garrison based in the region, the various engagements between the two forces helped enhance his son's reputation as a warrior and commander. So much so that in November 1832 when his father stood down as leader, Abd el-Kader was chosen by tribal elders as his replacement and given the title Amir al-Mu'minini (Commander of the Faithful). From the outset, and even though he signed two separate peace treaties with the French, his was a holy war against the French.[29]

The bedrock of Abd el-Kader's support was the Arab tribes of the Moroccan-Algerian borderlands and the Sufi Qadiriyya brotherhood.[30] However, during the course of his struggle against the French, he was also helped by tribes in other parts of the country. For example, in the winter 1845 the Beni-Djaad tribe of the Medea area in north-central Algeria rose in revolt at his behest. In the same year, so too did the tribes of Ouled Tebens, Ouled Deradj, and Ouled Ben Deigha of the Hodna area. Yet Abd el-Kader did not enjoy universal support among the tribes of west and central Algeria. During the course of his seventeen-year struggle against the French, he also fought against the tribes of Douira, Zmala, and Ouled Zeitoun of the Oran region, the Abel el-Nours and Ouled Bouaouns of the Batna area, and the members of the Tijaniyya brotherhood. But through a mixture of both co-option and coercion, Abd el-Kader was able to extend his authority over a large territory that covered much of western and central Algeria.

Abd el-Kader won perhaps his greatest victories in the period between the two treaties. The Desmichels treaty of 1834 consisted of two distinct parts. The first was written in both French and Arabic and was intended for French political and public consumption. The second was written in Arabic only and its existence kept secret from Paris and the French public. The discrepancies and contradictions between these parts meant that the cease-fire it brought into effect was unsustainable. According to the first part of the treaty, Abd el-Kader accepted French control over the region of Oran and free trade within it. In actual fact, under the terms of the second part of the treaty, he was granted a monopoly over all commerce that passed through the port of Arzew and permitted to insist that all French citizens passing through the region carry travel documents issued by him.

Alarmed by the growth of Abd el-Kader's power and influence and his insistence on certain commercial rights, in accordance with the second, secret part of the Desmichels treaty, Paris urged its commanders in the Oran region to deal with him militarily. On 28 June 1835, a column of two thousand French troops under General Camille Trézel engaged Abd el-Kader's forces at Macta.[31] The outcome was a humiliating defeat for the French. Paris responded by dispatching Marshal Clauzel back to Algeria in the capacity of governor-general. After occupying the cities of Tlemcen and Mascara, his forces were defeated at Sidi Yacoub and found themselves besieged at their base at Rachgoun. Clauzel's embattled troops were relieved by a column led by General Bugeaud, who went on to defeat another of Abd el-Kader's forces at Sikkak on 6 July 1836. Yet despite these set-backs, Abd el-Kader remained in control of much of the west of the country. Even more worrying for the French, areas that were supposedly pacified and under their control were repeatedly attacked and penetrated by hostile tribes allied to him.

In an effort to regain the initiative in the east of the country, a new army under the leadership of Governor-General Bertrand was dispatched to capture the city of Constantine. But with inadequate supplies and hindered by appalling weather conditions, the expedition was a disaster. Not only did Clauzel fail to take Constantine, but he lost one thousand men trying. Following this disaster, he was replaced as governor-general by General Charles-Marie comte de Damrémont. To prevent any further reckless adventures, Damrémont was given strict instructions by Premier Molé to limit France's occupation to certain coastal areas—Algiers, Bône, and Oran. And to help ensure the security of these enclaves, Molé sent General Bugeaud to negotiate a truce with Abd el-Kader.

Under the terms of this agreement, or the Treaty of Tafna as it was known, Bugeaud formally granted Abd el-Kader sovereignty over most of western and central Algeria, while France retained authority over the cities of Algiers, Arzew, Mostaganem, Mazagran, and Oran, and slices of the Sahel and Mitidja. The Treaty of Tafna represented the high-water mark of both the size of the territory controlled by Abd el-Kader and his power. Yet, like the Desmichels treaty before it, the Treaty of Tafna proved unworkable and was broken by both sides.

The French, under General Sylvain Charles comte Valée,[32] used the truce to occupy the city of Constantine and extend their rule in the regions of Oran and Titeri. Valée's seizure of this territory, in seeming contradiction with both the Treaty of Tafna and the policy of limited occupation, inevitably brought him into conflict with Abd el-Kader. War was resumed in the winter of 1839 when, after repeated warnings to Valée, Abd el-Kader sent his forces into the Mitidja. The following spring Valée responded by dispatching his troops to find and destroy Abd el-Kader's forces. Their failure to do so, allied to Valée's initial and misguided belief that it would be possible, resulted in his removal from office. In February 1841, Bugeaud was sent back to Algeria as governor-general by Premier Soult, leading to the start of a new phase in the struggle against Abd el-Kader. With renewed political support, Bugeaud initiated a scorched-earth policy whereby the harvests and livestock of tribes loyal to Abd el-Kader were systematically and, if necessary, repeatedly destroyed. These *razzias,* or raids, not only restricted the resources available to Abd el-Kader but put pressure on his coalition as tribes were forced to reassess their support of him.

The razzias proved to be very effective. So much so that in the summer of 1843, Abd el-Kader was forced to seek sanctuary in Morocco. For the next few months, he confined himself to launching raids across the border against French garrisons in the Oran region. Then in the spring of 1844, he returned to Algeria at the head of a new army made up mostly of Moroccan troops. But this latest campaign was ill-starred. Shortly afterward, the French launched a series of military strikes against Morocco to force the Sultan to withdraw his support for Abd el-Kader. To begin, in July 1844, the French navy, under the command of François d'Orléans, the prince de Joinville, bombarded the cities of Tangier and Mogador. Then a month later, on 14 August, Bugeaud fought and defeated the Sultan's army on the banks of the River Isley.

As a result of this military pressure and faced with mounting discontent among his own people, Abderrahmane capitulated. On 10 September 1844 he signed what became known as the Treaty of Tangier, which required him to outlaw Abd el-Kader and stop his using Morocco as base to launch raids against French forces in Algeria. Although Abd el-Kader continued to stimulate insurrections in various parts of Algeria, without the backing of the Sultan and with tribal support on the wane because of the razzias, he was unable to stop Bugeaud from extending and entrenching French rule. On 23 December 1847, shortly after Bugeaud had been replaced as governor-general, Abd el-Kader finally surrendered to General Louis de Lamoricière.

His submission, however, did not bring with it an end to Algerian resistance. Throughout the mid-1840s the regions of Oran, Algiers, and Titeri were gripped by numerous uprisings organized and led by Bou Maza. He claimed to be the *mahdi* and to have returned to drive the infidels from Algeria. Between autumn 1844 and winter 1845, Bou Maza repeatedly inspired the tribes in the Mina, Flittas, Ouarenseris, and Darah areas to wage holy war against the French. Each time the revolts were put down, but a lack of resources prevented the French from either capturing Bou Maza or defeating him decisively. But this changed in November 1845 when French forces under the command of Lieutenant-General Bourjolly and Colonel St. Arnaud followed Bugeaud's lead and launched a series of razzias against the recalcitrant tribes.[33] Bou Maza was finally captured in 1846.

The final insurrection of note to occur in the nineteenth century took place in the Constantine region. On 14 March 1871, the head of the Mukrani tribe, Mouhammed el Mukrani, attacked the local garrison with the aim of reclaiming the rights, privileges, and freedom of action enjoyed by his father. Since the late 1850s, as the French tightened their grip on the countryside, these liberties had been steadily eroded. Although Mukrani was supported by a few other local tribes, his insurrection amounted to little more than a small-scale revolt. To increase its size and enhance its effectiveness, Mukrani approached the head of the Rahmaniyya brotherhood, Mouhammad el Haddad, for help and support. On 8 April 1871 Haddad urged his followers to wage *jihad* on the French and conferred the title of Amir al Mujahidin (commander of the holy warriors) on Mukrani. With Haddad's support, around one hundred and sixty thousand Kabyle peasants flocked to join Mukrani, transforming his limited uprising into a major revolt.

Over the next seven months, Mukrani's army attacked villages and pieds noirs' farms throughout eastern Algeria.[34] One such attack occurred on the 21 May 1871 against the village of Palestro around 50 miles (80 kilometers) southeast of Algiers. A force of about six thousand assaulted the houses of pied noirs settlers, killing several of them.[35] But as summer turned into autumn, French forces were able to gain the upper hand. By the winter of 1871 Bu Mazraq's army had been decisively defeated and its members either killed, taken prisoner, or forced to flee. Bu Mazraq was finally caught on 20 June 1872. During the course of the rebellion, over 2,500 European settlers were killed. Their deaths help explain the severity of the punishment imposed by the French on the tribes in the Constantine region. Not only were they obliged to pay reparations, but they also had much of their land confiscated.

For the next fifty years, Algerian resistance to France remained unorganized and ineffective and was unable to halt the steady expansion of French rule. During that time, in keeping with the foreign policy objectives of the newly established Third Republic, successive governors-general extended the border of Algérie française ever southward to incorporate the central highlands of the Grand Erg Occidental, the Grand Erg Oriental, and the Plateau du Tademaït along with the northern fringes of the Sahara. By the early 1930s, this border reached as far as the Ahaggar Mountains and Tamanrasset, nearly 1,000 miles (1,600 kilometers) south of Algiers.

Yet, despite the extension and consolidation of French rule, at no point was the flame of Algerian resistance ever fully extinguished. While, at times, it amounted to little more than a spark, it endured and, in the early decades of the twentieth century, burst into life to consume the colonial state. But Algerian opposition of the twentieth century was fundamentally different from that of earlier times. France's enemies and adversaries of the nineteenth century fought and resisted the expansion of her power for a variety of reasons: loyalty to the Ottoman Empire and Grand Porte; religion and a determination to liberate Muslim lands; and a desire to preserve a vanishing way of life. None of them, however, was motivated by nationalist sentiments, by a desire to help Algerians achieve national self-determination.

Hajj Ahmed's resistance was spurred by his commitment to the multiethnic, polyglot Ottoman Empire. He did not declare Algeria's independence from Istanbul, nor did he seek to. Rather, he wanted to preserve its status as part of the Ottoman Empire. Abd el-Kader, similarly, did not confront the French in order to win independent sovereign statehood for the Algerian nation. And even though he continues to be hailed as the first Algerian nationalist, he fought France in the name of Islam, not on behalf of the

Algerian nation. It was religious fervor and a desire to chase the infidels out of Algeria that also drove Bou Maza. His was a holy war against the French, not a nationalist struggle. Neither was that mounted by Mouhammed el Mukrani and Bu Mazraq. Their rebellion was waged to safeguard a dying social, political, and economic order, not to ensure the liberty of the Algerian nation. In stark contrast, many of the individuals and groups who opposed and resisted French rule during the first half of the twentieth century were inspired by nationalism, by a belief that the Algerian people constituted a nation fully deserving of independence and statehood.

Assimilation and the Mission Civilisatrice: Turning Algerians into Frenchmen

As well as enabling France to consolidate its authority over an ever-increasing area, Bugeaud's scorched earth strategy laid the foundations for the establishment of a settler community and was one of the first acts in the pursuit of the doctrines of assimilation and Mission Civilisatrice in Algeria. As elsewhere, the French viewed the local population as inferior beings, at once primitive and degenerate, vice ridden and innocent, repulsive and fascinating. Such sentiments were expressed by countless politicians, soldiers, explorers, anthropologists, and commentators both in support of the extension of French rule over Algeria and its withdrawal from there.

French views of the local population were profoundly influenced by Algerians' commitment to Islam, their religiosity, and their lack of nationhood. From the outset, Islam was seen as the defining characteristic of Algerians' cultures and identities. That most Algerians were Muslims was believed to be both a manifestation and cause of their savagery and a major barrier to their becoming civilized. Such views were given official sanction through legislation like the Sénatus-Consulte of 14 July 1865. Under its provisions, Muslim Algerians were granted the right to apply for French citizenship (in accordance with the doctrine of assimilation) but could only do so once they had renounced their personal status as Muslims. Through this clause, the French government made citizenship conditional upon Muslim Algerians committing apostasy. And even if they were prepared to do so, the government offered no guarantees that their applications would be successful. Through legislation like this, the French authorities established a direct link between ethnicity and culture and political and civil rights.

In so doing, the authorities not only ignored the strict separation of church from state demanded by republicanism but they once again exposed for all to see the racist foundations on which the edifice of Algérie française was being built. In stark contrast to the Sénatus-Consulte of July 1865, that of June 1889 granted automatic French citizenship to any child born in

Algeria of European parents. Citizenship, in this instance, was not dependent on either the child or its parents first renouncing Christianity. And Algeria's Jews were all granted unconditional citizenship under the terms of the Crémieux Decree of October 1870. It was discrimination such as this that played a significant role in stimulating the development of Algerian nationalism from the early 1900s onward.

It was not just Muslim Algerians' practice of Islam that betrayed them as barbarians; it was also their high level of attachment to it. The scale and strength of this commitment was highlighted by the small number of Algerians who applied for French citizenship after the introduction of the Sénatus-Consulte granting them the right to do so. Between July 1865 and the repeal of the legislation in 1954, only around two thousand Algerians were willing to sacrifice their Muslim personal status in return for French citizenship. The widespread reluctance among the local population to give up their religion was taken by many in the Parti Colonial who were opposed to any increase in the political and civil rights granted to Muslim Algerians as evidence of the futility of pursuing assimilation. But even for those Parti members who remained favorably disposed to the doctrines of assimilation and Mission Civilisatrice, the Muslim masses' reluctance to abandon their religion was seen as a major impediment to their being assimilated and becoming civilized.

Although most Algerians were thought by the French authorities and European settlers to display an unhealthy attachment to Islam, some were believed to be more attached than others. As the French consolidated their rule over Algeria, there developed what has subsequently been identified as the Kabyle Myth.[36] The Kabyles were the largest ethnic group within the Berber community, leading to the term Kabyle being used in reference to the Berber population as a whole. According to this myth, the Kabyles were the descendents of the territory's original Christian inhabitants, the ancestors of the ancient Carthaginians. The myth developed as a result of French ethnographers' and anthropologists' beliefs that Kabyle society, unlike its Arab equivalent, bore several marked similarities to that of the French during medieval times.

In keeping with the linear understanding of civilization outlined in the Mission Civilisatrice, the French authorities placed the various ethnic communities in Algeria into a hierarchy of civilization. Although not explicitly included in this *échelle sociale* (social ladder), at the very top were the French against whose civilization Algerians were judged and categorized. The Arabs were viewed as an inferior race to the French because they were perceived to be greedy, fickle, and cowardly, while the Kabyles were presumed to be superior to the Arabs because they bore more similarities to the French. In light of this discovery, the Kabyle Myth contended that the task of civilizing the Kabyles would be far easier than that of civilizing the Arabs.

The third measure against which the French compared and evaluated the degree of civilization achieved by the Algerian population was nationhood. For the French, the nation-state was the most civilized unit of sociopolitical organization and governance. The French were a nation and were civilized. And the measure of their civilization was the achievements of its artists and musicians, poets and writers, scientists and engineers. Algerians were not members of a nation, but divided into a plethora of tribes, "separate centres, living independently of one another, without code, without law,"[37] and seemingly without accomplishment. Algerians' lack of nationhood was both a manifestation and a cause of their barbarity, a daunting hurdle that the French would have to help them overcome if they were to succeed in their mission of bringing civilization to North Africa.

To traverse this obstacle, and all the others barring the path to the assimilation and civilization of Algeria, the French embarked on a policy of breaking up the tribes. Tribal units had no place in the political and administrative structure the doctrine of assimilation recommended imposing on Algeria. And Algerians would never become civilized as long as such units were allowed to endure because civilized peoples were organized into nation-states, not tribes.

But the disorganization also received the wholehearted support of those Parti Colonial members, most notably the European settlers and their supporters in France, who opposed assimilation and did not wish to see any increase in the rights granted to the Algerian masses, or were uninterested in the civilizing goals of French colonization. They embraced disorganization as vital to the security and economic development of the territory. Unless the tribes were broken up, neither the European settlers nor France would be able to get access to Algeria's prime economic asset—land. And to work the land, the estate owners and managers required a pool of laborers from which to draw. The only way to ensure a ready supply of farmhands, willing to sell their labor for wages, was by destroying existing working structures and practices in the countryside.

The disorganization process, which began almost immediately after the 1830 invasion, passed through two distinct phases. During the first phase, the French authorities expropriated land from the tribes through a variety of means. Each tribe depended on its lands to graze its animals and raise crops, to produce the food it needed to support itself. After evicting a tribe from its lands, phase two of the disorganization process began. To prevent it from ever threatening the security of Algérie française in the future, the colonial authorities scattered its members across numerous new settlements called *douars-communes*. Modeled on the communes in France, each douar was inhabited by individuals and families drawn from many different tribes.

Between 1830 and the early 1870s, the main method for expropriating tribal lands employed by the French was military conquest. Through the campaigns it carried out against Hajj Ahmed, Abd el-Kader, Bou Maza, and the Mukrani tribe, the army seized hundreds of thousands of hectares. Much of this land was gained in the form of booty from the defeated Dey and Beys, from mosques and religious brotherhoods, and as war reparations. Indeed, following their failed uprising, the Mukrani tribe and its allies were forced to pay France 35 million francs and cede around 550,000 hectares of their remaining lands.

By the early 1850s, around 115,000 hectares of land had been distributed to 131,283 settlers.[38] Over the same period, successive governors-general established around 180 villages or *centres de colonisation* for the settlers to inhabit. As the number of settlers in the country increased, so too did their demand for land and insistence that the indigenous peoples be driven further away from the areas inhabited by Europeans.[39] But from the mid-1850s onward, it became increasingly difficult for the French to simply take land from the tribes by force. This was due partly to Napoleon III's determination to protect the local population from the avarice of the settlers and partly to the fact that the tribes had less land to cede.

As a consequence, the manipulation of property rights replaced military conquest as the main means by which land was transferred from the tribes to the settlers. One of the most important pieces of legislation to enable this was the Sénatus-Consulte of 1865. Ironically, this particular law was introduced to try to give the tribes some legal protection from the settlers. Yet it sought to do so by breaking up "every tribe of the Tell and other agricultural areas" and establishing "individual property" and distributing it "among the members of the douars."[40] In so doing, the Sénatus-Consulte hastened the disintegration of the tribes and left the new property owners vulnerable to exploitation at the hands of European developers and speculators.

This vulnerability was increased following the promulgation of the Warnier law a year after the collapse of the Mukrani rebellion. Named after its champion, Dr. Auguste Hubert Warnier, the law stipulated that all land transactions had to be conducted in accordance with French law, that land could not be held communally, and that all unproductive and uncultivated lands must be handed over to the Commissaires-Enqêteurs, the French office of colonization. In accordance with this law, tribes were forced to divide their lands among their members and register each plot as an individual holding. This often created plots that were too small to work, which encouraged the owners to sell to European speculators. Once a speculator acquired a plot, no matter how small, they could put it up for sale and, in so doing, force every other member of the tribe to do likewise. They were then free to buy up as many of the other plots as they wanted. Through this law the Commissaires-Enqêteurs acquired over 300,000 hectares of land, while speculators were able to buy around 500,000 more at below market value.

As well as enhancing the security of French Algeria and opening up the country to economic development and exploitation by the settlers and French businesses, the disorganization of the tribes helped advance the recreation of Algerians' cultures and identities. The changes that the disorganization affected forced Algerians to live and work within sociopolitical units introduced by the French, and in which they were afforded inferior political and civil rights. The long-term impact of these changes on the local population was made apparent by the development of Algerian nationalism during the early decades of the twentieth century.

Notes

1. Geoffrey Hawthorn, "'Waiting for a Text?': Comparing Third World Politics," in *Rethinking Third World Politics*, ed. James Manor (London and New York: Longman, 1991), p. 26; and Partha Chatterjee, *Nationalist Thought and the Colonial World: A Derivative Discourse* (London: Zed Books, 1986), p. 21.

2. Ernest Gellner, *Nations and Nationalism* (Oxford: Oxford University Press, 1983), p. 1.

3. Ernest Renan, *Qu'est que c'est une nation?* Conference presentation, Sorbonne, 11 March 1882, Paris, pp. 7–8.

4. Anthony D. Smith, *National Identity* (London: Penguin, 1992), p. 14.

5. Benedict Anderson, *Imagined Communities*, 2nd ed. (London and New York: Verso, 1991), p. 36.

6. Ibid., pp. 44 and 45.

7. Ibid., p. 116.

8. Anthony D. Smith, *State and Nation in the Third World* (Brighton: Harvester Press, 1983), p. 48.

9. Ibid., p. 51.

10. Basil Davidson, *The Black Man's Burden: Africa and the Curse of the Nation-State* (London: James Currey, 1992), p. 164.

11. Organisation of African Unity, OAU Charter (1963) available at www.africa-union.org/root/au/Documents/Treaties/text/OAU_Charter_1963.pdf, see Article III (accessed 23 July 2004).

12. Terrence Ranger, "The Invention of Tradition in Colonial Africa," in *The Invention of Tradition*, ed. Eric Hobsbawm and Terrence Ranger (Cambridge: Cambridge University Press, 1983), p. 212.

13. John A. A. Ayoade, "States Without Citizens: An Emerging African Phenomenon," in *The Precarious Balance: State and Society in Africa*, ed. Donald Rothchild and Naomi Chazan (Boulder, Colo., and London: Westview Press, 1988), p. 104.

14. Ibid.

15. Thomas Hylland Eriksen, "A Non-Ethnic State for Africa? A Life-World Approach to the Imagining of Communities," in *Ethnicity and Nationalism in Africa: Constructivist Reflections and Contemporary Politics*, ed. Paris Yeros (Basingstoke, UK: Macmillan, 1999), p. 47.

16. Clifford Geertz, *The Interpretation of Cultures: Selected Essays* (London: Fontana, 1973), p. 240.

17. Jaurès led the SFIO from its creation in 1905 until his assassination on 31 July 1914.

18. The Committee for Madagascar was established in 1895, and those for French Africa and French Asia in 1890 and 1901, respectively.

19. Robert Aldrich, *Greater France: A History of French Overseas Expansion* (London: Palgrave Macmillan, 1996), p. 101.

20. François Guizot, King Louis-Philippe's Minister of Foreign Affairs, cited in Aldrich, *Greater France*, p. 94.

21. Ferry served two terms as premier. The first lasted from 23 September 1880 to 14 November 1881 and the second from 21 February 1883 to 6 April 1885.

22. Algeria was incorporated under the terms of the 1848 French constitution.

23. The Crémieux Decree granted citizenship to the members of Algeria's Jewish community.

24. The Sénatus-Consulte of June 1889 granted citizenship to all children born in Algeria of non-French European immigrants.

25. Article 27 of the 1852 constitution stated that laws in Algeria and the colonies would be introduced by Senate decree.

26. Cited in Louis Vignon, *Un programme de politique coloniale* (Paris: Plon-Nourrit, 1919), p. 192.

27. Under the Ottomans Algeria was divided into four administrative regions—Algiers, Titeri, Constantine, and Mascara. Algiers was governed by the Dey and the remaining three regions by a Bey each.

28. This force was dispatched in November 1836.

29. The first treaty was signed 26 February 1834 with the French commander of the Oran region, General Louis-Alexis Desmichels. The second treaty, the Treaty of Tafna, was signed on 30 May 1837 with General Thomas Robert Bugeaud.

30. There were five such brotherhoods in Algeria at that time—the Qadiriyya, Darqawa, Rahmaniyya, Tayyibiyya, and Tijaniyya.

31. Trézel had replaced Desmichels early in the year after his double dealing came to light.

32. Valée was promoted to the position of governor-general after Damrémont was killed on 13 October 1837 in the battle to capture Constantine.

33. *The Times*, "The French in Algeria," 20 November 1845, Issue 19086, p. 7, col. C.

34. The term "pieds noirs," literally "black feet," was the name given to the European settlers in Algeria during the colonial era. Mukrani was shot and killed on 5 May 1871. He was replaced as leader of the insurrection by his brother Bu Mazraq.

35. *The Times,* "The Insurrection in Algeria," 31 May 1871, Issue 27077, pp. 9, col. E.

36. See Patricia Lorcin, *Imperial Identities: Stereotyping, Prejudice and Race in Colonial Algeria* (London: I. B. Tauris, 1999).

37. Capitaine d'Etat-Major Francois LeBlanc de Prebois, "Algerie," in *Du système de colonisation. Suivi par la France,* ed. M. A. T. Lachariere (Paris: Auguste Auffray), p. 1.

38. John Ruedy, *Modern Algeria: The Origins and Development of a Nation,* 2nd ed. (Bloomington: Indiana University Press, 2005), p. 69.

39. Indeed, by 1881 the ranks of the European population had swelled to 1.2 million people and, collectively, they owned 412,000 hectares of land. Ruedy, *Modern Algeria,* p. 69.

40. Henry Didier, *Le gouvernement militaire et la colonisation en Algérie* (Paris: E. Dentu, 1865), p. 15.

3

Algerian Nationalism and the War of Liberation

SIX HUNDRED MILES SOUTH OF Algiers, surrounded by the sands of the Sahara, sits the oasis town of El Golea. For centuries it had been a watering hole and rest stop for Arab merchants traveling south from the coast to trade with the desert-dwelling Tuareg and inhabitants of modern-day Mali and Niger. On 29 January 1930, however, it was the unlikely venue of the International Congress of Botanists and Agricultural Experts. The congress was the first of a series of events organized the length and breadth of Algeria celebrating one hundred years of French rule. The crowning glory of these festivities was a reenactment of the landing of the French expeditionary force at Sidi Ferruch.

Despite the many different types of celebration that were held— remembrance ceremonies, balls, concerts, parties, and statue dedications— the overriding mood was one of self-congratulation. French rule, the pieds noirs told themselves and the Muslim population, had done wonders for Algeria. The mosquito-ridden swamps of the Mitidja had been drained and turned into farmland. Algiers and Oran had been transformed from medieval ports into modern cities with grand buildings the equal of those of Marseilles, Toulon, and Nice. The number of deaths from diseases like malaria, cholera, and typhoid had been dramatically reduced with the introduction of vaccination programs and improvements in sanitation. And most impressive of all, the savage, warlike peoples who had resisted French rule for so long had been finally tamed and civilized. This was still a work in progress, of course, but now many of them spoke French, wore European clothes, and ceased to think of themselves as members of this or that tribe. A very few had even renounced Islam. To most European settlers, there appeared no significant obstacle barring French Algeria's path to a prosperous and glory-strewn future. As one British commentator who witnessed the celebrations firsthand wrote, "in the golden glow of the centenary there seem[s] no reason why the existing regime should not last indefinitely."[1]

Certainly few would have guessed that in just over thirty years French rule in the Maghreb would be at an end and Algérie française nothing but a memory.

The main cause of French Algeria's demise was the European settlers' dogged determination to prevent the introduction of reforms granting Muslim Algerians political and legal equality. Such reforms, the pieds noirs believed, would spell an end not only to their privileged position within Algerian society, but Algérie française itself. For the settlers, their fate was inextricably linked to that of the land they inhabited. Any increase in Muslim Algerians' rights would lead inexorably to the pieds noirs becoming politically, economically, and culturally subsumed. And if that happened, Algérie française would be swept away.

Yet it was actually this racist and zero-sum reasoning that led to French Algeria's demise. In the years immediately before and after World War I, various groups emerged dedicated to securing greater political and civil liberties for Muslims. These early committees and organizations were not opposed to French rule, far from it. They wanted France to fulfill its pledge to assimilate Algerians as part of the French nation. And they were prepared to wait. They did not expect the colonial authorities to extend full political and civil rights to *all* Algerians, just a select, sufficiently civilized few. Yet the response from the pieds noirs and their supporters in Paris was always the same: a shrill "*jamais*" ("never"). In the face of such intransigence, Algerians began turning their backs on groups preaching assimilation. They lent their support instead to organizations and individuals calling for independence from French rule, for the creation of a sovereign Algerian state. The longer the settlers refused to countenance any changes to the political, economic, and social status quo, the more determined selected groups of Algerians became to achieving independence.

This determination was strengthened further following the massacre of around fifteen thousand Muslims in the town of Sétif in May 1945. The killing was carried out by members of the police, gendarmerie, and army as well as groups of armed pieds noirs. The brutality of this event and cold-blooded collusion of the settlers and security forces not only increased the resolve of those wedded to the cause of Algerian independence, but persuaded some of them that it could only be achieved through violence. And so it was. On 1 November 1954, a group calling itself the National Liberation Front launched a series of small-scale raids against police stations and military barracks throughout the Algiers, Aurès, and Constantine regions. Its reasons for doing so were made clear in a statement issued by the organization's general secretariat in Cairo. It announced that the FLN was striving for nothing less than the "destruction of the colonial system" and "national independence" for Algeria.[2] Although the FLN's initial attacks achieved little, they started a seven-and-a-half-year military and political struggle that led to the death and displacement of hundreds of thousands of people.

Yet Algeria's independence was not won by force of arms alone. Equally important was the FLN's stimulation of Algerians' sense of nationhood and desire for political self-government. Algerians' growing belief that they constituted a nation deserving of independence made French rule increasingly difficult to maintain. While the French often defeated the FLN militarily, they needed the support of the people to be able to govern. Without this, French rule became increasingly dependent on military force, making it politically, economically, and morally unsustainable.

While the development of Algerian nationalism before and during the war of liberation heralded the end of French colonialism, it also signaled its enduring success. By using nationalism to articulate and express their grievances against colonialism, Algerians drew on an ideology that had been introduced to Algeria by the French and used to justify their rule. Although the war of liberation undoubtedly marked a watershed in Algeria's tumultuous history, it did not effect a complete break with the colonial past.

This chapter focuses on the development of Algerian nationalism from 1912 through the war of liberation and is divided into two main parts. In the first section, it examines the origins and development of Algerian nationalism in the twentieth century. The second section then charts the main contours of the war of liberation and how the FLN came to dominate the nationalist movement and stimulate Algerians' sense of nationhood.

Resistance and Nationalism in the Twentieth Century

Even though they failed to drive the French from their lands, the Algerians who resisted colonization throughout the nineteenth century did contribute to the liberation of Algeria, albeit in an unexpected way. They may not have fought the French in the name of the Algerian nation, to free it from the yoke of a foreign power, but that has not prevented them from being hailed as the first Algerian nationalists. Abd el-Kader, in particular, continues to be revered as the Algerian nation's greatest hero and the man who created the first independent Algerian state. Quite unintentionally, he became an icon of the nationalist movement as his efforts and achievements helped convince later generations of Algerians that they were indeed members of a nation and provided them with the legends that have become so vital to Algeria's national story. Through his struggle against the invaders, Abd el-Kader gave inspiration and succor to the Algerian nationalists of the 1950s and 1960s, the men and women who eventually drove the French from Algeria.

The Algerian nationalist movement of the twentieth century consisted of three distinct factions—the assimilationists, anticolonialists, and armed insurrectionists. Although the sequence in which these factions emerged and achieved prominence was broadly chronological, they did not constitute separate phases of the nationalist movement. For example, those who preached assimilation and closer ties with France coexisted and struggled for influence with those demanding outright independence. And all that separated the anticolonialists and armed insurrectionists was the means they adopted to achieve independence for Algeria. Neither did each of these factions constitute homogenous groups. They were each made up of a variety of different organizations. Yet, the development of the anticolonialists and armed insurrectionists came about because of the inability of the groups before them to significantly improve the political, economic, and social lot of the Algerian population.

From around 1910 until the FLN gained control of the nationalist movement in the late 1950s, a spiral of Algerian action and pieds noirs and French reaction drove the development of the nationalist movement. The assimilationists strove for the complete integration of Algeria with France but were repeatedly blocked by the European settlers and their metropolitan French allies who were opposed to it. This reaction contributed to the development of the anticolonialist faction, while its failure to affect the desired changes as a consequence of pieds noirs and French resistance helped lead to the emergence of those committed to violent opposition. Every attempt by the pieds noirs and their supporters to prevent any enhancement of the political and civil rights of the Algerian masses pushed the nationalist movement a little further down the spiral by contributing to the growth in numbers and commitment of those who believed that meaningful change could only be achieved through violence.

The first Algerian nationalist organization to emerge was the assimilationist Young Algerian (Jeune Algérien) group. It comprised and reflected the views and aspirations of a small group of well-educated, middle-class, French-speaking Algerians. On 8 June 1912, the group issued its manifesto, which called for increased representation of Algerians in the French National Assembly, the instigation of a fairer taxation system, and a more equitable distribution of resources between Europeans and non-Europeans.[3] Given their well-to-do and professional backgrounds, the Young Algerians were pro-French and elitist. They did not demand independence for Algeria, and the majority of the improved rights they sought were not intended for the uneducated many, just the privileged few.

In the summer of 1927 the Young Algerian movement evolved into the Federation of Elected Muslims (Fédération des élus des musulmans). It was so called as it was established by Muslim members of the Délégations financières.[4] Although only a decade had passed since the proclamation of the Young Algerian manifesto, the group no longer sought the total and absolute assimilation of Algeria with France, that Algeria be culturally subsumed by France. Instead they demanded equality and cultural pluralism. At a meeting of its constitutive congress on 11 September 1927, the Federation outlined its key aims: representation of the Muslim population in the National Assembly; equal pay and conditions with their European counterparts for Muslim civil servants; standardization of the length of military service, making it the same for Muslims and Europeans alike; freedom of travel for Muslims between Algeria and France; the development of education and training programs for Muslims; the full extension of French social law to Algeria; the suppression of the *code de l'indigénat*[5]; and the reformation of the electoral process in the *communes mixtes*.[6]

Despite its aim of gaining greater political and civil rights for Algerians without them having to abandon their culture and religion, the Federation remained committed to preserving and strengthening Algeria's union with France. One of the main reasons for this, as the young Ferhat Abbas was to declare, was that they did not believe in the existence of an Algerian nation.[7] They considered themselves Frenchmen, Muslim Frenchmen, and as such they wanted the rights and freedoms that were accorded Frenchmen. Partly because of this attitude, partly because of its commitment to work in and through existing political structures and abide by the law, partly because of the superior education of its members compared with the rest of the Muslim population, and partly because the pieds noirs and French found the other Algerian organizations even less palatable, the Federation became the primary interlocutor with whom the authorities in Algiers and Paris discussed issues relating to the non-European population.

That did not mean, however, that these authorities were eager to negotiate with the Federation or willing to do what it wanted. This was particularly true of the pieds noirs and their supporters who remained hostile to any reforms that might have given the Muslim populace more political, civil, and economic rights. The Federation and its members enjoyed more support though, from the left-wing parties and organizations in metropolitan France—the socialists, communists, and radicals. In 1936 these parties united and contested the legislative election of May that year as the Popular Front. The Front's victory gave the Federation and its members renewed hope that their agenda would be given greater consideration. These hopes were raised further when, in December 1938, Premier Léon Blum and his minister of state, Maurice Violette, sponsored a law to grant full citizenship to certain groups of Algerians without their having to renounce their Muslim personal status.

The proposed law was a response not only to the pressure exerted by the Federation but also the sociopolitical instability that gripped Algeria in the early 1930s. The self-congratulatory centenary celebrations of 1930 had humiliated and angered many Muslim Algerians. In the years that followed, sections of Algerian society that had previously had little to do with one another united to organize a series of protests, demonstrations, strikes, and boycotts. This volatile situation was made even more unstable by the reaction of the minister of the interior, Marcel Régnier, who, in March 1935, extended the hated code de l'indigénat. Although this measure was welcomed by the pieds noirs, it inflamed Algerians' sense of injustice and fortified the Federation's resolve to bring about change.

Almost overnight, Algerians' tempers were assuaged by the Popular Front's electoral success and Blum's appointment of Violette as his minister of state. To exploit the opportunities made available by the Popular Front's ascension to power, the Federation agreed to enter into an alliance with other groups keen to secure greater rights and freedoms for Algerians, the French Communist Party (Parti Communiste Algérien, PCA), and the Association of Algerian Muslim Ulama (Association d'Ulama Musulman Algérien, AUMA). In June 1936, at its first meeting in Algiers, the newly-formed Algerian Muslim Congress (Congrès Musulman Algérien, CMA) issued a charter of demands. These included the suppression of all discriminatory laws; the full administrative integration of Algeria with France; universal suffrage; Muslim representation in the French National Assembly; the preservation of non-Europeans' Muslim personal status; the separation of church and state; the promotion of Arabic; the expansion of education for Muslims; the improvement of public health care; the removal of pay discrepancies between Europeans and Muslims; and land redistribution.[8] The charter was taken to Paris and presented to Blum by a CMA delegation on 24 July 1936.

In the wake of this visit, the Blum government set about drafting new legislation to increase the number of Muslim Algerians allowed to vote in French parliamentary elections. The outcome was the so-called Blum-Violette law, which advocated enfranchising veterans, university graduates, civil servants, and professionals, and increasing the number of representatives Algeria returned to the Chamber of Deputies. In all, the law proposed adding around 22,000 Muslims to the electoral roll. This figure fell far short of the universal suffrage called for in the charter of demands. Nevertheless, the CMA gave the law its unequivocal support.

The CMA reaffirmed its backing for the law and the Popular Front government at a second conference held in July 1937. But by then cracks within the Congress were beginning to show. As the excitement that surrounded the drafting of the Blum-Violette law died down, it became increasingly apparent to the Federation, AUMA, and the communists that they had little in common with one another either ideologically or politically. The Federation and AUMA differed fundamentally over the desirability of Algeria's integration with France; the AUMA and the communists were at odds over the role religion should play in shaping Algerian politics and society; the communists and the Federation clashed on issues of class; and the AUMA and the Federation disagreed with the communists over the urgency with which changes to Algeria's political, economic, and social structures and practices should be introduced—the former were impatient for them to be implemented as soon as possible, while the latter wanted to wait so that France could concentrate on meeting the fascist challenge at home and abroad. In the end, the barriers dividing the CMA's various partners proved to be insurmountable and by the summer of 1938 it had ceased to exist as a meaningful entity.

In an attempt to contain the political storm whipped up by the law, Blum and the Popular Front premiers who followed him decided not to pass it by decree.[9] Instead, they placed it before the National Assembly and set to work trying to generate support for it in the Chamber of Deputies and Chamber of Peers. However, in so doing they gave the pieds noirs and their allies the opportunity to marshal their forces against it. Throughout the winter of 1937 and spring of 1938, the settlers stepped up the pace of their campaign against the law. In early 1938, Algeria's mayors and National Assembly members threatened to resign en masse if the law was passed, while a steady procession of prominent pieds noirs denounced the government for considering it in the first instance. Encouraged and given voice by the right-wing press, the settlers effectively stymied the government's efforts to get the law through the assembly. In late 1938, the pro–pieds noirs faction in the Chamber of Peers defeated the proposed law when it was submitted to the vote, while their allies in the Chamber of Deputies ensured that it remained bogged down in committees and was never placed before the House. In light of these setbacks and overwhelmed by the strength and vehemence of the settlers' opposition, the government gave up.

The collapse of the campaign to get the Blum-Violette law enacted sounded the death knell for the assimilationist movement. Yet again the Federation had been unable to persuade the National Assembly to enhance the political and civil rights of even a minority of the Algerian population. And yet again their efforts to do so had been thwarted by the pieds noirs and their supporters. This disappointment not only highlighted the continued intransigence of the European settlers, but it also confirmed the limitations of the assimilationists' influence and abilities and cast significant doubt on their claim that the existing political, economic, and social systems could be reformed.

The law's failure and the decline of the assimilationists' standing among the Algerian population contributed to the growth in popularity of another nationalist faction: the anticolonialists. One of the groups that increasingly fell within this camp was the AUMA. Since its creation in May 1931, the AUMA had trodden an ambiguous line in its relations with the Federation. At times, it was hostile. Two months after Abbas had published his article denying the existence of the Algerian nation, Abd el-Hamid Ben Badis, who had founded the AUMA along with Tayyib el-Okbi and Badir el-Ibrahimi, responded by declaring that the "Muslim population is not France; it cannot be France, it does not want to be France . . . it possesses its fatherland whose frontiers are fixed."[10] On other occasions, the AUMA worked with the Federation, as it did when the two organizations founded the CMA and cowrote the charter of demands in 1936.

The complexity of the AUMA's relations with the Federation reflected its uncertain attitude toward France. Whereas the Federation tried to embrace France in the hope that its members' affections might be returned, the AUMA was far more circumspect. For a start, as Ben Badis made clear, it believed Algerians to be a people and nation distinct from the French with their own "culture . . . customs . . . [and] habits with all that is good and bad in them."[11] The AUMA did not believe that Algerians were French or that they could, or should, attempt to become so. And yet, despite this position and again unlike the Federation, the AUMA vowed to eschew "all political discussions, as well as any intervention in politics."[12] Instead, it defined itself as an "association for moral education."[13]

Even though the AUMA viewed the French as foreign nonbelievers, it refused to get engaged in politics or enter the political arena. Or so it claimed. There were occasions, such as the support it gave the Blum-Violette law, when the AUMA knowingly broke its own pledge. And more generally, as it carried out its supposedly nonpolitical activities, it struggled to avoid commenting, either verbally or through its actions, on French policies in Algeria. From the outset, therefore, the AUMA's attitude toward and relationship with the colonial authorities was defined by its failing attempts to remain politically neutral.

The AUMA's efforts to remain neutral were driven by the *salafist* tendencies of its founders and early leaders.[14] The *salafiyya* or reformist movement had first emerged in Egypt at the end of the nineteenth century. Its ideas were transported to Algeria by key thinkers, such as Mohammed Abduh, who visited the country in 1903, and Algerians returning after living and working in the Middle East. And even though the salafist movement spanned the Islamic world and was introduced to Algeria from outside, the AUMA incorporated it as part of an Algerian nationalist agenda. This was reflected in the group's maxim—"Islam is my religion, Arabic is my language, Algeria is my country."

Salafism asserted that the failings of Muslim societies, their political, economic, and technological subservience to the European powers, were the result of the corruption of Islam. Their regeneration, therefore, depended on and indeed first required the reinvigoration of Islam. And this could only be achieved by returning to the ways of the earliest Muslims, and reexaminng the Quran and sunna. For the salafists of the AUMA, politics was not only of secondary importance to religion, it was an unwelcome distraction. It was not politics that was going to regenerate Algeria. And engagement in it reduced the time members of the AUMA and Algerians could spend doing what really mattered—attempting to live as their Muslim forefathers had.

The AUMA's primary objective was to facilitate the regeneration of Algerian society by instigating religious and social reform. Accordingly, the group set out to combat "alcoholism, gambling, laziness [and] ignorance" among the Algerian population.[15] Perhaps the most serious of these sins, as far as Ben Badis and the other leaders were concerned, was ignorance, and it was to countering this that they devoted their greatest energies. Ignorance, for them, did not only manifest itself as an inability to speak Arabic and a lack of understanding of the Quran and sunna, it also appeared as a belief in superstition. In addition to improving Algerians' linguistic and religious learning, the AUMA sought to end their veneration of saints, support for *marabouts,* and membership of religious brotherhoods. The AUMA considered saints, marabouts, and brotherhoods to be un-Islamic.

As part of its regeneration of Islam, the AUMA created a network of schools, madrassas, and intellectual societies where it taught Arabic and gave instruction in the Quran to Algerians of all ages. These establishments lay beyond the direct scrutiny and control of the colonial authorities, thereby enabling the AUMA to promote its ideas and beliefs unimpeded. To help disseminate its message to an even broader audience, AUMA members helped found and contributed articles to a number of journals and newspapers such as *Al Shihab* (The Meteor), *Al Basair* (Visions of the Future), and *Al Sharia al Mutahhara* (The Purified Law of God). They also made good use of the pulpit to propagate their views and generate popular interest in their concerns and support for their demands.

The AUMA's contribution to the Algerian nationalist movement was both complex and mixed. On the one hand, the uncertainty of its relations with the Federation and colonial authorities dulled its message and blurred its position. The hesitancy with which it both supported and admonished the Federation and the French, combined with its reluctance to get directly involved in the political process, limited its popular appeal as it was not totally clear what the organization stood for or offered. Yet, despite these limitations, the AUMA also helped advance the nationalist movement in two distinct ways. First, regardless of the ambiguity that defined its relations with the Federation and France, the AUMA was unequivocal in its assertion that Algerians constituted a nation separate and distinct from the French. Second, through its emphasis of Islam and Arabic, the AUMA identified characteristics that defined the Algerian nation and distinguished Algerians from the French and pieds noirs. This definition was embraced by other nationalist groups, including the FLN and the country's postindependence political leaders.

The European settlers and their conservative allies had not been alone in their opposition to the Blum-Violette law. It had also been condemned, albeit for very different reasons, by an Algerian group called the North African Star (Étoile Nord-Africaine, ENA). In an address to a CMA rally on 2 August 1936, the ENA's secretary-general, Messali Hadj, rejected the charter of demand's call for the full administrative integration of Algeria with France and pledged that his organization would honor the Algerian people's "hope for national freedom."[16]

The Blum-Violette law and the desirability of Algeria's union with France were not the only issues to divide the ENA from the other nationalist organizations. The ENA was also set apart by the makeup of its core constituency, the ideological beliefs of its founders and leaders, and its political objectives. Unlike both the Federation and AUMA, the ENA was not based in Algeria but Paris. It was established there in the summer of 1926 by Messali and Hadj Ali Abd el-Kader, the group's first president,[17] to defend the "material, moral, political and social interests" of the 100,000 or so North Africans who lived in the city.[18] The ENA's membership was made up of North African émigrés working in industrial plants such as the Renault factory at Boulogne-Billancort just to the west of Paris. Not only did the ENA's supporters live in France, but they were members of the industrial proletariat, unlike those of the Federation, who were middle class, and those of the AUMA, who were mostly agricultural laborers.

The ENA quickly established itself as the dominant group within the North African community in France. Its left-wing doctrine, allied with its recognition of the unique challenges confronting North African workers, gave it an appeal that no other organization, either Algerian or French, could match. By 1928, the group had as many as four thousand members while its newspaper, *El Ouma*, reached a circulation of around forty-four thousand by 1934. The ENA also benefited from a close working relationship with the French Communist Party (Parti Communiste Français,PCF) and its affiliated union, the General Confederation of United Labour (Confédération Générale du Travail Unitaire, CGTU). The ENA was able to draw on these organizations' support as Messali had been a member of them both. Throughout the winter of 1926 and 1927 the PCF not only provided the ENA with funding and access to meeting rooms but gave it advice on how it could organize and structure itself and increase its membership.

In early 1927, however, this relationship began to turn sour. The ENA leadership suspected the PCF of trying to turn the ENA into a subsidiary organization, little more than a wing of the PCF. And some of the ENA's more recent members, who had joined because they had been attracted by the group's nationalist objectives, did not support or want to advance the PCF's agenda. In February 1927, Messali asserted the ENA's independence and individuality by outlining the group's aims and demands in a speech to the League Against Colonial Oppression (Ligue conte l'oppression colonial,

LCOC) in Brussels. In it, Messali called for Algerian independence; the withdrawal of all French troops from Algeria; the creation of an Algerian national army; the confiscation of the large farming estates and the nationalization of the forests; the abolition of the indigénat; an amnesty for all those imprisoned for breaking the indigénat; freedom of the press and association; the same political rights for Algerians and French alike; the replacement of the Délégations financières with a parliament elected by universal suffrage; the election of municipal assemblies also by universal suffrage; an increase in access to education and the creation of Arabic language schools; the application of French social laws; and an increase in credit access for peasant farmers.[19]

Although some of Messali's demands appeared contradictory, such as his call for Algerian independence and the extension of French social laws to Algeria, by emphasizing the ENA's nationalist agenda he drew a clear distinction between the ENA and the PCF, and the Federation and AUMA. As a result of its anticolonialist and nationalist stance, the ENA was outlawed by the French authorities in 1929. In 1933, the group was relaunched as the Glorious North African Star (Glorieuse Étoile Nord-Africaine, GENA). However, the French authorities were unconvinced that the GENA was sufficiently different from the ENA and it, too, was quickly banned and Messali imprisoned.[20]

Upon his release, Messali left France for Geneva. During his time there he came into contact with the prominent Arab nationalist thinker and writer Shakib Arslan. This encounter had a profound effect on Messali as he turned his back on communism and rejected many of his earlier beliefs and views and, instead, embraced revolutionary Arab nationalism wholeheartedly. This shift in thinking brought with it the final decisive break between Messali and the PCF. In 1937, taking advantage of the amnesty granted by the Blum government, Messali ended his self-imposed exile and returned to France where he quickly set up a new organization—the Party of the Algerian People (Parti du Peuple Algérien, PPA).[21]

Despite the changes that Messali's thinking had undergone, the PPA's agenda bore many similarities to that of the ENA. Like its predecessor, the PPA continued to offer a blend of nationalist and socialist principles. Given that the lowest echelons of Algerian society were overwhelmingly made up of non-Europeans, the two doctrines complemented each other. Land reform, for example, was simultaneously a class and a race issue. Their combination also helped give the PPA popular appeal. Unlike the Federation, which represented a narrow constituency made up of many of the most privileged parts of Muslim society, the PPA appealed to working class Algerians on both sides of the Mediterranean. And unlike the AUMA, its references to Islam did not form part of a broader intellectual debate on religion, but were intended to help mobilize the Muslim population and emphasize their distinction from the pieds noirs.

The PPA's objectives were first outlined in the "Declaration of the Political Bureau of the Party of the Algerian People," published in *El Ouma* in the spring of 1937. After charging itself with the task of "improving the moral and material well-being of Algerians," it declared assimilation to be a chimera and that it would work instead toward the "emancipation of Algeria."[22] Although the language used was less inflammatory than that adopted by the ENA, and even though promises were made to represent and fight on behalf of all Algerians regardless of race, religion, and class, its core message was still the same—that Algeria must gain independence from France and that Algerians constituted a nation distinct from the French.

Also like the ENA before it, the PPA's members were harassed and its meetings broken up by the police. In August 1937, Messali was arrested for a second time, in accordance with the Régnier decree, and sentenced to two years in prison. Upon his release in August 1939 he was arrested yet again. In March 1941, because of his continued refusal to cooperate with the colonial authorities, he was sentenced to sixteen years' hard labor. Yet, despite Messali's imprisonment, the PPA remained the most popular of the Algerian groups. It was also the best organized and most dynamic. Its robust structure and ability to mobilize its supporters resulted from Messali's putting into practice the lessons he had learned from the PCF and CGTU. The group's dynamism stemmed from the youth of many of its members and their desire for action. All these attributes were highlighted to the Algerian people, the colonial authorities, and the other nationalist groups when the PPA successfully organized a march of its three thousand members through the streets of Algiers on 14 July 1937. The organization was subsequently outlawed in 1938 and operated clandestinely until 1946.

The first four years of World War II were a bleak time for the nationalist movement and Algerian population as a whole. Confronted by the challenges of first defending and then liberating France, the government in Paris and its successors in Vichy and London refused to countenance making any changes to Algeria's relationship with France. Until the national emergency was over, the rival governments and authorities in Algiers considered any such demands not just inappropriate, given the circumstances, but unpatriotic and even treacherous. Those nationalist newspapers that did not voluntarily cease publication or exercise self-censorship were closed down. And all the while, Algerians suffered growing hardships. Algeria's economy, so heavily dependent on French markets, finance, and manufactured goods, was severely disrupted by Germany's occupation of France. The unemployment, inflation, and shortages that ensued were exacerbated by the failure of successive harvests and increased demand for Algerian wheat in metropolitan France.

It was not until US and British forces landed in the west of Algeria in November 1942 that the nationalists were again able to gain any interest in their cause. In a bid to exploit US support for liberation movements and its political, economic, and military influence over the French, Abbas, Ben Badis, and representatives from the PPA met in February 1943 to draft a joint declaration of demands. The following month they produced the Manifesto of the Algerian People, which they presented to Governor-General Marcel Peyrouton. At its core were a series of demands: for an end to colonial rule, the recognition of Arabic as an official language, freedom of press and association, universal education, an end to all discrimination, and the release of political prisoners.[23]

Peyrouton responded by establishing a committee to consider potential reforms to improve Muslim Algerians' socioeconomic well-being. However, he also ensured that most of the members of the committee supported Algeria's assimilation into France. Suspecting Peyrouton of trying to derail their agenda, the drafters of the manifesto attempted to force his hand by persuading the twenty-one non-European members of the Délégations financières to propose a supplement that was more belligerent in both tone and content than the original manifesto. One of the demands made in the supplement was that "at the end of the hostilities . . . an Algerian state [be created] equipped with its own constitution . . . developed by an Algerian parliament whose members are elected by universal suffrage of all Algeria's inhabitants."[24] By involving the Délégations financières' representatives and by making their demands more extreme, the drafters hoped to frighten the governor-general into accepting the manifesto. The plan proved to be a partial success.

On 5 June 1943, Peyrouton was replaced as governor-general by Georges Catroux. Appointed to the post by the French Committee of National Liberation (Comité français de libération nationale, CFLN),[25] Catroux convened a new manifesto committee. This time he ensured that its membership was more representative. While both he and de Gaulle were sympathetic to the socioeconomic plight of many ordinary Algerians, they refused to contemplate the issue of Algerian independence. In that regard, the drafters failed in their attempts to force the colonial authorities to accept their program. However, they did succeed in frightening de Gaulle and Catroux into trying to reclaim the initiative.

In a speech delivered at Constantine on 12 December 1943, de Gaulle outlined the findings of Catroux's manifesto committee. They consisted of a series of reforms aimed at giving Muslim Algerians more political and legal rights. Three months later, on 7 March 1944, de Gaulle implemented these recommendations. As a result, French citizenship was granted to around sixty thousand non-Europeans without requiring any change in their personal status; Muslims were given the right to apply for any rank or position within the armed forces and Algerian civil service, and the right to vote in elections for the second non-European college was extended to all Muslims

over the age of twenty-one; Muslim representation in the Délégations financières was increased to 40 percent; and the despised *code de l'indigénat* was
finally abolished, ending all legal discrimination against Muslims. By introducing this legislation through decree, de Gaulle succeeded where Blum,
Chautemps, and Daladier had failed.

But for Messali, Ibrahimi, Abbas, and their respective supporters, the
decree of 7 March was too little too late. Even though the reforms it implemented were the most sweeping for a generation and went further than
those outlined in the Blum-Violette law that Ben Badis and Abbas had supported, the trials and hardships endured by the Algerian people during
World War II meant that many in the nationalist movement considered the
decree too limited. Only the archassimilationist Mohamed Ben Djelloul
hailed it as a triumph.

On 14 March 1944, Abbas created a new political organization, the
Friends of the Manifesto and of Liberty (Amis du Manifeste et de la
Liberté, AML). Intended to act as a popular front by incorporating like-
minded individuals and groups, its aim was to "make familiar the idea of an
Algerian nation, and to make desirable the creation in Algeria of an independent republic federated to a revived French Republic."[26] By the autumn
of 1944, the AML had over 300,000 members and its newsletter, *Egalité*,
was circulated to around half a million subscribers. Its popularity stemmed
partly from the chord it struck with the frustrated and increasingly impoverished Algerian masses and partly from the endorsements it received from
the AUMA and Messali. Only Ben Djelloul decried the new group.

Yet not all the AML's members or readers of its newspaper supported
either the group's agenda or Abbas. By the winter of 1944, tensions were
emerging between those loyal to Abbas and those faithful to Messali and the
outlawed PPA. Over the next six months events were to leave both Abbas
and Messali struggling to retain their positions as the preeminent leaders of
the nationalist movement.

In the spring of 1945, social instability in Algeria grew. Food was in
short supply, manufactured and consumer goods were scarce, the economy
was in an appalling state, and unemployment was rife. Both AML factions
organized demonstrations and rallies throughout the country to protest the
intolerable and worsening situation. As they grappled with these disturbances, the colonial authorities increasingly believed that, despite his
imprisonment, Messali was fanning the flames of discontent. To stop him
from doing so, Governor-General Yves Chataigneau ordered that he be sent
to the French Congo.[27] Once news of Messali's deportation filtered out,
demonstrations were held throughout Algeria on 1 May with more planned
to coincide with the VE-Day celebrations of 8 May.

In the little towns of Sétif and Guelma in the Constantine region the
police tried to break up the demonstrations as members of the crowd were

waving replicas of Abd el-Kader's outlawed standard. Incensed by the actions of the police and the deaths of some of the demonstrators, nearly 45,000 Muslims gathered and attacked government buildings and the homes of European settlers. By sunset, around one hundred pieds noirs had been killed and a further one hundred injured, mutilated, raped, and abused by the Muslim crowd. The response of the authorities and settlers was swift and pitiless. Around ten thousand troops flooded into the area and, with the support of police and gendarmerie units and armed gangs of settlers, indiscriminately killed and arrested thousands of Muslims. Over the course of the next week between 1,500 and 50,000 non-Europeans were killed. By the onset of winter, a further 5,500 Muslims had been arrested, hundreds of whom were sentenced to death or life imprisonment. Many of those who were killed or arrested had played no part in either the initial demonstrations or the murders of the Europeans that followed.

As news of what had happened at Sétif and Guelma spread throughout Algeria, Europeans and non-Europeans alike were outraged—but for very different reasons. To the pieds noirs, Sétif was a vindication of their opposition to any increase in Muslims' political and legal rights and a warning of what would happen if the government continued along that path. To many Muslims, the severity and indiscriminate nature of the authorities' and pieds noirs' response brought into stark relief the unjustness of the existing sociopolitical system. Despite all the improvements de Gaulle's 7 March decree introduced, and the advancements that its implementation implied were still to come, genuine equality appeared to be a long way off.

Perhaps unsurprisingly, given its effect on Algerian society as a whole, Sétif had a profound impact on the nationalist movement. In the short term it resulted in Abbas's imprisonment and the disbandment of the AML. In the long term it led to the emergence of a small group of men committed to dismantling Algérie française by whatever means necessary. Despite opposition from the settlers, Governor-General Chataigneau attempted to placate the Muslim population by pushing through a series of political and economic reforms. New agencies and schemes were set up to help the rural poor by improving the quality of the land they farmed. The old communes mixtes were replaced with new *centres municipaux* (municipal centers), governed by elected Muslim councils. And, on 17 August 1945, the second non-European college was permitted to send the same number of representatives to the French National Assembly as the European college. Yet the larger question of Algeria's relationship with France remained unanswered and, as far as Abbas, Messali, and the other nationalists were concerned, unresolved.

In October 1945 elections were held for the first Constituent Assembly whose task it was to draft a constitution for the new Fourth Republic. Under the terms of the recently introduced reforms, Muslim Algerians were entitled to take part in the vote to decide its membership.

But both Abbas and Messali instructed their supporters not to participate. As a result the Muslim Algerian contingent of the newly elected Assembly was made up of assimilationists like Mohamed Ben Djelloul. They proposed merging the two Algerian colleges, but even this recommendation was rejected. For the elections for the second Constituent Assembly in June 1946, Abbas reversed his earlier position and participated with a new organization, the Democratic Union of the Algerian Manifesto (Union Démocratique du Manifeste Algérien, UDMA). Winning eleven of the thirteen seats available to Muslims, Abbas advocated creating an Algerian parliament, elected by universal suffrage, that would have authority over all areas of policy except foreign affairs and defense, which would continue to be determined by Paris. Perhaps unsurprisingly, given the failure of Ben Djelloul's far-less-radical proposal, Abbas's plan was rejected by the Assembly.

The Assemblies' unwillingness to adopt either Ben Djelloul's or Abbas's schemes not only damaged the reputations of those who represented the most moderate elements of the nationalist movement, it also left Algeria's status unclear. Accordingly, Abbas urged Muslim Algerians to abstain from voting in the referendum of 27 October 1946 to approve the constitution drawn up by the Constituent Assembly. Shortly before the vote took place, Messali was finally released from prison. Almost immediately he set about creating a new organization, the Movement for the Triumph of Democratic Liberties (Mouvement pour le triomphe des libertés démocratiques, MTLD), to contest the election to appoint the first National Assembly of the Fourth Republic. With an agenda similar to that of the still outlawed PPA, the MTLD won five of the fifteen seats in the non-European college.

One of the tasks confronting the new National Assembly was sorting out Algeria's constitutional status. Of the seven draft proposals that the Assembly considered, none advocated either assimilation or outright independence. That was because the groups that supported these positions, the pieds noirs deputies and MTLD, refused to submit any recommendations. The seven proposals that were examined all advocated increasing Algeria's political autonomy by varying degrees. The decision finally taken by the government on 20 September 1947 disappointed even moderate Muslim deputies.

Under the terms of this statute, Algeria was defined as a collection of *départements* with financial independence. The Assemblée financière, formerly the Délégations financières, was renamed the Assemblée algérienne and its powers increased slightly, although they still fell far short of what Abbas and the UDMA had campaigned for.[28] All laws passed by the new assembly had to be approved by the governor-general, while its proposed budgets required the authorization of both the minister of finance and the minister of the interior as well. And Paris retained authority over all policy relating to the legal system, customs, land use and distribution, elections, the Algerian civil service, and defense.

French control of the Algerian Assembly was augmented by the power of the pieds noirs within it. The statute dictated that the Assembly would have sixty members, thirty from each of the two colleges. And for a law to receive the Assembly's official backing and be passed to the governor-general for signing, it needed the support of two-thirds of all members. In this way, the Europeans could veto any legislation discussed by the Assembly that they did not approve. And while the Muslim members could do the same, they could not prevent the National Assembly in Paris from introducing laws that they opposed.

Through its instigation of these rules and procedures, the statute maintained the unequal political relationship between the European and Muslim communities. The European college was elected by pieds noirs and those Muslims with French citizenship only. In 1947, this amounted to around 500,000 people. The members of the non-European college, on the other hand, were chosen by all other Muslim voters, of whom there were about 1.5 million. For this reason alone, the statute was rejected and denounced by the UDMA, MTLD, AUMA, and many Muslim Algerians. It was also condemned by the settlers who thought that it gave far too much to the Muslims.

The promulgation of the statute dashed the hopes of many moderate nationalists. Although they had not been wholly satisfied with the reforms introduced by de Gaulle, Catroux, and Chataigneau, they felt that progress was being made albeit perhaps not quickly enough. Yet the statute ended even this hope as it ensured that the pieds noirs, despite their unhappiness, would retain their privileges and control of Algerian society at the expense of the Muslim masses. Certainly there were reasons to rejoice. The abolition of the code de l'indigénat represented one such highlight. But the overall power relations between Muslims and the pieds noirs, Algeria and France, remained the same. Moreover, it was difficult to retain any hope that they would soon be changed.

The despondency that gripped the nationalist movement added yet more impetus to the process that was already under way and that was leading to the emergence of a new type of anticolonialist, one who was prepared to use violence to liberate Algeria. In March 1950, the Algerian police successfully smashed a group called the Special Organization (Organisation Spécial, OS). Established as the paramilitary wing of the MTLD-PPA, it first came to light in the late 1940s after some of its members stole around 2.8 million French francs from the Oran post office. The money from this robbery was intended to help pay for the training and equipping of the one thousand fighters recruited by the OS leadership since the mid-1940s to wage war on the colonial authorities. While the OS never came close to fulfilling its goal of liberating Algeria from French rule, its emergence marked the start of a new phase in the development of the nationalist movement. Furthermore, the experience gained by the OS's leaders and members of building a clandestine organization dedicated to armed struggle proved to be useful. Indeed, three of those arrested—Ahmed Ben Bella, Mohamed Boudiaf, and Hocine Aït Ahmed—later helped found another organization, the National Liberation Front.

By the end of 1950, the MTLD-PPA-OS had become the preeminent nationalist organization. With around twenty thousand members made up mostly of young men of working and middle-class, urban and rural backgrounds, it dwarfed the UDMA. Yet, the MTLD's large size and the speed with which it grew came at a cost as the group was wracked by internal disagreements and divisions. In the immediate aftermath of the dissolution of the OS, rival factions struggled for power in a wave of tit-for-tat killings. One of the main sources of disunity was Messali himself, who tried to concentrate all authority in his own hands. The question of Messali's position within the organization came to a head in the summer of 1954. After being deported from Algeria to France in 1952, Messali held a congress in Belgium in July 1954 at which the assembled delegates awarded him the presidency of the MTLD for the rest of his life. Still in Algeria, the central committee, led by Ben Youssef Ben Khedda, organized its own congress in August 1954 and promptly expelled Messali from the party.

Disillusioned by this internecine bloodletting and frustrated at the inactivity it imposed on the MTLD, Ben Bella, Boudiaf, Aït Ahmed, and six other like-minded young men founded a new group in March 1954—the Revolutionary Committee for Unity and Action (Comité Révolutionnaire d'Unité et d'Action, CRUA).[29] Dedicated to the violent overthrow of Algérie française, they spent the summer of 1954 making preparations for an armed insurrection against the colonial state. Some of them focused on planning the campaign while others concentrated on promoting their cause abroad. Finally, after renaming themselves the National Liberation Front on 10 October, they set a date for the start of their rebellion—All Saints' Day 1954.[30]

The foundation of the FLN and its subsequent declaration of war represented a tragedy for France in more ways than one. Most obviously, it signaled the start of a conflict that was to last seven and a half years, cost tens of thousands of lives, lead to the loss of a vast territory, and drive France to the brink of civil war. But, in addition, it marked its final rejection by a group of men who should have been among its staunchest supporters. And perhaps no one person better epitomized this loss than Ben Bella himself.

A decorated war hero who twice volunteered to serve in the French army, he fought in the battle for France, for which he was awarded the Croix de Guerre. After being demobilized in 1940, he joined a regiment of Moroccan *tirailleurs* (riflemen) and fought with the Free French in the

Italian campaign, during which he was promoted to the rank of warrant officer and given the Médaille Militaire. Not only had he demonstrated his loyalty to France time and again on the battlefields of Europe but, as a veteran, he enjoyed more rights than most other Muslim Algerians. Yet neither they nor his past were enough to dissuade him from the course of action he now took.

Ben Bella was not the only one to have fought under the French army's colors. So, too, had Belkacem Krim, his trusted lieutenant Omar Ouamrane, and the wily Ramdane Abane. As well as bringing with them a wealth of experience that helped the insurrectionists plan and organize their rebellion and train the recruits who increasingly flocked to their cause, their personal opposition to France sent out a powerful message. If men such as these with their political privileges and extra rights, who had once fought for France and had been prepared to make the ultimate sacrifice on its behalf, had lost faith in Algérie française, then for how much longer could the union between the two peoples endure?

The War of Liberation

The insurrection began in the early hours of the morning of 1 November 1954. At Biskra, Batna, Blida, and over twenty other locations scattered throughout Algeria, small groups of poorly armed FLN fighters attacked an array of targets with mixed results.[31] The organization enjoyed its greatest successes in Kabylia where Belkacem Krim and his men cut telegraph wires and destroyed stores of tobacco. But elsewhere the outcome was less encouraging. In Algiers, all operations were called off as those charged with carrying them out panicked and refused to continue. In Biskra also, nerves got the better of the FLN agents. Their premature assault on the gendarmerie barracks led to the declaration of a state of alert throughout the area, forcing their comrades in nearby Batna to beat a hasty retreat before they had fulfilled their mission. But more serious than the failure of these individual raids to accomplish their immediate objectives was the failure of the insurrection as a whole to trigger a groundswell of support for the FLN among the Muslim population. Winning and maintaining the allegiance of the non-European masses remained one of the FLN's most pressing tasks throughout the war of liberation.

Despite the limited impact of these attacks, the reaction of the pieds noirs was predictably hysterical—it always was when Europeans were killed. The following day, the conseil-général for the département of Algiers voted unanimously that order must be restored quickly and firmly; that the guilty, once caught, be made an example of; that no weakness could be tolerated; and, that French policy must not pander to the insurgents and their sympathizers in any way.[32] A similar tone was adopted by the senator for Algiers, Henri Borgeaud, who demanded that "the evil must be pursued where it is to be found . . . [and] security measures must be reinforced."[33] To appease this clamor for action and dispel any lingering notions that the forces of law and order had been caught off guard, the authorities in Algeria and the government in Paris did what the pieds noirs demanded of them.

In a foretaste of what was to come, Paris spent the week following the attacks increasing troop levels in Algeria and rounding up suspects—both real and imagined. On 2 November three additional companies of soldiers were flown from France to Algeria to help with the search for the culprits.[34] During the course of the manhunt dozens of those involved in the raids were arrested. So too were numerous MTLD members, and the organization was outlawed on 7 November.[35] But it was not just the guilty who suffered; many innocent people were also imprisoned. These arbitrary arrests helped win the FLN more support and sympathy among the Muslim population than the actual raids themselves. Finally, on 12 November, the government gave voice to the policy it was pursuing. In a speech before the National Assembly, Premier Mendès-France declared that between the Algerian departments and "Metropolitan France there [could] be no conceivable secession," that neither his government nor any that followed would "yield on this fundamental principle."[36]

While Premier Mendès-France's combative speech gained him the temporary backing of the National Assembly and the pieds noirs, it won him few friends among the Muslim Algerians. His uncompromising stance, allied to the actions of his security forces, reinforced the view held by a growing number of Algerians that their country remained France's subservient satellite and that the authorities would go to any lengths to mollify the pampered settlers. But more significantly, he committed France to a path from which no government could easily stray, no prime minister could simply retreat. Less than two weeks after the FLN's initial raids, Mendès-France had committed France to a policy the pieds noirs would never allow to be abandoned and whose objectives stood in polar opposition to those of the FLN.

The FLN's position and aims were made clear in its first proclamation, broadcast by Egyptian state radio hours before the attacks began and reproduced in a pamphlet distributed throughout Algeria. In addition to restoring the Algerian state, the FLN promised to eliminate "the last vestiges of . . . [political] reformism," which it blamed for Algeria's current woes, to liquidate "the colonial system," and to internationalize "the Algerian problem."[37] From the outset, the FLN's core objective was to dismantle the French Algerian state. But it also identified a series of subsidiary aims, some of which were vital stepping-stones to achieving the liberation of Algeria and others that formed part of the FLN's broader political agenda.

Gaining the support of the international community was essential to the FLN's cause. Without it, the FLN would lack the necessary materials, finance, and diplomatic credibility to sustain its struggle. And without any external pressure being exerted on France, the challenge of forcing her to the negotiating table would be even more difficult. On the other hand, the FLN's aim of dominating the nationalist movement, of achieving preeminence over all other groups and organizations was not essential to the liberation of Algeria. But it was vital to the FLN's aims of becoming the primary partner with whom the French negotiated and of governing Algeria once independence had been won.

To achieve these objectives, the FLN waged separate yet interrelated campaigns against the security forces; the French and Muslim populations in both Algeria and France; the political leaders in Paris and Algiers; other nationalist groups; and the international community. It mounted these campaigns along multiple lines of operation—military, political, economic, cultural, and ideological. And it did so in order to convince everyone—the French, non-Europeans, and world alike—that the preservation of Algérie française would cost France far more than it was willing and able to pay in blood, treasure, economic development, and international reputation.

In the months immediately following the 1 November attacks, both sides struggled to formulate effective responses to the new security environment. The French army's efforts were undermined by its use of tactics and weapons that were inappropriate for both the terrain in which it had to operate and the type of conflict in which it was now embroiled. French commanders soon discovered that the columns of troops they sent to track down and apprehend the small bands of FLN fighters were too slow and unwieldy for the task. They also found out that they were unable to fully exploit their technological superiority and greater firepower as their tanks, artillery pieces, and other armored vehicles could not stray far from the roads and tracks. And they could prize little useful intelligence as to the whereabouts of FLN operatives out of the inhabitants of the villages their men passed through.

Despite the inadequacies of the initial French counterinsurgency efforts, the FLN still found itself put under real pressure by the security forces. In addition to the dozens of fighters who were arrested in the police roundups that followed the 1 November raids, other key personnel were either captured or killed by the recently deployed army units throughout the course of the winter. By early December two of the FLN's most senior figures, Belkacem Grine and Mohamed Sbaihi, had been shot and killed by French paratroopers, while a third, Ben Boulaid, the overall commander for the Aurès region, had been arrested. Many FLN fighters also died from hunger and cold as they were forced to retreat ever deeper into the inhospitable mountains of Algeria's remoter regions. And they could not always rely on the support of local villagers. Some welcomed the insurgents and gave them food and other supplies. But others did not out of loyalty to or fear of the local *caid*,[38] or concern that the starving FLN fighters might steal what little food they had. Such hostile villages either turned a cold shoulder to any FLN fighters who arrived or betrayed them to the French authorities.

By Christmas 1954, the FLN had been reduced to just 350 fighters.[39] With so few men and with the struggle to survive the number one priority, the FLN all but ceased operations. But the arrival of spring brought with it renewed hope and a steady flow of fresh volunteers. Whether motivated by the excesses of the security forces or a newfound respect for the FLN, these recruits remained impervious to the reforms being introduced by the new governor-general, Jacques Soustelle. With a greatly expanded budget, Soustelle set about removing some of the political inequalities that Muslims found most egregious and trying to improve the standards of living of the rural masses.

In particular, provisions were made to significantly increase the number of Muslim civil servants and promote more non-Europeans to positions of greater responsibility. The hated communes mixtes were finally abolished and replaced with a new type of commune in which authority lay with an elected council. The school building program was doubled in size, and Arabic language tuition was made compulsory in all Muslim schools. Around $150 million was set aside to fund new public works schemes and some limited agricultural reforms were implemented. But perhaps the most ambitious of the measures introduced by Soustelle was the creation of a new service dedicated to helping the peasant population and improving the links between them and the colonial authorities. This Special Administrative Section (Section Administrative Spécialisée, SAS) comprised around four hundred junior officers. Sent out into remote rural communities throughout Algeria, their responsibilities included everything from administering justice to planning and building irrigation systems.

During his first months in office, Soustelle had tried to steer a middle course between the extremists on both sides. This included resisting the pressure that was quickly brought to bear on him by the pieds noirs and their allies. His reluctance to unquestioningly side with them, combined with his socialist background and his reform package, won him the hostility of many in the settler community. But both Soustelle's views and his relations with the pieds noirs changed dramatically in August 1955.

Strengthened by the arrival of spring and a host of new recruits, the FLN was able to resume operations in early 1955. As spring turned into summer, the number of raids, ambushes, and assassinations carried out by its fighters and operatives steadily increased. Under pressure from the pieds noirs to stem the rising tide of attacks, Soustelle responded by sanctioning the policy of collective responsibility whereby whole communities were made to pay for the crimes committed by some of their members. But instead of weakening the FLN, this unjust measure boosted its recruitment further. And to strike back at Soustelle, the army, and the pieds noirs, the commanders of wilaya two,[40] Youssef Zighout and Lakhdar Ben Tobbal, planned an attack on the small town of Philippeville. On 20 August, FLN fighters supported by local inhabitants armed with knives and staves, descended on the settlement and made for those parts inhabited by Europeans. In a matter of hours, over one hundred of the townsfolk had been killed, many of them settlers.

This massacre made a deep and lasting impression on Soustelle and from that point on he sided unequivocally with the pieds noirs. So much so that when he left Algiers for Paris after being replaced as governor-general in January 1956, he was given a hero's departure by the settlers. Yet the tragedy of Philippeville did not end with the murder of its inhabitants and Soustelle's change in attitude. Like Sétif and Guelma before, the Philippeville massacre was followed by the most appalling reprisals, carried out by pieds noirs vigilantes in conjunction with the security forces. Thousands of Muslims, both guilty and innocent alike, were arrested or summarily executed. These deaths not only helped fortify the FLN's determination to pursue its cause, they also widened the breach between the European and Muslim populations and between the governing authorities and the non-European community. This was precisely what the FLN wanted.

Integral to the FLN's efforts to drive the French from Algeria was turning popular Muslim opinion against Algérie française. The FLN's military operations helped achieve this shift by demonstrating to Muslim Algerians its powers, fortitude, longevity, and willingness to strike blows against the French on their behalf. Such operations, even those that failed, helped inspire non-European Algerians and win the FLN the allegiance of some. Its military activities also resulted in retribution from the security forces and pieds noirs, the viciousness and excessiveness of which drove many Muslims into its arms. The indiscriminate and merciless nature of the reprisals that greeted many FLN attacks made a mockery of official efforts to eradicate discrimination against Muslim Algerians and improve their standards of living. It also reinforced the FLN's claims that only in a liberated Algeria would Muslims enjoy the political and civil rights and economic prosperity they deserved.

Yet the FLN was not supported by all non-European Algerians, even when its victory seemed assured. Tens of thousands of Muslims remained loyal to France. From the outset, the FLN was determined to gain the support of a majority of Muslim Algerians—by any means necessary. While it did inspire and win the devotion of many non-Europeans, it also terrorized and eliminated anyone who resisted and rejected it. Many of those assassinated and murdered by the FLN in the early years of the war were Muslim men and women who worked for, supported, or were sympathetic toward the French. In late November 1954, the French garrison at T'Kout awoke to find the body of a Muslim policeman, his throat cut and eyes gouged out, lying a short distance beyond the main gate to their barracks. On his chest was pinned a piece of paper with "FLN" scrawled on it. This unfortunate policeman was one of the first of thousands of Muslim Algerians to be killed by the FLN.

And not all of those who opposed French rule pledged their allegiances to the FLN. Throughout the war of liberation, several rival nationalist groups were established, each with its own members and followers. The ruthlessness with which the FLN subsumed rival organizations is evidenced by its treatment of the Algerian Communist Party (Parti Communiste Algérien, PCA) and Algerian Nationalist Movement (Mouvement Nationaliste Algérienne, MNA).[41] Despite its leadership's declarations of support, the FLN forced the PCA to dissolve itself on 1 July 1962. The FLN's treatment of the MNA, which, unlike the PCA, challenged its control of the nationalist movement, was far more brutal. On 29 May 1957 at the village of Mélouza, FLN fighters shot, hacked, and stabbed to death three hundred MNA-supporting villagers. The Mélouza massacre followed that of Guenzet where the FLN, led by the wilaya three commander Ait Hamouda Amirouche, attacked and killed nearly five hundred MNA fighters.

Since the start of the war, most of the fighting had taken place in the countryside surrounding the towns and cities and in the vast, rugged hinterland. As a consequence, the main brunt of it had been borne by the rural population. Overwhelmingly Muslim, this populace found itself caught between the FLN, the security forces, and various other nationalist guerrilla groups. During the course of the war, hundreds of thousands of peasants were killed in the attacks and reprisals carried out by the different sides. Around 300,000 more were imprisoned in the internment camps built by the French army from the summer of 1955 onward. And of those who remained, many were forcibly relocated by the security forces.

In 1956, as part of its efforts to separate the FLN insurgents from the rest of the population, the army initiated a policy of *regroupement*. This involved resettling the residents of villages in areas in which the FLN was known to be active in *centres de regroupement*, newly constructed settlements located in regions pacified and controlled by the army. These centers usually lacked even the most basic facilities and were often situated a long way from the land worked by those who were made to move. This made it difficult for them to continue working the land on which they and their families depended.

The policy of regroupement complimented that of *quadrillage*. This entailed dividing the country into a series of small military districts, each of which could then be systematically combed by the army. In the border areas, rather than resettle the villagers and nomadic herders they came across, the army simply drove them into neighboring Morocco and Tunisia. Their expulsion made space for two electrified fences, one running the length of the Algerian-Moroccan border and one the Algerian-Tunisian border. When these barriers became fully operational in September 1957, they altered the nature of the conflict. Instead of taking place in the interior, the bulk of the fighting shifted to the borders as ALN troops in Tunisia and Morocco tried desperately to get into Algeria.

In September 1956, the FLN opened a new front against the French in the city of Algiers. This time, the main targets of FLN operations were not soldiers, gendarmes, policemen, or pro-French Muslims, but pieds noirs civilians. This move, which was decided on at the Soummam[42] conference, was intended to make the settlers suffer and endure some of the hardships that had been inflicted on the Muslim population in the countryside. Moreover, the FLN's leaders realized that the assassination of European civilians would generate far greater awareness of their cause in metropolitan France, Europe, and North America than would the deaths of yet more French troops and Algerian Muslims.

One of the earliest actions of, what became known as, the Battle of Algiers was a string of bomb attacks. In the evening of 30 September, two explosions ripped through the Milk Bar and the Cafétéria, killing three people and injuring another forty. Most of the victims were young Europeans. These blasts were followed by other bomb and gun attacks. Policemen were shot dead from behind and even the mayor of Boufarik, Amédée Froger, was gunned down. Shortly before the funeral procession escorting his body arrived at the cemetery where he was to be buried, another FLN bomb exploded. On learning this, the already emotional pieds noirs crowd went wild. Young European men attacked Muslims in the streets. By the end of the battle, such *ratonnades* (rat hunts), as they were called, had become an established part of life in Algiers. This polarization of the European and non-European populations was precisely what Abane, M'hidi, and Yacef wanted to achieve.

With the police unable to stem the rising tide of FLN attacks, the resident minister, Robert Lacoste,[43] gave responsibility for restoring law and order to General Jacques Massu and his paratroopers. Over the course of the next year, Massu used a range of measures to break the FLN network in Algiers. Key to his success was intelligence—its acquisition and speedy exploitation. One of the most important sources of intelligence was that sweated out of suspects. Massu's interrogators frequently used torture to extract information from prisoners. It was then acted upon immediately to maximize the chances of seizing those who had been implicated. Massu also gained intelligence from the network of Muslim agents recruited by Captain Christian Léger and his commanding officer, Colonel Yves Godard, as well as the neighborhood wardens who were managed by Colonel Roger Trinquier as part of the Urban Protection System (Dispositif de Protection Urbaine, DPU).

While the methods adopted by Massu and his subordinates were highly controversial, they were also effective. One by one the various terror cells were liquidated, and Massu inched ever higher up the chain of command toward those at the top. Finally, on 24 September 1957, Yacef was captured. Two weeks later, on 8 October, his most notorious lieutenant, Ali la Pointe, was cornered at 5 Rue des Abderames in the casbah. After he refused to surrender, Massu's men blew up the house and its occupants. Ali la Pointe's and Yacef's elimination marked the end of the Battle of Algiers.

The battle formed part of the FLN's broader campaign to focus international attention on Algeria. This campaign had begun before the first shots of the war of liberation had even been fired. Until his capture in October 1956,[44] Ben Bella had hurried from one country to another throughout Asia and Eastern Europe asking for money and arms. But not all of the externals' efforts were focused on getting weapons and funding for the armed struggle. They also undertook diplomatic missions to try to persuade foreign governments to support them against the French.

One of the FLN's greatest triumphs was gaining an invitation to the Bandung Conference in April 1955. The conference was attended by delegates from twenty-nine African and Asian countries. The FLN was represented by Ben Bella and Muhammed Yazid, who attended as unofficial observers. That did not prevent them from petitioning the official delegates, most of whom promised financial assistance. The conference also passed unanimously a motion proposed by the Egyptians demanding an end to France's occupation of Algeria. But perhaps most valuable of all were the pledges of diplomatic support Ben Bella and Yazid gained. This support was vital to the achievement of one of the FLN's main diplomatic objectives— stimulating debate on the Algerian war in the United Nations (UN).

On 28 January 1957, while the Battle of Algiers was still raging, the FLN organized an eight-day general strike of all Muslim workers to coincide with the opening of the UN session in New York. It was intended "to bestow an incontestable authority upon . . . [the FLN] delegates at the United Nations in order to convince those rare diplomats still hesitant or possessing illusions about France's liberal policy."[45] Although the strike was eventually broken by Massu's paratroopers, it did contribute to the FLN's longer-term aim of having the Algerian question placed on the General Assembly's agenda for debate. On 20 September 1957, the FLN's representative at the UN, Muhammed Yazid, finally achieved this. And even though this discussion did not lead to any resolutions or declarations of official UN support, for the FLN it was another important step along the path of internationalizing the Algerian conflict and of forcing France to acknowledge that it was not solely a domestic issue.

Eventually, Yazid's patient and skillful diplomacy bore fruit. With the support of the governments of the newly independent African and Asian countries and the nonaligned movement, he succeeded in having the Algerian question placed on the agenda once again in December 1960. This time, France failed to stymie the debate and, after its delegates walked out, a motion was passed recognizing Algeria's right to self-determination.

The FLN's efforts to win international support were helped by the mistakes made by the French government. In November 1956 British and French troops landed in Egypt as part of a joint operation with the Israelis to seize control of the Suez Canal. Despite gaining control of the area surrounding the canal, Britain and France were forced to withdraw after the invasion was roundly condemned by the United States and other foreign governments. France was denounced again by the international community after its bombers leveled the Tunisian village of Sakiet Sidi Youssef in February 1958. In stark contrast to the successes enjoyed by the FLN, France only managed to alienate its allies and tarnish its international reputation.

Yet despite these setbacks, France made some progress in improving its standing among the Algerian people over the summer of 1958. The catalyst for this upturn was de Gaulle's return as prime minister on 1 June 1958.[46] Four months after he had taken office, on 3 October, he outlined a range of sweeping economic reforms in a speech at Constantine. As part of his Constantine Plan, de Gaulle pledged to create around 400,000 new jobs, build 200,000 new homes, distribute 250,000 hectares of land to Muslim peasant farmers, raise Muslim wages to the same level as those in metropolitan France, and ensure that two-thirds of non-European children attended primary school.[47]

The popularity of the plan and the high esteem in which many Muslims held de Gaulle alarmed the FLN, which feared it was losing its grip on the masses. To prevent any further loss of influence, its leaders decided to step up their armed campaign and redouble their diplomatic efforts. In so doing, they hoped to impress the people sufficiently to win back any support that may have been lost. So in December 1958, Ben Khedda led a diplomatic mission to China, where he extracted promises of weapons and other military support from his hosts. And in so doing, he killed two birds with one stone by securing the arms the FLN needed for its military campaign and international support of its cause.

At the end of his speech in Constantine, de Gaulle appealed directly to the FLN's recently created Provisional Government of the Algerian Revolution (Gouvernment Provisoire de la République Algérienne, GPRA).[48] In return for agreeing to a cease-fire, he offered a "peace of the brave." The GPRA did not reject de Gaulle's offer of a cease-fire immediately but ensured that negotiations would never take place. On 28 September 1958, it announced that it was prepared to enter into talks with the French government but only if it was represented by Ben Bella and the other external leaders seized by the French in 1956. Their selection was totally unacceptable to the Élysée Palace. It was to take two more years of fighting before representatives of the FLN and French government met around the negotiating table.

The plan was also greeted with skepticism and outright hostility by many senior army officers and the pieds noirs, largely because of the significant progress the security forces were making in their struggle against the insurgents. At the same time that Massu's paratroopers were defeating Yacef's bombers in Algiers, the army was inflicting a series of heavy defeats on the FLN's forces of the interior. These units found it increasingly difficult to recover from the casualties they suffered and equipment they lost as the sealing of the borders and policy of *regroupement* severely reduced their access to fresh supplies and new recruits.

The scale of these victories increased during the first half of 1959 with the introduction of the Challe Plan. Devised by General Maurice Challe, who was appointed commander in chief of the French forces in Algeria on 12 December 1958, the plan set out to take the fight to the ALN. The main strength of the quadrillage system was its limitation of the ALN's freedom of movement. However, it relied on the army having a presence throughout the country. As a consequence, the army's resources and manpower were constantly spread very thinly. This made it virtually impossible for it to build up the troop concentrations it needed to launch counteroffensives. And such counteroffensives were further hampered by the lack of uniformity in how the French units in each of the seventy-five military districts conducted operations. No common tactical procedures existed, meaning that when larger operations were carried out involving units from various districts, days of preparations were required to ensure that they understood one another. By the time their preparations were complete, the initiative had often been lost.

To overcome these difficulties, the Challe Plan created a new rapid deployment force called the Commandos de Chasse to track and engage ALN units and a general reserve to provide overwhelming force against these units once they had been pinned down. Rather than simply contain the ALN, as had happened under the quadrillage system, the French army was placed on the offensive; it was reorganized so that it could actively seek out and destroy the enemy. In addition to establishing the Commandos and general reserve, the Challe Plan also called for the number of *harkis*—Muslim Algerian soldiers serving in the French armed forces—to be increased from 25,000 to 60,000. These local troops were intended to lead the searches for ALN units.

On 22 July 1959, Challe's offensive against the insurgents reached its apogee with the conclusion of Operation Binoculars. This final act was the crowning glory of a campaign that had decimated the FLN's forces within Algeria. Virtually all of its companies had been smashed and their members either killed or forced to operate in much smaller units. Those fighters who remained at liberty were in a poor state, lacking food, ammunition, sufficient weapons, and other vital supplies.

The overall success of Operation Binoculars and the Challe offensive made de Gaulle's offer of Algerian self-determination all the more unpalatable to the army and the pieds noirs. In a radio address to the French nation broadcast on 16 September 1959, de Gaulle outlined three different paths along which Franco-Algerian relations could proceed. The first was outright secession for Algeria, an option that de Gaulle condemned as "incredible and disastrous." The second was integration, the complete union of the two countries and the accordance of the same political, civil, and human rights to all regardless of race, culture, or religion. The final option was association with the possibility of self-determination. Under this alternative, if the Algerian people chose it, Algeria would have its own government that would work closely with Paris militarily, politically, and economically.

To both the army and the pieds noirs, de Gaulle's offer of self-determination was tantamount to capitulation to the FLN and a betrayal of those Algerians, European and non-European alike, who remained loyal to Algérie française. Challe expressed what many in the army felt when he complained to Prime Minister Michel Debré[49] that, "one does not propose to soldiers to go and get killed for an imprecise final objective."[50] The pieds noirs were similarly hostile. To them, self-determination would turn them into a politically and culturally marginalized minority, stripped of all the privileges they currently enjoyed.

Goaded by the GPRA's declaration that the promise of self-determination was a step in the right direction, and appalled by de Gaulle's sacking of Massu, the savior of Algiers, after he criticized the government's proposal, the pieds noirs ultras tried to force de Gaulle from office. On 24 January 1960, European youths and members of the shadowy French National Front (Front National Français, FNF) threw up barricades across Algiers' main streets, cutting off the city center. When a unit of the loathed Republican Security force (Compagnies Républicaines de Sécurité, CRS) attempted to drive its way through and disperse the demonstrators, they were fired on. For five days the ultras manned the barricades as an uneasy stillness descended on the city. Unlike the CRS, the troops sent onto the streets were generally welcomed by the demonstrators—so long as they did not try to disperse them.

But there were two crucial factors working against the pieds noirs. The first was de Gaulle himself. He delivered a speech that gave heart to his supporters and asserted his authority over those who opposed him.[51] The disgruntled pieds noirs had no contender who could seriously challenge him. The second factor was the huge support de Gaulle enjoyed in metropolitan France. This split between Frenchmen of the northern and southern shores of the Mediterranean had been confirmed shortly after de Gaulle's self-determination declaration. Unlike their compatriots on the other side of the water, the metropolitan French gave de Gaulle their wholehearted support. And this included the political echelons as, on 16 October 1959, he won a vote of confidence in the Assembly with a huge majority. For the pieds noirs, Barricades Week, as it became known, ended in bitter disappointment.

Over the months that followed, all sides fumbled to formulate a coherent strategy. The ultra leaders contemplated how best to confront the twin threats of the FLN and de Gaulle. The army, while still loyal to de Gaulle, remained suspicious and uncertain as to what his true intentions were. And the GPRA struggled to formulate an adequate response to de Gaulle's self-determination offer of the previous September. Under continued pressure from the French army, weary of the war that had entered its sixth year, and tempted by de Gaulle's proposal, the more moderate elements in the CNRA and GPRA favored making a positive response. But the hardliners resisted and refused to countenance anything less than Algeria's immediate and complete independence from France. Not for the last time, they ensured that the GPRA rejected de Gaulle's overtures.

The dilemmas facing the various camps were kept alive when, on 14 June 1960, de Gaulle made a televised address. As with his speech in Constantine, it ended with a direct appeal to the GPRA to help him find an "honorable" resolution to the conflict. The army was once again angered by this fresh approach to an organization over which it had gained the upper hand on the battlefield. As were the pieds noirs, to whom this latest address provided more evidence of de Gaulle's untrustworthiness and determination to sell them out. And yet again the GPRA was forced into deciding how it should react. Unlike before, however, its response was both swift and positive.

Between 25 and 29 June 1960, representatives of both the French government and GPRA met at Melun. The outcome was a resounding defeat for de Gaulle. In addition to being fruitless, these discussions bestowed political legitimacy on the FLN. Just as the French fratricidal wrangling of Barricades Week had done, the Melun negotiations helped the FLN win the support of many Muslims who remained undecided. Melun seemed to confirm that the FLN was the true representative of the Algerian people; that it was the favored negotiating partner of the French government; and that it was succeeding in its struggle as it had forced France to respect and acknowledge its demands. The swiftness of the GPRA's response was also a masterstroke as it made de Gaulle choose between Si Salah and the GPRA.[52] De Gaulle abandoned one set of negotiations, which had the potential to cripple the FLN, in favor of another from which he gained nothing.

The occurrence and failure of the summit at Melun was to have another significant consequence—it helped heighten the resentment that a significant number of French officers felt toward de Gaulle. In April 1961, this bitterness finally boiled over. Between 20 and 26 April, a military junta led by Challe seized power in Algiers in a bid to ensure that Algeria remained French.[53] From the outset though, the putsch struggled to gain the support it needed among the armed forces in Algeria. Although some units did side with Challe, most notably the 1st Foreign Legion Parachute Regiment (Régiment Étranger Parachutistes, REP) and the 14th and 18th Parachute Regiments (Régiment de Chasseurs Parachutistes, RCP), most did not. The damage this inflicted on the putsch was exacerbated by the basic errors made by the rebels and the uncertainty of their aims.

The putsch finally collapsed shortly after de Gaulle instructed the French public "to block the road everywhere" to the rebels, and forbade "every soldier" from executing any of their orders.[54] Ironically, and as Bernard Tricot noted, the failed putsch "made even more inevitable the result which it had wanted to prevent, at the same time reducing the chances of attaining it under acceptable conditions."[55] The deep divisions between the government and the army, the metropolitan French and the pieds noirs, and within the army itself, combined with the purges of the officer corps that were now required, greatly weakened de Gaulle's negotiating position. Confronted by the specter of civil war and unable to wholly rely on or trust the loyalty of the army, de Gaulle had little option but to abandon his hope of achieving his favored settlement of Algeria's association with France. The FLN entered the next round of negotiations in a position of notable strength.

Notes

1. These comments were made by the journalist Mary Motely. Cited in Alistair Horne, *A Savage War of Peace*, rev. ed. (New York: New York Review of Books, 2006), p. 36.

2. Front de Libération Nationale, *Appel au peuple algérien* (1954).

3. Cited in Claude Collot and Jean-Robert Henry, *Le mouvement national algerien: Texts 1912–1954* (Paris: L'Harmattan, 1978), p. 24.

4. The Délégations financières was created through a series of presidential decrees between 1898 and 1900. It had sixty-nine members—forty-eight Europeans elected by the pieds noirs community and twenty-one Muslims elected by the country's Muslim constituency.

5. The code de l'indigénat, often referred to simply as the "indigénat," was a series of thirty-three laws that applied to all Muslim Algerians who were not French citizens. These laws were introduced between 1834 and the 1889.

6. Cited in Collot and Henry, *Le mouvement national algerien*, p. 41. By the early twentieth century, the communes mixtes system was despised by Algerian nationalists of all hues as it placed a tiny number of unelected European administra-

tors in charge of tens of thousands of Muslims. These units of government were established in those parts of the country where Muslims were numerically dominant (except the Sahara, which remained under military rule). Each commune was governed by an unelected European administrator.

7. In an article published in 1936, Abbas declared: "had I discovered the Algerian nation, I would be a nationalist . . . However, I will not die for the Algerian nation, because it does not exist." Cited in John Entelis, *Algeria: The Revolution Institutionalized* (London and Sydney: Croom Helm, 1986), p. 38.

8. Cited in Collot and Henry, *Le mouvement*, pp. 72 and 73.

9. There were four Popular Front premiers between 1936 and 1938—Blum (4 June 1936–22 June 1937); Camille Chautemps (22 June 1937–13 March 1938); Blum (13 March 1938–10 April 1938); and Édouard Daladier (10 April 1938–21 March 1940).

10. Cited in Charles-Robert Ageron, *Modern Algeria* (Trenton, N.J.: Africa World Press, 1991), p. 95.

11. Cited in Entelis, *Algeria: The Revolution Institutionalized*, p. 44 and Ageron, *Modern Algeria*, p. 95.

12. Cited in Collot and Henry, *Le mouvement*, p. 45.

13. Ibid., p. 44.

14. The term *salaf* translates as "ancestor."

15. Cited in Collot and Henry, *Le mouvement*, p. 45.

16. Ibid., pp. 83 and 84.

17. Messali became president in 1927.

18. Cited in Collot and Henry, *Le mouvement*, p. 39.

19. Ibid., p. 39.

20. The ENA was dissolved by presidential decree on 26 January 1937.

21. The PPA was established on 11 March 1937.

22. Cited in Collot and Henry, *Le mouvement*, pp. 91 and 92.

23. Ibid., pp. 163 and 164.

24. Ibid., p. 168.

25. The CFLN took charge of Algeria on 2 June 1943. It was presided over by Generals Charles de Gaulle and Henri Giraud. De Gaulle became the sole leader on 9 November 1943.

26. Cited in Collot and Henry, *Le mouvement*, p. 186.

27. Chataigneau replaced Catroux as governor-general on 8 September 1944 and served until 11 February 1948. Messali was deported to the French Congo on 25 April 1945.

28. The Assemblée financière had replaced the Délégations financièrs in September 1945.

29. The other six founders of the CRUA were Mohamed Khider, Rabah Bitat, Belkacem Krim, Larbi Ben M'Hidi, Mourad Didouche, and Mostefa Ben Boulaid. Along with Ben Bella, Boudiaf, and Aït Ahmed, they became known as the Nine Historics.

30. The CRUA continued to function as the FLN's governing executive.

31. The FLN's armed force consisted of the fighters of the various wilayas and the troops of the Armée de Libération Nationale (ALN) who were based in Morocco and Tunisia.

32. Cited in Horne, *A Savage War*, p. 97.

33. Ibid., p. 97.

34. *The Times*, "Violence Spreads to Algeria," 1 November 1954, Issue 53078, p. 4, col. C.

35. *The Times*, "Algeria Party Dissolved," 7 November 1954, Issue 53083, p. 6, col. A.

36. Cited in Horne, *A Savage War*, p. 98.

37. FLN, *Appel au people algérien*.

38. Caids were local Muslim governors, appointed by the region's European administrator.

39. Horne, *A Savage War*, p. 103.

40. The FLN divided Algeria into six wilayas or military districts.

41. The MNA was founded by Messali in November 1954.

42. Held in August 1956 in the Soummam Valley in the Kabylia region of Algeria, the conference was a summit meeting of FLN leaders. From it emerged the Soummmam Platform, which set out, among other things, how the FLN and ALN were to be organized and the war against the French prosecuted. The main organizer of the conference was Ramdane Abane. Abane was part of the CRUA and became one of the members of the five man Coordination and Execution Committee (Comité de Coordination et d'Exécution, CCE) that was established at the conference. The CCE was the executive of the National Council of the Algerian Revolution (Conseil National de la Révolution Algérienne, CNRA), which acted as a shadow parliament with thirty four elected delegates. Together, the CCE and CNRA replaced the CRUA.

43. The post of resident minister was created on 2 February 1956 and replaced that of governor-general. Lacoste was the first person to be appointed to the position. He replaced Georges Catroux, who had replaced Soustelle in January 1956.

44. Ben Bella was captured along with Boudiaf, Khider, Aït Ahmed, Bitat, and Mostefa Lacheraf on 22 October 1956, when their flight from Morocco to Tunisia was intercepted by French security forces.

45. Cited in Horne, *A Savage War*, p. 190.

46. On 13 May 1958, Algiers was paralyzed by a new pieds noirs demonstration. In place of Resident-Minister Robert Lacoste, who had returned to France in late April, a Committee of Public Safety was formed under the leadership of Raoul Salan, the Commander-in-Chief of the French armed forces in Algeria. After two weeks of frantic negotiations in Paris, President René Coty invited de Gaulle to form a government on 29 May.

47. Ageron, *Modern Algeria*, pp. 118–19.

48. The GPRA was established on 19 September 1958.

49. Debré was premier from 8 January 1959 to 14 April 1962.

50. Cited in Horne, *A Savage War,* p. 347.

51. De Gaulle's speech to the nation on 29 January 1960 brought the protests to an end.

52. In June 1960, de Gaulle met secretly with Si Salah and his two lieutenants, Si Mohamed and Si Lakhdar, to discuss the possibility of a ceasefire between France and wilaya four (the wilaya Si Salah commanded). Given that these negotiations, known collectively by the French as Operation Tilsit, had got so far as to see Si Salah visit the Élysée Palace, there seemed every reason to hope that they might succeed.

53. Challe had been replaced as commander in chief of the French forces in Algeria on 23 April 1960 by General Crépin.

54. Cited in Horne, *A Savage War,* p. 453.

55. Ibid., p. 462.

4

Independence and the Challenges of Nation Building

ON 20 MAY 1961 IN the little French town of Évian close to the Swiss border, negotiations began between the French government and the FLN over ending the war in Algeria. The main purpose of these talks was to arrange a cease-fire and set out the process for transferring power to an Algerian government. At times the negotiations came perilously close to collapse as one or other set of delegates refused to back down over a particular issue. Yet after ten months of intermittent discussion an agreement was finally reached. And on 18 March 1962, representatives from both sides signed what quickly became known as the Évian Agreements.[1] At noon the following day a general cease-fire was declared, bringing to an end the seven-and-a-half-year war between France and the FLN.

Although the agreements initially led to an upsurge in violence, they represented a remarkable triumph for the FLN. Against seemingly insurmountable odds, it had outthought, outfought, and outmaneuvered a great power to lead Algeria to the promised land of independence. And during the course of the negotiations at Évian and Lugrin, its delegates systematically forced their French counterparts to make other major concessions.[2] Time and again the FLN got its way on such issues as sovereignty over the Sahara, the pieds noirs' right to dual nationality, and the length of time France could lease the Mers-el-Kébir naval base and other military installations. While Krim was accused by some of his colleagues of conceding too much, he and his team achieved a highly favorable settlement.

The FLN's ability to do so was due in no small measure to the strength of their negotiating position. By the time the talks started, it had total control of the nationalist movement, international support for its cause, the backing of most Muslim men and women, and an army of some 20,000 to 30,000 troops. Yet despite these appearances, all was not as it seemed. Without doubt the FLN was in a stronger position than the French government; the General's Putsch had helped see to that. But it still needed the war to end quickly, if for no other reason than to relieve the massive internal pressures that were threatening to blow it apart.

This explosive situation was the result of the toxic relations that had come to exist between key members of the FLN's leadership. Aït Ahmed hated Ben Bella, Ben Bella hated Krim, Krim hated Boumedienne, and Boumedienne hated Ben Khedda. In truth, such rivalries had always existed and were to be expected given the strength of the personalities involved, what it was these individuals were trying to achieve, and the circumstances in which they were operating. But over the course of the war, what had often started out as mild dislike steadily had given way to fear and absolute loathing.

Yet remarkably, all this was kept hidden from the outside world as those involved agreed, for the sake of the greater good, to preserve the appearance of unity. For year after long year, the FLN's leaders successfully maintained the illusion. But with the signing of the Évian Agreements, their need to do so suddenly vanished. The rapid breakdown in relations this ushered in was made all the more complete by the competition for power and influence in the new state that quickly arose. And the closer the country edged toward independence the more intense and acrimonious this struggle became. So much so that within days of its declaration on 3 July 1962, fighting had broken out between rival factions.

The internecine violence that marked the country's birth as a sovereign state has remained a tragic constant until the present day. Indeed, since independence every president has had to ward off an armed challenge to his authority. To counteract these threats and the broader sociopolitical instability that has given rise to them, each man has tried to create and fortify the internal connections between himself and the general population, to strengthen the bonds that bind him to the people. And each has sought to do so through a process of nation building. It is this process—what it is and what it entails—that is the primary focus of this chapter. After charting the nature and extent of the violence that confronted Algeria's first three presidents, it considers how they each defined the nation; the reasons for their incorporation of Islam, Arabism, and socialism; and how they attempted to ensure their definitions achieved hegemony.

A House Divided Against Itself

In Algeria, independence was greeted with unrestrained joy as ordinary people celebrated both their freedom from colonial rule and the end of the war that had claimed so many lives. But their jubilation was short lived. As the summer wore on, the nationalist slogans chanted by the crowds that

thronged the streets of Algiers gave way to a single, heartfelt declaration—
Baraka saba'a sanin, seven years is enough. The cause of their anguish was
the continued fighting between armed groups in and around the capital as
various factions attempted to seize control of the newly independent state.
Largely as a result of these clashes, which lasted throughout July and
August 1962, around fifteen thousand people lost their lives.

The roots of this new conflict lay in the deep cracks that riddled the
FLN leadership. Unlike other anticolonial and nationalist organizations,
such as the Neo-Destour Party in neighboring Tunisia, the FLN was not
founded by one person but nine. As a result, it was subject—at least in the
beginning—to the authority of them all. And while the influence and standing of the original Historics waxed and waned during the course of the war,
the principle of leadership by committee they helped establish endured.
Undoubtedly, this saved the FLN and its war effort from the whims and
excesses of any one person. Yet it also encouraged competition between the
members of the various committees—the CRUA, CNRA, CCE, and
GPRA—that governed it, as they each looked to preserve and enhance their
influence.

This competition was itself fueled by the geographical separation of the
group's leaders. Operating clandestinely throughout Algeria and various
foreign lands, many of them lived and worked in near perfect isolation from
one another. The freedom of action this allowed—notwithstanding the limits imposed by the French security forces—encouraged them to build personal fiefdoms and accuse each other of not doing enough to further the war
effort. And the divisive effect of these power bases was often magnified by
their ethnic composition as individuals looked to their own kin for help and
support. In so doing, and by promising to champion their ethnic groups'
interests, these notables further weakened the unity of both the FLN and the
country as a whole.

In the weeks and months between the declarations of cease-fire and
independence, the various internal and hitherto largely unseen forces tearing
at the FLN were gradually released. This process was hastened along by
events at the CNRA congress held in Tripoli in late May and early June
1962. The main purpose of this gathering was to give the FLN's leaders the
chance to hammer out a political and economic strategy for Algeria once it
became independent. Yet from the moment it opened, the congress descended into bitter wrangling and acrimony as the assembled delegates took the
opportunity to pick sides and harangue their opponents. And even though
they eventually succeeded in drafting the so-called Tripoli Program, it only
fanned the flames of disagreement because of its strident criticism of the
GPRA and wilaya commanders.[3]

During the course of the congress, one contest had begun to take center stage—that between Ben Khedda (the leader of the GPRA) and Ben Bella (the architect of the Tripoli Program). At stake was the right to shape Algeria's political future. For the time being, and in accordance with the Évian Agreements, the country was under the nominal authority of the Provisional Executive.[4] But its mandate to govern scarcely extended beyond organizing the referendum to ask Algerians whether they wanted independence or not.[5] So the question as to who would finalize the country's postindependence political order—its institutions and practices— remained open. Ben Khedda argued that the authority to decide these matters rested with the GPRA as it, after all, was the provisional government. But Ben Bella disagreed and called for the creation of a new body, a Political Bureau to take charge of the process. Whoever prevailed would be in the best position to become Algeria's first head of state once it finally became independent.

In the face of Ben Bella's accusations of incompetence and megalomania, Ben Khedda left Tripoli early and headed for Tunis. In his absence, Ben Bella took the opportunity to push through his version of the Tripoli Program and to announce the names of those who would sit on the Political Bureau. Along with himself, they included Hocine Aït Ahmed, Rabah Bitat, Mohamed Boudiaf, and Mohamed Khider (Ben Bella's fellow prisoners from Château d'Aulnoy), and colonels Hadj Ben Alla and Mohamedi Saïd of the ALN.[6] There was seemingly no room for either Ben Khedda or any other member of the GPRA.

Unsurprisingly, Ben Khedda dismissed the idea of a Political Bureau out of hand and immediately set about trying to undermine Ben Bella's position. It was at this point that he made his most serious mistake. Over the previous few weeks it had become apparent that Ben Bella enjoyed the support of Colonel Houari Boumedienne who, as the military's most senior officer, brought with him the armed might of the National Popular Army (Armée Nationale Populaire, ANP).[7] But rather than attempt to persuade Boumedienne to shift his allegiance to the GPRA or simply remain neutral, on 31 May 1962 Ben Khedda tried to dismiss him and majors Ali Mendjli and Ahmed Kaïd from their posts on the general staff. Boumedienne responded by refuting Ben Khedda's authority to issue such orders and committing himself fully to Ben Bella's cause.

The loss of Boumedienne to the other side dealt Ben Khedda a serious blow. But it was not yet fatal, and on 5 July 1962 the GRPA and its allies— the commanders of wilayas two, three, and four, and the leaders of the General Union of Algerian Workers (Union Générale des Travailleurs Algériens, UGTA) and the Federation of France of the National Liberation Front (Fédération de France du Front de Libération Nationale, FFFLN)— made Tizi Ouzou their provisional capital.[8] Over the next week, talks between what became known as the Tizi Ouzou Group and Ben Bella were held in Rabat to try to diffuse the situation but to no avail. Then on the evening of 12 July, Ben Bella left Morocco for the city of Tlemcen in the west of Algeria where, over the next few days, he was joined by the other members of the Political Bureau, the ANP's general staff, Abbas, and other allies.

Ben Khedda's and Ben Bella's choices of Tizi Ouzou and Tlemcen as the respective capitals added a new danger to their rivalry. In full knowledge of what they were doing, they ranged the country's Berber and Arab populations against one another and turned what had started out as an essentially political struggle into an ethnic one. Now communal pride was at stake and, arguably of greater importance, control of the central government and the state apparatus. For both sides were nearly homogenous in their makeup, with the Tizi Ouzou Group including virtually no Arabs, and the Tlemcen Group no Berbers.

By the end of July, Ben Khedda's position was looking increasingly precarious. In truth, the forces ranged against him were formidable. And if the Political Bureau had wanted to assert its claim militarily, there would have been little he could have done to prevent it. But what finally beat him was the mounting discontent within the Tizi Ouzou Group itself, as ever more of his allies grumbled about his leadership. With dwindling support that made it even harder for him to oppose Ben Bella, he finally capitulated on 28 July 1962 and recognized the Political Bureau's primacy. But that was not the end of the country's protracted crisis of succession as the day before Ben Khedda's surrender, Krim and Boudiaf announced the formation of a new committee for the "defence of the Algerian revolution and the restoration of unity,"[9] made up mostly of wilaya three fighters.

In early August, Krim and Boudiaf's committee members, along with fighters from wilaya four who had occupied Algiers, engaged several ANP units as they entered the country from their bases in Tunisia and Morocco. To avoid any further bloodshed, Ben Bella attempted to negotiate a ceasefire with the commanders of the recalcitrant wilayas. But when they refused, on the grounds that the terms he was offering were unacceptable, he ordered the ANP, on 30 August, to occupy Oran and Algiers. To help the army restore order, he called on the cities' inhabitants to rise up against the occupying forces of the rebel wilayas.[10]

The willingness and, in some instances, eagerness of the wilaya three and four fighters to make a stand was fueled by the mounting resentment they felt toward the ANP. It had been simmering away for a number of years as they and the other *marquisards* of the interior continued to seethe at the ANP's refusal to help them more during the war of liberation. It had been they, after all, who had fought the French day after day while the ANP remained safe in its camps in Tunisia and Morocco. And their reward, so it seemed, would be dissolution, integration—or reconversion as the Tripoli Program called it—into the ANP. It was unfair, so the wilaya three and four commanders argued, to ask their men "to go back to barracks to become a conventional service after seven years" of struggle.[11] Besides, they still had a duty to the people, to safeguard their interests and keep a careful eye on the new state.

Finally in early September they got their chance to exact their revenge. But events did not go according to plan. After coming under sustained heavy fire from the ANP units sent against them, the wilaya four men were forced to withdraw from their redoubts in the town of Boghari and the Algiers' casbah to La Chiffa canyon some twenty-five miles to the south of the capital. To cover their retreat and slow the pursuing troops, they blew up the bridge on the road south of La Chiffa. Yet they still could not prevent the ANP forces from surrounding them. After holding out until 9 September, the wilaya four commanders finally capitulated and agreed to a cease-fire. In a gesture of reconciliation Ben Bella allowed them, along with the heads of the other five wilayas, to contribute men to the Algiers garrison.

With its primacy now confirmed, the Political Bureau drafted a new, shorter list of 195 candidates to stand in the National Assembly election. Submitted to the Algerian electorate on 20 September for their approval, it was endorsed by around 85 percent of them. Perhaps unsurprisingly, voter turnout was at its lowest—64 percent—in Algiers, the heart of what had until recently been wilaya four territory.[12] With the new Assembly now in place, the Provisional Executive and GPRA formally surrendered their powers to it on 25 September. Four days later, its deputies voted, almost to a man, to make Ben Bella the country's first prime minister.

The Nation-Building Process Under Ahmed Ben Bella

Yet those who hoped that Ben Bella's appointment would bring about the peace and stability so desperately wanted by ordinary Algerians were to be sorely mistaken. Indeed, it took less than six months for the first armed challenge to his authority to be made. Outraged by the government's pursuit of reconversion, on 9 February 1963 Major Si Larbi—the military commander of the Constantine region—banned Mohamed Khider, the minister of finance and information and secretary-general of the FLN, from setting foot in his region. And to make good his threat, he issued instructions to his forces to arrest Khider if he tried to do so.[13] Anxious not to be seen as weak,

Ben Bella responded by dismissing Larbi from his post and ordering his immediate return to Algiers.

Rather than force the issue, Larbi backed down. But Ben Bella was not so fortunate with his next challenger, his erstwhile ally Aït Ahmed. In June 1963, Aït Ahmed resigned his post as deputy for Michelet before denouncing Ben Bella as a dictator. Shortly afterward, he left Algiers for his native Kabylia, where he set about organizing boycotts of both the referendum on the proposed national constitution and the presidential election in which Ben Bella was standing as the only candidate. Indeed, it was Ben Bella's refusal to allow anyone else to participate that prompted Aït Ahmed's actions. Although the constitution and Ben Bella's candidacy were approved by around 97 percent of those who voted, turnout in Kabylia was substantially lower than in other parts of the country. Official figures claimed that 52 percent of the region's electorate went to the polls. Unofficial reports, however, based on checks of polling booths carried out by journalists, suggested that the true figure was far lower.[14]

Buoyed by the success of the boycott, on 29 September 1963 (the first anniversary of Ben Bella's appointment as prime minister) Aït Ahmed announced the creation of a new opposition group called the Socialist Forces Front (Front des Forces Socialistes, FFS). Led by himself and Colonel Mohand Ou el-Hadj—the wilaya three commander—its goal was nothing short of overthrowing the government. In most parts of the country Aït Ahmed's call to arms went unheeded due to war weariness and suspicions that the FFS was a vehicle for Berber nationalism. But within Kabylia itself, it attracted significant support, leading to the deployment of ever more ANP troops in the region.

The first clashes between the two sides took place on 10 and 11 October 1963 near Medea and Michelet.[15] Yet within a few days a ceasefire was declared, as the FFS fighters joined the ANP in repelling the several thousand Moroccan troops who had crossed the border into Algeria two days earlier. The invaders' goal was to capture and hold the western portion of the Algerian Sahara, which, they claimed, had formed part of the Cherifian Kingdom before it was seized and added to Algeria by the French. During the war of liberation, the GPRA had promised to establish a joint Algerian-Moroccan commission to investigate Morocco's territorial claims as soon as Algeria gained its independence. But Ben Bella refused to honor this agreement and instead called on Rabat to adhere to the Organization of African Unity (OAU) founding charter, which asserted the inviolability of Africa's colonial borders.

On 15 October, Ben Bella issued orders for the mobilization of all war veterans as the fighting spread to engulf the whole border region.[16] He also called on the international community to condemn Morocco. To that end he tried to arrange an extraordinary meeting of the OAU and sent Hadj Smaine—his minister of justice—to petition the Arab League when it met in Cairo in late October. Eventually a cease-fire was declared on 20 February 1964, although, by that time, most of the fighting had long since stopped. And since neither side had been able to defeat the other, despite some ferocious fighting in the desert around Hassi Beida, the border remained where it was.

With the passing of the Moroccan threat—at least for the time being—the FFS felt free to resume its campaign against the government. So in February 1964, its fighters carried out a series of hit-and-run raids against ANP forces stationed in Kabylia, and made a half-hearted attempt to assassinate Ben Bella. Then from the start of summer onward, it concentrated its efforts on organizing a boycott of the National Assembly election scheduled to take place on 20 September. While it enjoyed some limited success in Kabylia, where only 55 percent of the region's voters took part, its pleas were largely ignored in the rest of the country, where turnout averaged around 85 percent.

As preparations for the election were taking place, another rebellion broke out also in the east of the country. Leading it was Colonel Mohammed Chabani, commander of wilaya four and member of the Political Bureau. Yet from the moment this new uprising began, it ran into difficulties as it struggled to attract the popular support it needed to sustain itself. After limping along for a few weeks, it was finally crushed in mid-August when ANP forces routed Chabani's small force. He himself was captured and, after a quick trial, executed by firing squad on 3 September 1964.[17]

The FFS too was irrevocably damaged when on 17 October 1964 Aït Ahmed was also apprehended.[18] Like Chabani, he was sentenced to death after being tried by a special revolutionary court on 10 April 1965. And Khider and Boudiaf received similar sentences in absentia for their roles in antigovernment activities since March 1962. Lawyers working for Aït Ahmed in France challenged the court's legality on the grounds that it sat in camera and had no appeals process apart from a petition to the president for clemency.[19] Partly as a result of these pressures, which sparked an outcry in France, and partly to assuage popular opinion in Kabylia, Ben Bella commuted Aït Ahmed's sentence to life imprisonment. He eventually escaped from prison in 1966 and fled to Switzerland.

Although none of the attempts to overthrow Ben Bella came very close to succeeding, the frequency with which they occurred painted a worrying picture for him and his government. He may have been loved and adored by many Algerians, but he remained the object of revulsion for thousands more. And there was no denying the ethnic division within the country.

Most of those who opposed Ben Bella—Ben Khedda, Aït Ahmed, Ou el-Hadj, Khider, and Boudiaf—were Kabyles, and their ability to make nuisances of themselves rested in no small part on the willingness of many other Berbers to follow them. And, to a certain extent, Ben Bella had no one to blame for their hostility but himself. Indeed, his desperation to see off the GPRA had helped create the situation that now confronted him.

In an effort to undo what he had done and, in the process, make his own position less precarious and the government of Algeria a little easier, Ben Bella tried to heal some of these rifts by embarking on a program of nation building. To begin with, he set about defining the Algerian nation, identifying the core characteristics of Algerian national identity. And what he focused on were Islam, Arabism, and socialism. Islam had first been exclaimed as central to the Algerian character by the FLN in its "Appeal to the Algerian People" made on 1 November 1954.[20] Its emphasis of Islam was driven by its need to identify a feature that was common to most non-Europeans, but which distinguished them from the pieds noirs. Indeed, it had been the FLN's ability to convince Algerians of the intractability of the differences between the various communities that had held the key to their campaign.

Given his need to unify the country, Ben Bella reiterated Islam's centrality to Algerian nationality in both the 1963 constitution and the Algiers Charter.[21] In so doing, he attempted to bring the country together by emphasizing a cultural theme that was common to the vast majority of Algerians and predated French colonization. The constitution and charter also stressed the "Arab . . . essence of the Algerian nation,"[22] as well as its commitment to socialism.[23] While Ben Bella never fully explained his understanding of socialism, for him the ideal Algerian was a Muslim Arab socialist.

To ensure this definition achieved primacy, Ben Bella and his government set about trying to control the discourse on national identity. They did so by placing limits on the opportunities individuals and groups had to discuss and promote alternative understandings. As part of this process, they systematically extended their authority over the country's media, political system, and social space. Control of the press was achieved in part through censorship. During the first months of independence, domestic news outlets had exercised self-censorship to avoid adding to the violence and bloodshed. Yet after a while, more concrete limits were introduced by the government so that by 1965 all news reports were subject to heavy restrictions. These measures were supplemented by the creation of an FLN-controlled union that all journalists had to join.

At the same time it was busy curtailing the media's freedom of action, the government also set about extending its control over the political system by increasing its power at the expense of other institutions, most notably the

National Popular Assembly (Assemblé Populaire Nationale, APN). The erosion of the Assembly's autonomy and legislative functions began with the Political Bureau's selection of the 195 candidates who were elected as its first deputies. Finalized in September 1962, just as the Bureau was confirming its triumph over the GPRA and fighters of wilaya four, the list of candidates submitted to the Algerian electorate was drawn up solely by Ben Bella and his allies. In so doing, they denied the electorate any choice in who they voted for as each candidate stood unopposed. By selecting who could become a deputy, Ben Bella and the other members of the Bureau ensured that the Assembly was filled with their supporters, each of whom was dependent on the Bureau for his or her position.

Throughout the summer of 1963, the government reinforced its primacy by subverting the Assembly's legislative authority. This subversion began with the drafting of the country's first constitution, a responsibility afforded the National Assembly under the terms of the constitutional referendum of 20 September 1962.[24] Ben Bella initially confirmed this mandate, stating that it was the Assembly's task to "give the country a constitution."[25] In response, the president of the Assembly, Ferhat Abbas, set up a Special Constitution Commission that, by April 1963, had two drafts to consider. By that time, however, Ben Bella had changed his mind, arguing instead that sovereignty and legislative authority rested with the party. To substantiate this claim and ensure that it was codified in law, Ben Bella began preparing his own version of the constitution. Once his draft was complete, in July of that year, he sent it to party officials around the country for their approval. This they gave at a meeting in Algiers on 31 July 1963.[26]

Although the party officials' ratification of Ben Bella's constitution was not legally binding, Abbas had little choice but to accept it as neither of the two drafts being prepared by the Assembly was yet finished.[27] With no other constitution with which to challenge Ben Bella's, Abbas resigned as the Assembly's president on 14 August 1963. In his final speech before it, he launched a scathing attack on the content of the Ben Bella constitution and the disregard it paid to the Assembly's authority. Abbas was particularly concerned that it made Ben Bella "the head of state, party, and Government" and that it placed the Assembly "under the thumb of a man who dominates ministers and who chooses deputies by party trickery."[28]

The constitution's concentration of power in Ben Bella's hands was achieved through Articles 23 and 24. Article 23 made the FLN the only legal political party, and Article 24 gave it responsibility for making policy and overseeing both the National Assembly and the government.[29] As the governing executive of the FLN, the Political Bureau was granted authority over the government and National Assembly, and as secretary-general of the FLN, Ben Bella had power over the Political Bureau.[30] His authority over the Algerian political system was reinforced further by the other positions that he held. By October 1963, he was commander in chief of the armed forces, prime minister, and president of the republic.

Ben Bella exploited Abbas's resignation to strengthen his influence over the National Assembly still further by engineering the appointment of Hadj Ben Alla as its new president. As a member of the Political Bureau and ally of Ben Bella, Ben Alla curtailed what little remaining independence the Assembly's deputies had, ensuring that they were unable to mount any serious opposition to the government's policies. Indeed, one of his first actions was to make sure that Ben Bella's draft of the constitution passed the Assembly without any alteration.

On 24 August 1963, Ben Bella's draft, or the "official draft from the conference of FLN leaders" as it was formally known,[31] was submitted to the Assembly for ratification. During the four-day debate that followed, none of the various amendments proposed by different deputies were incorporated. Then, on 28 August, 139 deputies of the 170 present voted to adopt it. This endorsement was confirmed in the national referendum held on 8 September 1963.[32] Through the extension of its authority over Algeria's political system, the Political Bureau reduced the opportunities for individuals and groups to debate its definition of the nation. The Bureau also denied them access to the country's main political platforms from which they could have legally challenged its vision of the nation.

To limit these opportunities further, the Political Bureau also set about occupying and controlling the country's social space. By gradually extending its authority over key civil society groups, the bureau prevented them from becoming forums in which alternative definitions of the nation could be discussed. Moreover, through the extension of its control, it also decreased the ability of these groups to promote competing definitions of the nation.

The first and arguably most important civil society group that Ben Balla sought to gain control of was the UGTA. Along with the ANP and FLN, the UGTA was one of the most politically powerful organizations in Algeria. Its influence stemmed from a variety of sources including the size of its membership, its organizational cohesion, the discipline and professions of its members, the astuteness of its leaders, and its financial strength.

By the time Algeria gained independence, the UGTA had established itself as the country's largest trade union with 250,000 members.[33] The dues they and the members of its affiliate, the General Association of Algerian Workers (Association Générale des Travailleurs Algériens,

AGTA) paid,[34] gave the UGTA an income that was neither controlled by, nor dependent on, the government. And the cohesiveness and discipline of its cadres meant that its leaders, who were among the most competent in Algeria,[35] were able to mobilize tens of thousands of people in either support of or opposition to government policy. Moreover, given that this membership was made up of mostly skilled and semiskilled urban workers, the UGTA leadership had enormous influence over the most modern parts of Algeria's economy. This influence was increased further following the departure of nearly the entire pieds noirs population during the final twelve months of the war of liberation. The exodus of almost the whole of the European community deprived the country of most of its professional workforce, raising the importance of those skilled and semiskilled workers who remained.[36]

During the war the FLN and UGTA had worked closely together. One of the most important contributions the UGTA had made to the FLN's war effort was its organization of strikes by Algerian workers, no easy feat given the severe restrictions placed by the French security forces on the movement and congregation of non-Europeans. These strikes played a vital role in the anticolonial struggle as they helped generate solidarity among the Algerian population and damaged the French economy. And perhaps more importantly, they helped focus the attention of metropolitan France and the world in general on events in Algeria.

Yet, despite the closeness of its working relationship with the FLN during the war of liberation, the UGTA remained a distinct organization with its own leaders, resources, procedures, and structures. The UGTA's separateness was confirmed by the exclusion of all but one of its leaders from the FLN's governing bodies. With the exception of its first secretary-general, Aïssat Idir, none of the UGTA's leaders sat on the CCE, CNRA, or GPRA. Relegated to a supporting role, the union had little choice but to nurture its own resources and strengthen the organization and cohesiveness of its cadres. Only by doing so could it effectively contribute to the struggle against the French and maximize its influence within the nationalist movement. Ironically, therefore, the FLN's wartime treatment of the UGTA encouraged it to develop the autonomy that Ben Bella and Khider later wanted to undermine.

By excluding the UGTA's leaders from its governing bodies, the FLN failed to curb their syndicalist tendencies. Before the UGTA was created, several of those who later became its leaders were members of the PCF trade union, the CGTU. The CGTU was guided by the doctrine of syndicalism, which emphasized direct action on the part of union members, such as boycotting the goods produced by certain companies and taking part in general strikes. Syndicalism also dictated that unions must retain their freedom of action by remaining independent of all other organizations including political parties.[37] While the CGTU never fully conformed to these strictures, it was in syndicalism that a number of the UGTA's future leaders were schooled. Idir, for example, was a member of the CGTU from 1944 until he helped establish the UGTA in February 1956.[38]

The ideological differences between the UGTA and FLN were reinforced by the political divisions that existed between the two organizations. These differences came to a head once Algeria achieved independence. The UGTA's leaders, like many of its rank-and-file members, were further to the left of the political spectrum than Ben Bella and the rest of the Political Bureau. This divergence was made apparent by the UGTA's criticisms of Ben Bella's economic policies and, in particular, the lack of support he initially gave the *autogestion* committees. Indeed, its leaders argued that state socialism, unlike autogestion, limited the workers' control of the economy by allowing "the petit-bourgeois spirit to persist."[39]

Perhaps unsurprisingly in light of their differences, the UGTA's leaders resisted Ben Bella's and Khider's efforts to bring them under the Bureau's control. Their resistance began in earnest shortly after the Bureau confirmed its political primacy over the GPRA. In October 1962, Ben Bella and Khider initiated a three-pronged campaign to weaken the UGTA's resolve by hampering its activities, enticing away its members, and challenging its dominance of the trade union movement. In early October, the Bureau prevented the UGTA's secretary-general from contacting his regional coordinators in Constantine and Annaba. Later that month, the Prefect of Algiers seized a special edition of the UGTA's newspaper, *L'Ouvrier Algérien*, before it was distributed to its members. Then, in November 1962, Khider tried to persuade the UGTA coordinator at Kolea to defect with his two thousand members to the newly created FLN unions. On each of these occasions, the UGTA rebuffed the pressure exerted on it. In fact, so successful was it in doing so that, on 21 December 1962, the Political Bureau signed an agreement pledging to respect the union's autonomy, and freedom of action.[40] This agreement expanded the promise made by Ben Bella and the FLN in the Tripoli Program to allow the union to concentrate on defending the workers' material and cultural interests.[41]

Despite these assurances, it was not long before Khider and Ben Bella renewed their efforts to gain control of the UGTA. In January 1963, they used the occasion of the UGTA's first congress to engineer the election of new, pro-FLN union leaders. In his opening address to the assembled delegates and foreign observers,[42] Ben Bella rescinded the Political Bureau's earlier promises. He declared that all trade union activity must be situated within the framework of "a single form of political thought" devised and controlled solely by the FLN.[43] Over the next two days, Ben Bella and his supporters reiterated the party's right to primacy over the UGTA both publicly to the congress as a whole and privately to individual delegates. Yet on each occasion they were unable to persuade either the UGTA's leaders or a majority of its members to surrender to the Political Bureau's authority.

In the face of this intransigence, Ben Bella and Khider changed tactics. On the final day of the congress, as the delegates returned for the last few sessions, they were prevented from retaking their seats by members of the Algiers' branch of the FLN. Having seized control of the congress, the new "delegates" promptly voted Secretary-General Boualem Bouriba out of office before electing Rabah Djermane in his place. The rest of the UGTA's Executive was also removed from power and replaced with men favoring unification with the FLN.[44] Shortly afterward, these new leaders issued a statement announcing that the union would "mobilise their [members] energy, devotion, and technical skill in the active service of the nation through the rapid and conscientious execution of the orders of the party."[45] Ben Bella and Khider had won. And although the UGTA did recover some of its lost autonomy during the final years of Ben Bella's premiership, it never fully regained the freedom of action it possessed prior to its first congress.[46]

The UGTA was not the only civil society organization over which the Political Bureau attempted to force its authority. Another was the General Union of Muslim Algerian Students (Union Générale des Étudiants Musulmans Algériens, UGEMA), arguably the second most important union in Algeria after the UGTA. Like the UGTA, the UGEMA was keen to remain autonomous of the FLN and the pro-FLN National Liberation Front Youth (Jeunesse du Front du Libération Nationale, JFLN) and Muslim Scouts (Scouts Musulmans Algériens, SMA). As with the UGTA, Ben Bella chose his moment carefully to assert the Political Bureau's authority.[47] Exploiting the heightened nationalist sentiments within the country created by the Algerian-Moroccan war of October 1963, he persuaded the UGEA's leadership to unite with the JFLN and the SMA under the umbrella of the National Youth Committee that was supervised directly by the Political Bureau.

In fact, Morrocco was just one in a series of enemies the Political Bureau told the Algerian public to unite against. The vilification of this and other countries and groups advanced the nation-building process by enabling the government to encourage and frighten Algerians to accept and come together behind its leadership. While Morocco was clearly identifiable as an enemy of the Algerian people, at least for the period that the War of the Sands lasted, the other foreign powers denounced by the Political Bureau were those assumed to have neocolonial designs on Algeria or any other African or Asian country. During the course of Ben Bella's premiership several states were accused of neocolonialism, but the two against which the charge was most often leveled were France and the United States. Ben Bella's preoccupation with neocolonialism was made clear in the Tripoli Program and noted by Robert W. Kromer of the US National Security Council staff. In a memorandum to President John F. Kennedy dated 13 October 1962, Kromer argued that the main reason for inviting Ben Bella to the White House was "to offset any misapprehensions he may have about 'neocolonialist' US policies."[48] Whether such denunciations were justified or not, Ben Bella used the threat of neocolonialism to unite Algerians behind his leadership. Only by remaining united could they ward off the threats posed by predatory foreign powers.

Yet it was not only foreign countries that were accused of trying to subvert the masses' interests; so too were certain groups within Algeria. The two most frequently identified as enemies of the Algerian people were the harkis and the bourgeoisie. The harkis were condemned and persecuted for collaborating with the French. Not only were thousands of them killed in the years immediately following independence, but legislation was brought in to seize property, goods, and money from anyone convicted of collaboration.[49] And the bourgeoisie was condemned for being "the bearer of opportunistic ideologies of which the principal characteristics [were] defeatism, demagoguery, alarmism, [and] contempt for the revolutionary principles" and for advancing "neo-colonialism."[50]

The role ascribed to Morocco, neocolonial foreign powers, the harkis, and the bourgeoisie by Ben Bella and the Political Bureau as the antagonistic "Other" against whom Algerians must unite was similar to that assumed by the colonial state and pieds noirs during the war of liberation. Once independence was achieved, the FLN was no longer able to unite the Algerian people behind its leadership in opposition to the exploitative colonial state as it did not exist. Neither could it unite Algerians against the privileged and culturally distinct pieds noirs as most of them had fled the country and those few who remained had had their privileges removed. By making these countries and groups the focus of popular hostility and opposition, Ben Bella was able to fill the void left by their demise.

The Nation-Building Process Under Houari Boumedienne

Since independence, Ben Bella had derived enormous benefits from his alliance with the ANP's most senior officer, Houari Boumedienne. Through this alliance, he had been able to call upon the ANP to resist the various armed challenges to his authority. Indeed, throughout the course of his premiership, the ANP fought and defeated on his behalf the forces of the GPRA, Major Si Larbi, wilaya three, wilaya four, Colonel Chabani, and the FFS. Yet the benefits Ben Bella gained from these victories came at a high political cost. With every ANP triumph, his reliance on Boumedienne and the military grew. And this dependence was increased further by Ben Bella's efforts to control Algeria's political system and social space. His erosion of the National Assembly's powers and the UGTA's autonomy undermined their ability to counterbalance the military's influence. As a consequence of his efforts, Ben Bella eliminated the very political institutions and civil organizations that could have helped him gain greater independence from the military.

To decrease his reliance on Boumedienne, Ben Bella tried to enhance his influence over the ANP's General Staff, curtail Boumedienne's power in the government, and create a new military force separate from the ANP. In October 1963 Ben Bella replaced Boumedienne as the ANP's chief of staff with Colonel Tahar Zbiri. And, over the next year, he set about replacing Boumedienne's supporters (who were collectively known as the Oujda Clan) in the government with men loyal to him.[51] During 1964 Cherif Belkacem, Ahmed Medeghri, and Ahmed Kaïd were all eased from their respective posts of minister of education, minister of the interior, and minister of tourism. As a result, Abdelaziz Bouteflika, minister of foreign affairs, and Boumedienne himself, minister of war, were the only members of the Oujda Clan still left in the government by the end of the year.

Then in early 1965, Ben Bella proposed the creation of a people's militia that would be entirely separate from the ANP and under the direct control of the president. His motives for establishing such a force were to reduce his dependence on the ANP and to have a body of armed men he could use against it, should the need ever arise. Although the militia was never raised, Ben Bella's proposal worsened his increasingly strained relationship with Boumedienne. It finally reached breaking point in early June 1965 when Ben Bella attempted to dismiss Bouteflika and rehabilitate Aït Ahmed.

In May 1965, preparations began for the second Afro-Asian conference which was being held in Algiers. Part of these preparations included negotiating with the governments of the attending African and Asian countries. Officially, it was the responsibility of the minister of foreign affairs to organize and oversee these talks. Yet as May wore on, Bouteflika found himself increasingly marginalized as Ben Bella assumed more and more of his duties. In early June, concerned that his one remaining ally in the government was being forced out, Boumedienne intervened. Ben Bella responded by threatening to fire both him and Bouteflika. And, to add insult to injury, it emerged shortly afterward that the man Ben Bella was planning to replace Bouteflika with was none other than Aït Ahmed, the former rebel leader. Ben Bella hoped that Aït Ahmed's inclusion in his government would increase his popularity among the Berbers. This represented a double affront to Boumedienne. Not only was Ben Bella threatening to remove one of his closest allies, but he was planning to replace him with the man Boumedienne had brought to justice and who had been responsible for the deaths of ANP soldiers.

On 19 June 1965, therefore, Boumedienne made his move. In the early hours of the morning ANP troops under the command of Zbiri seized control of the presidential palace and other key buildings in Algiers. During the hours that followed, scattered and small-scale demonstrations in support of Ben Bella broke out in urban centers throughout the country. But these protests were quickly and easily suppressed by the police and army.[52] Then, at noon, a Radio Algiers broadcast broke the news of Ben Bella's arrest and replacement by a group calling itself the Council of the Revolution (Conseil de la Révolution, CR).[53] Supported by the ANP, the Council pledged to bring an end to "personal power" and put in place "a democratic and responsible state."[54]

But Boumedienne's seizure of power did not bring with it an end to the armed uprisings, revolts, and rebellions that had punctuated Algerian politics since independence. During the course of his fourteen years in power, he was confronted by several armed revolts. One of the earliest was launched by his erstwhile ally Colonel Tahar Zbiri. Despite being appointed by Ben Bella, Boumedienne allowed Zbiri to remain as the ANP's chief of staff. Yet in the years that followed the coup d'état, relations between the two men deteriorated. The main source of their disagreement was the role of the military in Algerian politics. Zbiri was keen to see the army withdraw from political life whereas Boumedienne wanted it to remain directly involved.

The situation between the two men eventually came to a head in December 1967. By that time, the political dust stirred up by the coup d'état had largely settled, leaving Boumedienne feeling sufficiently secure to finally remove Zbiri. In so doing, he hoped not only to silence his opponent once and for all but also to reestablish his total authority over the armed forces. Yet he underestimated Zbiri's resolve and desire for revenge. And by casting him into the political wilderness, he left him with little option but to take drastic action. Indeed, with no other cards left to play and with little left to lose, Zbiri moved to overthrow the government and oust the CR. To those ends, he spent the days immediately following his dismissal hastily gathering those units of the ANP still loyal to him and making ready to march on Algiers from his stronghold in the Aurès.

Yet Zbiri realized that his tiny force was no match for the main body of the ANP. His plan, therefore, was to generate public support for his cause by drawing the inhabitants of the towns and villages he intended to pass through to his standard. In this way, he hoped to transform his small band of followers into a mass movement whose collective will the government would find impossible to ignore or resist. Yet from the beginning, his uprising failed to capture the popular imagination. Most ordinary people were unwilling to join him because they were heartily sick of the ongoing instability. They were more concerned with rebuilding their lives after the bloodshed of the war of liberation and first months of independence. And many of Zbiri's former comrades were more loyal to Boumedienne than they were to him, and promptly pledged their allegiance to the government.[55] Zbiri failed, therefore, to get the men, guns, and public backing he so badly needed. And as a result, his small force was routed by the ANP on the outskirts of Miliana, some fifty miles southwest of Algiers.[56]

With the defeat of his forces, Zbiri returned to the Aurès, where he planned and organized assassination plots against Ahmed Kaïd, the secretary-general of the FLN, and Boumedienne.[57] Helping Zbiri in his efforts was Belkacem Krim who, in the autumn of 1967, had established another movement dedicated to the overthrow of the government. An attempt on Kaïd's life was made on 24 January 1968 but failed as the four men sent to kill him were arrested. The information they provided during their interrogations enabled the Algerian security forces to roll up the network created by Zbiri and Krim. As a result, its leader, Belkacem Lichani, was captured along with arms, ammunition, and a list of intended targets on 22 February 1968.

Despite this roundup, an attempt on Boumedienne's life was made on 25 April 1968. As he left Government House in the center of Algiers following a weekly cabinet meeting, a gunman opened fire on his car. Boumedienne sustained a cut to his upper lip while his driver, the only other occupant of the vehicle, was shot in the right shoulder. The assailant was killed, along with another man suspected of being his accomplice, at the scene of the attack by guards from Government House. Although neither assassination plot was successful, they, along with Zbiri's uprising, served to highlight the depth of opposition that existed to Boumedienne's rule.

And these were not the only armed challenges Boumedienne had to contend with. For, on 27 January 1976, Algeria and Morocco went to war again. The cause of this new conflict was Morocco's occupation of the Spanish Sahara. On 6 November 1975, over 300,000 unarmed

Moroccans had crossed the border as part of the Green March to support their government's claim to sovereignty over the territory. And even though it was still a Spanish possession, the border troops allowed the marchers to proceed unharmed.[58] To resolve the situation, Spain, Morocco, and Mauritania signed, on 14 November, the Madrid Accords, under which Morrocco received the northern two-thirds of the territory and Mauritania the southern third. In return, Spain was granted mining rights throughout the territory by both the Moroccan and Mauritanian governments.[59]

Regardless of Morocco's historic claim over the Western Sahara,[60] both the territory's inhabitants, the Sahrawi, and Algeria rejected the Accords. Led by the Popular Front for the Liberation of Saquia el-Hamia and Rio d'Oro (POLISARIO),[61] most Sahrawi wanted the territory to become an independent state.[62] Algeria supported POLISARIO, partly to prevent Morocco from acquiring more territory and influence in the region, and partly to gain access itself to the extensive phosphate and iron ore deposits recently discovered there.

So, in late January 1976 two battalions of Algerian troops crossed the border into the Western Sahara with the aim of nullifying the Madrid Accords by driving the occupying Moroccan and Mauritanian forces from the territory. They were engaged by Moroccan units at Amgala about 180 miles (290 kilometers) from the Algerian border. The battle that ensued lasted for around seventy-two hours and ended in the comprehensive defeat of the Algerian force. But, despite this setback, Algerian troops remained in control of parts of both the Western Sahara and northern Mauritania until a cease-fire was declared on 15 February 1976.[63] But the cessation of fighting between Algerian and Moroccan forces did not signal the end of POLISARIO's armed struggle. Nor did it mark Algeria's acceptance of Morocco's annexation of the Western Sahara. Throughout the late 1970s and much of the 1980s, Algeria gave POLISARIO weapons and diplomatic support. And, to this day, the sovereignty of the Western Sahara remains a significant source of tension between the two countries.

Boumedienne's ability to see off the various challenges that confronted him depended, to a greater extent, on his control of the military. It had, after all, enabled him to crush Zbiri's fledgling rebellion and Krim's terrorist network. And even before that, it had allowed him to quickly and bloodlessly remove Ben Bella from office. Indeed, it was the degree and directness of the control he enjoyed that separated him from his predecessor. As the ANP's architect in chief, its most senior officer, and the occupant of the ministry of defense since independence, he had unparalleled access to the army. Moreover, many of its officers, particularly its most senior, owed their commissions to him. As a result Boumedienne was able to command their almost unconditional loyalty.

To help preserve the ANP's loyalty, Boumedienne lavished money and attention on it as he set about building a modern fighting force. From the moment Algeria achieved its independence, he worked tirelessly to ensure that the armed forces received a sizable chunk of the national budget. And his efforts were greatly helped by the direct access he had to the treasury. Unlike his ministerial colleagues, he did not have to work through the minister of finance. In fact, he could, and frequently did, ignore the finance minister's calls for austerity. As a result, in 1963 Boumedienne secured for the ANP an annual budget of $100 million. And although that amount dipped to $34 million the following year, he got it increased year on year so that by 1965 it once again stood at $100 million.[64] Representing around 15 percent of the national budget, it remained at that level for the rest of the decade.[65]

Ensuring that the ANP was well financed helped Boumedienne keep both its officers and men onside, as did his lionization of their exploits during the war of liberation. With his encouragement, the ANP (or rather its predecessor, the ALN) was heralded as the vanquisher of the French, of being the vital instrument with which the Algerian people had fought for and won their independence. But more than that, it was portrayed as the keeper of the sacred flame of resistance and the guarantor of the people's continued liberty. Indeed, Boumedienne saw to it that the ANP occupied a privileged position within Algerian history and society, which resulted in the showering of much glory on its men and officers.

Yet Boumedienne did not secure the ANP's support by flattery alone; he also purged it of those elements that were hostile toward him. As part of the modernization process, he saw to it that many of the former wilaya commanders and fighters, who had been incorporated within the ANP during the first months and years of independence, were discharged. He suspected them, not unreasonably given the past behavior of the wilaya three and four fighters, of harboring the old prejudices of the internal faction. The most common of these held that, during the war of liberation, it had been the fighters in Algeria who had made the greatest sacrifice in the struggle against the French. In contrast, the units of the ALN had avoided danger by sheltering in their camps in neighboring Tunisia and Morocco. And as the ALN's commanding officer, Boumedienne had been, in their eyes, the man ultimately responsible for this cowardly strategy.

Although the armed challenges that confronted Boumedienne were never as serious as those faced by Ben Bella, their occurrence highlighted the continued existence of deep divisions within Algerian society. To overcome them and consolidate his authority, Boumedienne undertook a process of nation building. And just like that developed by Ben Bella, his definition of the nation centered on the three themes of Islam, Arabism, and socialism. The Algerian nation's Islamic and Arab character was reiterated in the new national constitution introduced by Boumedienne on 27 June 1976. It asserted, just as the 1963 constitution had done, that Islam was the state's sole religion and Arabic its only official language.[66] The 1976 constitution also declared that socialism was the "irreversible choice of the people" and the only way "of assuring the development of the country," "establishing social justice," and ensuring "the consolidation of national independence."[67] As it had been for Ben Bella, Boumedienne's ideal Algerian was a Muslim Arab socialist.

To try to ensure that this definition achieved dominance, the Boumedienne regime also attempted to control the discourse on national identity by limiting Algerians' ability to discuss or promote alternative definitions. Building on the measures already undertaken by Ben Bella, Boumedienne reinforced the government's control of the political and social spaces, used the education system to promote its definition of the nation, and identified common enemies to rally the people against.

Despite promising to transform Algeria into a "democratic and responsible state," the Boumedienne regime retained an iron grip on the country's political system. To begin, the CR suspended the APN, the institution through which the people were supposed to exercise sovereignty. And, although the APN's powers had already been compromised and severely restricted by Ben Bella, its abolition was symbolic of the continued decline in ordinary Algerians' political influence. In its place, Boumedienne established local (Assemblées Populaires Communales, APC) and regional (Assemblées Populaires des Wilayat, APW) assemblies. These bodies were supposed to form "the base of the state" and provide "the framework through which the popular will was expressed and democracy realised."[68]

But from the outset, the power and authority of these bodies was strictly limited as they were placed under the tight control of central government. Financially, the assemblies were dependent on the government-controlled National Bank of Algeria (Banque Nationale d'Algérie, BNA). And although elected, their membership was drawn from lists of candidates prepared by the FLN. Far from offering a counterbalance to central government, the APCs and APWs simply became channels through which its decisions were passed down to the people. On no account were they allowed to challenge or amend the government's policies or its definition of the nation.

And neither could the FLN, as it too was quickly subjected to the CR's authority. Indeed, one of the Council's first actions was to abolish the FLN's governing organs—the Political Bureau and the Central Committee—and replace them with a new supreme leader whom it selected. The man the CR chose to perform this role was Ahmed Kaïd, one of its own members and minister of finance in the new government. In line with the CR's primary goal of building a strong, highly centralized state, he was tasked with ensuring that the FLN worked in harmony with, rather than in opposition to, the government.

What this in fact meant, and what the CR aimed to achieve, was the subversion of the political authority granted the FLN by the Algiers Charter. Under its terms, the party was charged with the solemn task of overseeing the actions of the country's political leaders, of ensuring that they acted in the people's best interests and holding them to account if they failed to do so. The CR, through Kaïd, aimed to reverse this arrangement and turn the FLN into an organ of the state, if not in name then at least in function. As such, it was expected to follow and enact government policy unquestioningly and, by the same token, promote the definition of the nation developed by Boumedienne and his advisers.

In public, Boumedienne and his fellow CR members continued to pay lip service to the Algiers Charter. And to all appearances, the party did indeed occupy the privileged position marked out for it. In the official history of the war of liberation that was set down in the late 1960s and early 1970s, the FLN's achievements were celebrated unreservedly and to such an extent that to criticize or even question them was an act of heresy. And the FLN's seeming centrality to national life was reinforced as membership of it became an essential prerequisite to gaining access to certain jobs, houses, and other privileges. Perhaps unsurprisingly, therefore, its membership grew rapidly throughout the 1970s so that by the end of the decade it stood at around 300,000.

Yet despite such outward signs of health, vigor, and importance, the FLN was steadily relegated to the margins of the political process. For a start, neither the army nor any of the major departments of state allowed party activists to operate openly within their organizations. As a result, the FLN was unable to exert much direct influence over the members of these institutions or, by extension, the institutions themselves. But arguably of greater significance was Kaïd's effective curbing of the party's revolutionary instincts. Originally, the FLN had been founded to transform Algeria, first by driving the French out, and then overhauling its political and economic structures, culture, and society. Once the war of liberation ended, both Ben Bella and Boumedienne remained keen to effect this rejuvenation. But only in so far as it left their power and influence intact or enhanced. Indeed, and despite frequently speaking in terms of continuing Algeria's revolutionary transformation, Boumedienne was anxious to exercise strict control over the

FLN. So under Kaïd, the party was bureaucratized to such an extent that it was turned from being an active agent of revolutionary change into a monument to it.[69]

Kaïd's appointment also signaled the resurgence of the Oujda Clan. Following Ben Bella's removal from power, its various members were given important posts in the new administration. Just as Kaïd was made head of the FLN, so Belkacem was appointed minister of finance, Medeghri minister of the interior, and Bouteflika minister of foreign affairs. And Boumedienne himself occupied the posts of president, prime minister, and minister of defense. In this way, he and his closest allies, who were all indebted to him following his stand against Ben Bella, were placed in charge of the country's most important institutions and government departments. But Boumedienne's loyalty to them was not without limits and, in the early 1970s, by which time his position as head of state had become unassailable, he began dispensing with their services. In December 1972 Kaïd was summarily dismissed as head of the FLN. Then in 1974 Medeghri died in mysterious circumstances, supposedly by his own hand. Finally, in 1975 Belkacem was sacked from the government. The only member of the Clan to survive this purge was Bouteflika, arguably the most powerful and influential of them all save for Boumedienne himself.[70]

Boumedienne's treatment of his erstwhile allies gave clear warning of his ruthlessness as he was quite prepared to do whatever was necessary to safeguard his power and authority. With the help of the shadowy Military Security (Sécurité Militaire, SM), he eliminated two of his most implacable enemies—Mohammed Khider and Belkacem Krim. Both men had taken their struggles against the Algerian government abroad. Yet, as it turned out, even this was not enough to protect them, as first Khider and then Krim were murdered, presumably by SM operatives.[71] With these two dead, Ben Bella in prison, and Mohamed Boudiaf and Hocine Aït Ahmed living in exile, there was no one left with the stature or support to challenge Boumedienne. And, as popular affection for his presidency grew, the more secure his position became. So much so that by 1976 the CR had been allowed to dwindle to just nine members, and those who remained played little part in the decisionmaking process.

As well as being subjected to tight controls itself, the FLN was also used by Boumedienne to extend his authority over other civil society organizations. Shortly after taking power, he had clashed with the UGTA over autogestion. Since independence the union had strongly supported the creation of autogestion enterprises and advocated the expansion of that sector of the economy. The UGTA supported autogestion because it granted workers control of the means of production. Despite his declarations of support, Ben Bella had systematically undermined the autonomy of the worker-managed enterprises by increasing their financial and logistical dependence on the state. And, once in power, Boumedienne continued this process as he set about bringing the autogestion sector entirely under his control.

To extend the FLN's authority over the UGTA, Boumedienne and Kaïd adopted a tactic similar to that used by Ben Bella and Khider. In October 1968, Kaïd organized a conference to discuss the FLN's recent review into union activities. But rather than use the occasion to repair government-UGTA relations, Kaïd emphasized the review's various criticisms of the union. The most damning of these was its accusation that the UGTA was preoccupied with "wages and working conditions and class struggle" at the expense of the nation's interests.[72] So during its third congress in October 1968, Kaïd packed the meeting hall with loyal party members who duly voted the incumbent leaders out of office before electing a new executive that placed the union firmly under the FLN's authority.

As well as asserting his control over Algeria's social space, Boumedienne redesigned the country's education system, just as Ben Bella had started to before he was removed from office, to teach students that Algeria was a nation of Muslim Arabs who were innately socialist in their values and attitudes. Part of the redesign process included making Arabic, not French, the primary language of instruction in the country's schools, colleges, and universities, as only by rejecting the language of the colonizer in favor of their own mother tongue could Algerians be truly free from colonial domination. The Arabization of education was the first step of a much broader project to make Arabic the dominant language of Algerian public life. Ben Bella's and Boumedienne's commitment to achieving this was enshrined in the 1963 and 1976 constitutions.[73]

Under Boumedienne, both Arabic language tuition and the teaching of other subjects in Arabic were steadily increased. By 1965 pupils in the first year of primary school were taught exclusively through the medium of Arabic, while the time dedicated to Arabic language tuition increased from seven to ten hours per week for all age groups.[74] By the end of 1968 the second year of primary school had been completely Arabized and the time set aside for the teaching of Arabic increased to twenty hours per week for first and second year pupils, and fifteen hours for third and fourth year students. By the time of Boumedienne's death in 1979 all primary school pupils were studying in Arabic as were 52.6 percent of middle school and 57.1 percent of high school students.[75]

Although certain years (the final grades at high school) and selected subjects (mathematics and the sciences) continued to be taught mostly in French, by the end of Boumedienne's premiership Arabic was the primary language of instruction for most students. And the regime's use of education to promote its definition of the nation did not stop with Arabization. On 16 April 1976, the government passed ordinance 76-35, which detailed the aims and organization of the country's education and training systems. Article 2 of the ordinance stated that it was the education system's responsibility to develop citizens' characters, prepare them for active lives, provide them with scientific and technical knowledge, and stimulate their love of the fatherland "within the framework of Arabo-Islamic values and socialist conscience."[76] With the promulgation of this ordinance, all teachers in primary, secondary, and tertiary pedagogic institutions were obliged to teach their students syllabi that promoted the Boumedienne regime's definition of the nation.

Like Ben Bella before him, Boumedienne also exploited tensions between Algeria and other countries to advance the nation-building process. During the course of Boumedienne's premiership, Algeria's relations with France became increasingly strained. The main sources of tension were the treatment of French citizens in Algeria; the treatment of Algerian citizens in France; the exploitation of Algerian resources; and the Algerian government's nationalization of French-owned businesses, companies, and assets. On 18 November 1968 Dr. Augustin Dalmais was sentenced by an Algerian military court to twenty years imprisonment for spying. And two other French citizens, Eugène Gidon and Georges Vedel, were both given five-year prison terms for the same offense. The severity of Dr. Dalmais's sentence was in retaliation for the harsh sentences handed down to two Algerians convicted of industrial espionage in France.[77]

Franco-Algerian relations took another blow in January 1971 when the Algerian government increased the amount of tax French oil companies operating in the Sahara had to pay. And to show it meant business, the Algerian authorities prevented oil tankers belonging to two French companies from taking on loads at the port of Arzew. The Algerian government's aim was to back up its annulment of an earlier trade agreement between the two countries that granted French companies' preferential status.[78] Over the following three months, the quarrel escalated. On 16 April 1971 French delegates broke off their negotiations with the Algerian government over future joint exploitation of the Saharan oil fields.[79] The following day, Paris ended Algeria's privileged economic relation with France, which had been established as part of the Évian Agreements.[80] And, although France's foreign minister, Maurice Schumann, was keen to stress that this break did not rule out future economic cooperation, it nevertheless marked a significant worsening of relations between the two countries.

These relations were dealt another blow when, on 19 September 1973, the Algerian government suspended the migration of its citizens to France. It took this decision in response to a rise in the number of attacks against Algerians working in France and the French authorities' failure to either prosecute those responsible or guarantee their citizens' "security and dignity."[81] The increase in attacks was initially triggered by the murder of a tram driver by an Algerian youth in Marseilles the previous month. This resulted in the retaliatory murder of ten Algerians for which no one was brought to justice.

The suspension had serious political and economic consequences. For a start, it represented a vote of no confidence by the Algerian government in the judicial competence and racial impartiality of the French authorities. The suspension was introduced as a last resort and only after the French government's failure to respond satisfactorily to the numerous diplomatic approaches made by Boumedienne and his ministers. Furthermore, the suspension nullified an agreement signed by both governments the year before that allowed 25,000 Algerians to travel to and work in France each year.

The suspension also had significant economic ramifications. At that time, there were around 750,000 Algerian nationals working in France who sent remittances to family members still in Algeria. These payments, which amounted to hundreds of millions of dinars, were vital to both the millions of people who depended on them and the Algerian economy as a whole. The Algerian workers also made an important contribution to the French economy. In addition to spending at least part of their wages in France, they were an important source of cheap labor for French businesses and companies. The extent of the damage the suspension inflicted on both countries' economies highlights the seriousness with which the Algerian government viewed the attacks on its citizens and the French authorities' failure to prevent or respond adequately to them.

The damage caused by this row exacerbated that inflicted by the constant disagreements between the French and Algerian governments over Algiers' nationalization of French-owned businesses and assets. By the end of Boumedienne's time in office, many foreign-owned businesses, most of them French, had been nationalized. The process of nationalization had begun shortly after Ben Bella and the Political Bureau had seized power. In November 1962, Ben Bella had extended state control over all of Algeria's power companies, some of its mines and foreign trade. This was followed, during the course of 1963, with the seizure of French-owned hotels, shops, cinemas, factories, and land. In all cases, either no or insufficient compensation was paid to the dispossessed owners.

In December 1963 Ben Bella had founded the state oil and gas company, SONATRACH.[82] Under Boumedienne, SONATRACH took over the Algerian assets of all remaining foreign energy companies, including those of the Compagnie Française des Pétroles. Boumedienne also nationalized all foreign-owned mines, and fully nationalized the airline company, Air Algérie. Each new wave of nationalization was met with a flurry of protests and representations from Paris and other foreign governments.

Boumedienne's actions toward the French, along with his response to the Madrid Accords, formed part of the tough line he adopted in his dealings with the international community. The main aim of his foreign policy, throughout his time in office, was to oppose and resist colonialism in whatever forms it took. France's actions toward its Algerian community and Morocco's and Mauritania's occupations of the Western Sahara against the wishes of its inhabitants were taken as clear examples of colonial aggression. Algeria, therefore, had a duty to stand up to these countries on behalf of the underdog, be they Algerian citizens or the Sahrawi.

Boumedienne's stance on these and other foreign policy issues furthered the nation-building process in two distinct ways. First, it created international incidents that could be used to stir up nationalist sentiments, to encourage Algerians to unite and rally behind their leader against common adversaries. The denunciation of Morocco, Mauritania, Spain, and France helped generate a "them-and-us" mind-set among the population. Only by uniting, only by putting aside any superficial and unimportant differences they might have with one another, could Algerians defeat the challenges posed by these reprehensible foreign powers.

Second, Boumedienne's stance made a statement about what Algeria stood for, what values it believed in, and what type of people Algerians were. It demonstrated that Algerians were brave: they were not afraid to fight for what they believed. That Algerians had honor: they were prepared to stand up for the weak against the strong. And that Algerians were determined: they were prepared to do what was right even when it damaged their own interests. The stance the Boumedienne regime took against the Madrid Accords and in its relations with France provided evidence of Algerians' virtuosity, of the commendable characteristics that made up the Algerian national personality.

The Nation-Building Process Under Chadli Benjedid

On 27 December 1978 Boumedienne died of a rare blood disease after a short illness. Under him, Algeria endured armed rebellions, assassination attempts against members of the government, an interstate war, mass protests, and the serious deterioration of its relations with France. The fact that his premiership remains the greatest period of sociopolitical stability and economic prosperity that Algeria has ever known speaks volumes about the country's postindependence history.

Following his death, two candidates emerged as favorites to succeed him. The first was Abdelaziz Bouteflika, an original member of the powerful Oujda Clan and Boumedienne's minister of foreign affairs. He wanted to limit the FLN's influence and dismantle the country's socialist economy by introducing liberal economic reforms. This stance earned him the support of the country's small middle class and the technocrats who managed the economy and raged against its inefficiencies. The second front-runner was Mohamed Salah Yahiaoui. He was deeply committed to socialism and wanted to raise the FLN's political profile by transforming it into a tool for the mobilization of the masses. Perhaps unsurprisingly, he was the favored candidate of both the FLN leadership and the UGTA.[83]

But despite their political pedigree and the strength of their respective bases of support, neither man succeeded Boumedienne because they failed to win the backing of the country's most powerful political institution—the army. As far as its high command was concerned, neither man could be trusted with Boumedienne's legacy, to preserve what he had done and keep to the path he had laid out. Bouteflika was unacceptable because of his opposition to socialism. And Yahiaoui was similarly objectionable because he wanted to increase the FLN's political power and turn it into a rival to the military.

The man the high command preferred was Colonel Chadli Benjedid, commander of the Oran military district. To his fellow officers, he represented a safe pair of hands. He would not create instability by introducing any radical reforms, and neither would he threaten the military's interests and privileged position. Bringing all their considerable influence to bear, the high command persuaded the FLN to nominate Benjedid as its candidate in the forthcoming presidential election. And, on 7 February 1979, he was duly elected by 95 percent of voters after standing unopposed.

Despite being chosen as the man most likely to keep the ship of state steady, under Benjedid Algeria experienced some of its most dramatic upheavals. The first crisis to confront him emerged before he had even formally taken office. In December 1979 the University of Algiers was paralyzed by a two-month strike launched by Arabic-speaking students in protest of the better job opportunities available to their francophone peers. As a result of the speed with which the Arabization of the education system had taken place, the demand for Arabic-language teachers had consistently outstripped supply, leading to the appointments of less able and qualified people. French-language teachers and the learning materials they used, especially for the sciences, were invariably, therefore, of a higher quality.

And so, too, were the students they churned out, whom employers were keen to hire because of their dealings with French and other foreign businesses and companies.

To iron out some of these inequalities and prevent the protesters from falling under the sway of Islamic fundamentalists, Benjedid introduced a raft of political, economic, and social reforms. In particular, he created more jobs reserved exclusively for Arabic speakers, accelerated the Arabization of the education system and other public services,[84] and appointed Arabic speakers to key government posts. He even had French place names replaced with Arabic ones. But in sharp contrast to what he intended, Benjedid's efforts sparked further unrest, this time among the country's Berber minority. Indeed, immediately after announcing the acceleration of the Arabization process, the regime was confronted by widespread protests in Tizi Ouzou and parts of Algiers.

The spark that ignited these demonstrations was the governor of Tizi Ouzou's decision to prevent the celebrated Kabyle poet Mouloud Mammeri from giving a lecture at the local university center. On hearing this, the students went on strike, staging sit-ins in their classrooms and occupying other university buildings. Over the next few weeks the situation escalated as pupils in nearby schools also went on strike and large pro-Berber demonstrations were organized in Algiers on 16 March and 7 April. Then on 16 April Tizi Ouzou was brought largely to a standstill as workers at a number of industrial plants, including those operated by SONELEC, SONELGAZ, SONITEX, and the city's hospital, came out in support of the students and pupils. This strike was followed by another on 22 April and was matched with rallies in Paris and Ottawa.

The regime's response to these protests was very different from its reaction to those of the Arabic-speaking students. Rather than make any concessions, the authorities decided to meet the demonstrators with force, killing, injuring, and arresting dozens of them as it did so. For example, police broke the general strike of 16 April by storming the occupied buildings and plants and arresting the demonstrators inside. And, despite the regime's promises to consider the protesters' concerns, the FLN's Central Committee declared its unanimous support for the Arabization process after meeting in May.

The so-called Berber Spring, as the demonstrations of March and April 1980 became known, was a notable flashpoint in the long struggle for cultural recognition mounted by Algerian Berbers.[85] Demands that their culture be officially recognized were first made by Belkacem Krim during the war of liberation. But shortly after independence, leadership of the cause passed to Hocine Aït Ahmed and the FFS. Aït Ahmed's capture and the subsequent decline of the FFS as a military and political force left the

Berber movement weak and divided. And with few friends in high places, it struggled to gain the government's attention or affect the political agenda until the start of the 1980s.

Yet the torch of opposition was not extinguished altogether. In 1968 the Berber Cultural Movement (Mouvement Culturel Berbère, MCB) was created to petition for democracy and cultural pluralism. But despite its efforts, the MCB met with little tangible success because of pressure exerted on it by the security forces. As a result of the inhospitable political and cultural climate that prevailed under Boumedienne, the torch of Berber activism passed to the large Berber community living and working in France. It was in Paris in 1967 that the Berber Academy of Cultural Exchange and Research (Académie Berbère de l'Échange et de la Recherche Culturel, ABERC) was established. And it was also in Paris, in 1972, that the Berber Studies Group (Group d'Études Berbères, GEB) was founded. The main aims of both these organizations were to promote knowledge and understanding of Berber culture, traditions, and languages, and pressure Algiers and the other Maghreb governments to grant Berbers greater political, cultural, and linguistic freedoms.

Although the Berber Spring failed to win Berbers the rights they so desperately wanted, it was a seminal moment in their relationship with the state and Algeria's political development. Shortly afterward, a new organization called the Committee of the Children of the Martyrs (Comité des Enfants de Chouhada, CEC) was founded to channel Berber demands and grievances. It was followed, in July 1985, with the establishment of the Algerian League for the Defence of Human Rights (Ligue Algérien pour la Défense des Droits de l'Homme, LADDH). Together with the MCB and FFS, these organizations prevented the state from assuming the level of control over Kabylia it had enjoyed throughout the 1970s. Furthermore, by demanding more political and civil rights for individuals, these groups increased the pressure on the Benjedid regime to liberalize and democratize the country's political system.

Berber nationalists and Arabic speakers were not the only ones pressuring the Benjedid regime to introduce political, social, and cultural reforms and to reevaluate the postindependence definition of the nation. So too were Islamist groups. In fact, the first armed challenge to the regime was made by the Armed Islamic Movement (Mouvement Islamique Armé, MIA). The founder and early driving force behind the MIA was the perpetual rebel, Mustapha Bouyali. His life as a *maquisard* began when, still in his teens, he joined the FLN to fight the French. As a veteran of the war of liberation he was well placed to receive the various rights and privileges accorded *ancien combatants* by the country's postindependence leaders. But he was expelled from the FLN instead, after rallying to the

FFS's banner in the early 1960s. For the next ten years or so he kept out of trouble. Then in the late 1970s he experienced something of a religious epiphany after attending the El-Achour mosque in Algiers.[86] From that point on, he dedicated himself to the task of transforming Algeria into an Islamic republic.

To begin with, he worked largely within the existing legal-political framework. Most of his energy was spent either trying to unite the Islamist movement or pressuring the government to introduce conservative legislation like banning mixed sex education and outlawing the sale of alcohol. Yet within a couple of years, he had grown disillusioned with this approach due to its failure to bring about the unity or changes he wanted. The final straw eventually came in May 1981 when rival factions within the Islamist movement refused to take part in a demonstration he had organized. Convinced that the movement would achieve nothing unless it worked together but that its leaders were too selfish to do so, he determined to realize by force that which he had failed to accomplish by peaceful means.

So he set to work building a new organization to wage war on the Benjedid regime, finally establishing the MIA in July 1982. Yet shortly afterward, he was arrested by the security forces along with dozens of other MIA members. Luckily though, he was able to escape and flee abroad. But with him out of the country, the MIA struggled to mount any serious operations and all but ceased activity. Only with his return to Algeria in late 1984 did its campaign gather any sort of momentum. In August 1985, its militants stole the payroll from a factory just outside Algiers. And six days later they attacked the police station in the town of Soumma, killing one of the officers stationed there before making off with arms and ammunition.

The government responded by dispatching troops to sweep the countryside surrounding Larbaa, a small town on the southern edge of the Atlas Mountains. That this was Bouyali's main area of operations was no accident. He knew the region intimately from his time as a member of the wilaya four *maquis*. And for the next 18 months, he made good use of the skills and knowledge he had learned during the war of liberation to keep his pursuers at bay. Yet the ability of he and his men to evade capture for so long was not due solely to their own efforts. They also benefitted significantly from the support and good will shown them by the local inhabitants.[87]

Yet it all came to an end on 3 February 1987, when Bouyali was killed in an ambush. His death heralded the end of the MIA in its first incarnation. Shortly after, those few remaining fighters who had not been killed or captured already were quickly rounded up. Unlike before, the sentences handed down to them were harsh. Of the 202 people who were tried, only fifteen were acquitted, while 182 were given prison terms of varying lengths, and five were executed.[88] But the genie was out of the bottle. For while the MIA never came close to overthrowing the government or to transforming Algeria into an Islamic state, it heralded the birth of the militant Islamist movement.

The MIA rebellion though, was but one expression of Islamist hostility to the Benjedid regime. More frequently, this opposition manifested itself as protest marches against mixed-sex education, the continued sale of alcohol, women wearing Western-style clothes, the government's failure to introduce sharia law, the actions of the police, or some other issue close to the Islamist movement's heart.[89] Invariably these rallies centered on the University of Algiers, either taking place on its campus or involving its students. So it was on 12 November 1982 when around 100,000 people gathered at the university mosque to condemn the arrest of 400 Islamist students a few days earlier. And again on 12 April 1984 when the funeral cortege for Shaykh Abdellatif Soltani passed through the university's grounds.

The Benjedid regime's response to this unrest and the various challenges posed by Arabic speakers, Berber nationalists, and Islamists emphasized his commitment to the process of nation building. Under him, it took place in two distinct phases. During the first phase, which lasted from when he took office until the mid-1980s, the regime promoted a definition of the nation similar to that of its predecessors. During the second phase, which lasted from the mid-1980s until Benjedid was forced to resign in 1991, the definition of the nation was significantly altered. Moreover, the political, economic, and social reforms Benjedid introduced gave the population far more opportunity to debate what it meant to be Algerian. These changes were the result of the extreme political, economic, and social pressures exerted on the regime.

At the heart of the definition promoted by the Benjedid regime during the first phase were Islam, Arabism, and socialism. Not long after taking office, Benjedid declared that Algeria was irreversibly committed to the path of Arab socialism outlined in the National Charter.[90] And he demonstrated this commitment by accelerating the Arabization process and refusing to grant the Berbers any more cultural or linguistic rights. Although his commitment to socialism appeared less strong, the economy remained state centered until the mid-1990s and the introduction of the International Monetary Fund (IMF) and World Bank–sponsored Structural Adjustment Programs (SAP).

And, even though the regime had cracked down hard on Islamist groups, Islam remained integral to its definition of the nation. Its commitment was demonstrated by its initiation of a mosque and madrassa-building program. From 1982 onward Benjedid raised the level of state funding for

Islamic schools and *imam* training programs and set about increasing the number of preachers in the country. By the end of the decade around 160 madrassas, fifty cultural centers, two academies, and three scientific colleges had been built, and the vast Emir Abdelkader University for Islamic Sciences was finally completed.

These efforts also formed part of the regime's attempts to occupy and dominate the social space by giving it control over the country's mosques. The religious schools and centers that it built were intended to replace the unofficial mosques that it was steadily shutting down. Only imams trained at state-run colleges and universities approved by the minister of religious affairs were allowed to preach in the official mosques. As well as having sole authority over the placement of preachers, the minister also organized the annual *hajj*, seminars, conferences, publications, and the programming of religious broadcasts on television and radio. Through these measures, the regime sought to eliminate the pulpit as a platform from which Islamist preachers could criticize the state and promote their definition of the nation.

Benjedid also tried to outmaneuver the Islamists by introducing a Family Code on 9 June 1984. The Code met many of the demands frequently made by Islamists, including making it illegal for Muslims to wed non-Muslims; making a woman the charge of her family until she was married and her marriage was consummated (at which point she became the charge of her husband); and making divorce an almost exclusively male right.[91] The regime hoped that by passing the code it could pacify the more moderate elements of the Islamist movement and drive a wedge between them and the hardliners. It also aimed to regain the loyalty of those sections of society that were sympathetic to the Islamist agenda but were appalled by the behavior of some of the movement's activists and groups.

The processes of nation building pursued by the postindependence regimes of Ahmed Ben Bella, Houari Boumedienne, and Chadli Benjedid were profoundly shaped by Algeria's colonial experiences. For a start, each man was unswervingly committed to the logic of the nation-state, the idea and belief that nation-states were the most natural and legitimate units of political, economic, social, and cultural organization and governance. This logic was brought to Algeria and imposed on the population by the French in the name of the Mission Civilisatrice. And, even though Ben Bella, Boumedienne, and Benjedid rejected completely France's assertion that Algeria was not a nation and should not become independent, they accepted and embraced as their own the ideology of nationalism.

Colonial rule also had a significant impact on the definition of the nation developed and promoted by Algeria's postindependence leaders. Their emphasis on Islam, Arabism, and socialism was driven by the effects this rule had on the Algerian people. Islam was identified as a defining characteristic for four main reasons. First, it was something that clearly separated the non-European population from the pieds noirs, the exploited and abused majority from the privileged and brutal minority. Religion had been the main determinant of the allocation of political, economic, and legal rights in French Algeria as Muslims were denied certain liberties precisely because they were Muslim. Second, Islam was one of the few cultural characteristics that most members of the non-European population shared. Regardless of age, gender, and ethnicity, most Algerians were Muslims and had suffered for being such under colonial rule.

Third, Islam pre-dated French colonization. This was important, as it enabled Ben Bella, Boumedienne, and Benjedid to trace the Algerian nation's roots back to antiquity. Their ability to identify the nation's ancient past was vital to creating the impression that the nation had always been. And, the glories of Islamic civilization helped them counteract the denigration that had been heaped on Muslim Algerian cultures and achievements by the colonizers. Far from being the barbarous savages that the French had always said they were, Algerians were members of a vast and glorious civilization, the achievements of which continued to beguile and enrich humanity in equal measure.

It was for similar reasons that the Ben Bella, Boumedienne, and Benjedid regimes emphasized the Arab dimension. The Arab people's history was as ancient as it was glory strewn. And, the conquest of North Africa and the advancement of Islam throughout the region formed an important part of this history. While the emphasis of this dimension through the Arabization program alienated Algeria's Berber minority, it undoubtedly helped unite and lionize the Arab majority.

Socialism was selected because it was a modernist ideology critical of capitalism. Capitalism, as far as the leaders of the FLN were concerned, was one of the principal forces that had driven France's invasion and conquest of Algeria. Egged on by the merchants of Marseilles, France had colonized Algeria to provide its industries with a new market for its goods and to gain exclusive access to the territory's natural and human resources. Socialism, by comparison, offered economic, political, and social development without the "exploitation of man by man."[92] And as a modernist ideology it presented a path to future prosperity and glories, and reminded Algerians that, by remaining united, they could achieve great things.

Socialism was also emphasized because, so the postindependence regimes asserted, Islam was inherently socialist.[93] Like the leaders of other African countries that had recently won their freedom, Ben Bella, Boumedienne, and Benjedid drew parallels between socialism and traditional, pre-French cultural and religious practices. According to them,

Muslims were, by virtue of the religion they practiced, good socialists. Far from being an alien doctrine imported to Algeria from abroad, socialism had been in the country all along. Simultaneously, therefore, socialism offered the Algerian nation a pathway to the future while tapping into traditions, values, and habits that were ancient.

The success, such as it was, of the Ben Bella, Boumedienne, and Benjedid regimes' nation-building programs rested in part on the appeal of the definitions they developed. Although opposition to the themes of Arabism, Islam, and socialism clearly existed in certain quarters, they were also embraced by large swathes of the population. Part of their appeal resulted from developments in the international arena. Throughout the late 1950s and early 1960s, much of the Middle East was aflame with pan-Arabism, which spread quickly throughout the region and gripped the imagination of many of its inhabitants. And from the late 1940s onward, Soviet intervention in Africa increased markedly as it set about carving out a sphere of influence in the continent. These developments helped give the themes of Arabism and socialism a dynamism and vigor that boosted their appeal among ordinary Algerians.

Arguably the principal architect and primary promoter of pan-Arabism was the Egyptian president, Gamel Abdel Nasser, who, from the moment it began, was a major influence on the Algerian war of liberation. It had been in Cairo that the FLN had formally announced to the world the commencement of its armed struggle to liberate Algeria from French rule. And although much of the material support Nasser promised the FLN never materialized, his pledges were enough to persuade France to join Britain and Israel in invading Egypt in November 1956. It was hardly surprising, therefore, that Ben Bella and Boumedienne should incorporate the theme of Arabism within their definitions of the Algerian nation. And Nasser's various triumphs, starting with France's humiliating withdrawal from Egypt in December 1956, helped turn Arabism into something positive.

Even the various blows dealt to the cause of pan-Arabism failed to significantly damage Algerian support for it. Arguably one of the most serious of these was the humiliating reverse suffered by the Arab armies at the hands of Israel in the Six Day War of June 1967. The magnitude of this defeat dealt a severe blow to Nasser's prestige and led to a loss of faith in pan-Arabism throughout the Middle East—except in Algeria. But this was not because of anything Nasser did, but rather was the result of Boumedienne's dignified and uncompromising response. Through his unwavering support for the Palestinian cause (which included committing troops to the Arab army) and willingness to keep supporting it (even to the extent of breaking off diplomatic relations with the United States),

Boumedienne won considerable acclaim from ordinary Algerians. His stance not only helped generate popular support for his presidency, but it also Algerianized Arabism, gave it a local hue.

By this time, the chief armorer, political supporter, and financial backer of Egypt and a number of other Middle Eastern and African states was the Soviet Union. Since the end of World War II, a new scramble for Africa had begun as France, Britain, and the United States on one side, and the USSR and its Warsaw Pact allies on the other, set about currying favor among the continent's governments. Of course many of these governments cooperated with both camps as they attempted to beat their own paths as part of the nonaligned movement. And Algeria was not alone in maintaining strong economic links with its former colonial master while simultaneously accepting military support and financial aid from the Soviet Union. And in so doing, Algiers was able to gain a modicum of leverage over and independence from Paris and Moscow by exploiting their fears that it might embrace their rival more fully if they refused to cooperate.

Yet such machinations aside, the Ben Bella and Boumedienne regimes were naturally empathetic toward the Soviet Union. For a start, it had supported the FLN politically and militarily during the war of liberation. And once that was over, its strident anticolonialism, which was designed to weaken its Cold War enemies, chimed with the two Algerian leaders' own views and foreign policy objectives. Through *Pravda,* the Communist International, and Radio Moscow, the USSR maintained a steady stream of invective against French and British colonial rule and American capitalism and neoimperialism. At the same time, the various African nationalist and anticolonial movements agitating for independence were presented as being socialist in both outlook and objectives.

The validity of such claims notwithstanding, the Soviet Union was seen by many Africans as a potential ally in their struggle against colonial rule and a benevolent benefactor as they tried to adjust to life following independence. In this way, the USSR and socialism were seen to promise a better future, while France and Britain offered nothing but more of the same. And socialism's appeal was further strengthened by the example of the Soviet Union itself. Surrounded by enemies and in highly unfavorable circumstances, it had transformed itself into a superpower. Just like Arabism, socialism came across to many Algerians as a dynamic alternative to the staid and exploitative doctrine of capitalism.

Notes

1. Belkacem Krim signed the agreements for the FLN and Louis Joxe, Robert

Buron, and Bernard Tricot signed on behalf of the French government.

2. The Évian Agreements were the outcome of three rounds of negotiations. The first round took place at Évian from 20 May 1961 to 13 June 1961. The second occurred at Lugrin from 19 July 1961 to 28 July 1961, and the third at Évian from 7 March 1961 to 18 March 1961.

3. John Ruedy, *Modern Algeria: The Origins and Development of a Nation*, 2nd ed. (Bloomington: Indiana University Press, 2005), p. 191.

4. Led by Abderrahmane Farès, the Executive had twelve members—three Europeans, representing the pieds noirs community; six Muslims (including Farès), representing the nationalists; and three Muslims, representing those parts of the population that were supposedly neutral.

5. The referendum was held on 1 June 1962 with 5,975,581 people voting in favor of independence and just 16,534 against (*The Times*, "France Hands Over Power in Algeria," 4 July 1962, Issue 55434, p. 12, col. E).

6. Reda Bekkat, *El Watan*, "Algérie 1962: la Grande Dérive," (4 August 2005) available at www.elwatan.com/IMG/_article_PDF/article_24149.pdf, see p. 3 (accessed 23 February 2007).

7. This was the new name adopted by the ALN when Algeria gained its independence.

8. The FFFLN was established in 1957.

9. *The Times*, "Another Algeria Group Formed," 27 July 1962, Issue 55455, p. 8, col. B.

10. Henry Jackson, *The FLN in Algeria: Party Development in a Revolutionary Society* (London: Greenwood Press, 1977), p. 112; and Martin Stone, *The Agony of Algeria* (New York: Columbia University Press, 1997), p. 45.

11. *The Times*, "Army Moves to End Algeria Crisis," 25 August 1962, Issue 55479, p. 4, col. F.

12. *The Times*, "85 Per Cent Poll in Algeria," 22 September 1962, Issue 55503, p. 7, col. E.

13. *The Times*, "Algeria Military Leader Ousted," 11 February 1963, Issue 55622, p. 9, col. A.

14. *The Times*, "Berbers Rejection of Arabs as Usurpers," 3 October 1963, Issue 55822 p. 9, col. A.

15. *The Times*, "Algeria Rebels Confront Troops," 11 October 1963, Issue 55829, p. 9, col. G; and *The Times*, "Algeria Again Facing Civil War," 12 October 1963, Issue 55830, p. 98, col. D.

16. *The Times*, "General Mobilization in Algeria," 16 October 1963, Issue 55833, p. 12, col. D.

17. *The Times*, "Algeria Rebel Leader Executed," 4 September 1964, Issue 56108, p. 10, col. C.

18. *The Times*, "Leader of Algeria Revolt Captured," 19 September 1964, Issue 56146, p. 11, col. E.

19. *The Times*, "Death Sentences in Algeria," 12 April 1965, Issue 56294, p. 8, col. E.

20. The appeal states that one of the two goals of the FLN was "to achieve national independence by restoring the sovereign Algerian state, democratic and social within the framework of Islamic principles." Front de Libération Nationale, *Appel au people algérien*, 1954.

21. The Algiers Charter (*La Charte D'Alger*) comprised the motions adopted

by the FLN during their first congress, which took place in Algiers between 16 and 21 April 1964. It was drafted by Mohamed Harbi, Michel Raptis, and Souliman Lotfallah.

22. Front de Libération Nationale, *La charte d'Alger* (1964), chap. 3, para. 5.

23. The constitution stated that one of "the fundamental objectives of the Democratic and Popular Republic of Algeria [is] . . . the building of a socialist democracy." République Algérienne Démocratique et Populaire, *Constitution du 10 septembre 1963*, (1963), Article 10.

24. Eighty-five percent of the Algerian electorate voted in favor of this referendum, which also appointed the 195 candidates put forward by the Political Bureau to the National Assembly.

25. Jackson, *The FLN in Algeria*, p. 89.

26. Ruedy, *Modern Algeria*, p. 200.

27. Ibid.

28. Quoted in *The Times*, "Mr. Abbas Quits as Algeria's Speaker," 15 August 1963, Issue 55780, p. 8, col. G.

29. République Algérienne Démocratique et Populaire, *Constitution du 10 septembre 1963,* Articles 23 and 24.

30. Ben Bella replaced Khider as the FLN's secretary-general on 17 April 1963.

31. Jackson, *The FLN in Algeria*, p. 90.

32. Of the 5,122,828 Algerians who went to the polls, 98 percent supported the adoption of Ben Bella's draft.

33. Jackson, *The FLN in Algeria,* p. 112.

34. Based in France, the AGTA's membership comprised most of the large Algerian community living and working there.

35. Jackson, *The FLN in Algeria*, p. 112.

36. Mahfoud Bennoune, *The Making of Contemporary Algeria, 1830–1987* (Cambridge: Cambridge University Press, 1988), pp. 89–90.

37. Jackson, *The FLN in Algeria*, p. 113.

38. The UGTA was founded on 24 February 1956.

39. Cited in Ian Clegg, *Workers' Self-Management in Algeria* (London: Penguin Press, 1971), p. 117.

40. Ibid.

41. CNRA, *Projet de programme pour la réalisation de la révolution démocratique populaire* (1962), Annexe: Les organisations de masses.

42. Around 360 UGTA delegates and 62 observers from European trade unions attended the congress.

43. Cited in Jackson, *The FLN in Algeria*, p. 126.

44. The members of the new UGTA Executive were Mohammed Flissi, Press Secretary; Cheikh Benghazi, Organization Secretary; Mohamed Tahar Chafai, Finance Secretary; and Safi Boudissa, Secretary at Large.

45. Cited in Clegg, *Workers' Self-Management*, p. 117.

46. On 23 August 1964, Ben Bella issued a presidential decree giving the UGTA responsibility for organizing and operating worker training programs. These extra freedoms were added to in March 1965 when, at the second UGTA congress, union delegates were allowed to elect a new executive free from interference from Ben Bella.

47. At its fifth congress, held on 10 August 1963, the UGEMA changed its name to the General Union of Algerian Students (Union Générale des Étudiants Algériens, UGEA).

48. Memorandum from Robert W. Kromer of the National Security Council staff to President Kennedy, Department of State Conference Files, Lot 65 D 533, CF 2176.

49. Under this law, which was passed in July 1964 and came into force in October of that year, anyone convicted of collaboration had to leave their home immediately and wait to be resettled by the state. They also forfeited any money or valuables found on the property, any bank accounts they had, and any vehicles they owned. The law also applied to anyone who bought a property from a collaborator. *The Times*, "Algeria Penalizes 'Collaborators,'" 2 October 1964, Issue 56133, p. 7, col. A.

50. CNRA, *La révolution démocratique populaire*, section III, subsection B.

51. The Oujda Clan comprised six senior officers: Boumedienne, Cherif Belkacem, Abdelaziz Bouteflika, Mohamed Tayebi, Ahmed Medeghri, and Ahmed Kaïd. Its members met in 1956 when Boumedienne set up his headquarters in the town Oujda just over the border in Morocco.

52. *The Times*, "10 Deaths Reported in Algeria Clashes," 22 June 1965, Issue 56354, p. 12, col. F.

53. Ben Bella remained in prison until after Boumedienne's death in 1979.

54. *Annuaire de l'Afrique du Nord*, vol. 4 (1965), p. 627. The 26-man council was mostly made up of army officers and was tasked with advising the government. It was finally dissolved on 12 December 1976.

55. *The Times*, "Armed Rising in Algeria Fails," 15 December 1967, Issue 57126, p. 1, col. E.

56. The clash occurred on 14 December 1967. Ibid.

57. Kaïd was made head of the FLN on 11 December 1967.

58. The Spanish Cortes ratified the Accords four days later on 18 November 1975.

59. The Mauritanian government renounced its claim to the southernmost third of the Western Sahara on 5 August 1979, but then Moroccan troops annexed the region on 14 August 1979.

60. The Spanish Sahara was renamed the Western Sahara once Spanish sovereignty over it ended on 26 February 1976.

61. POLISARIO was established on 10 May 1973.

62. On 27 February 1976 POLISARIO declared the establishment of the Sahrawi Arab Democratic Republic (SADR).

63. Benjamin Stora, "Algeria/Morocco: The Passions of the Past. Representations of the Nation that Unite and Divide," *The Journal of North African Studies* 8, no. 1 (Spring 2003): p. 25.

64. Jackson, *The FLN in Algeria*, pp. 191 and 192.

65. David Ottoway and Marina Ottoway, *Algeria: The Politics of a Socialist Revolution* (Berkeley and Los Angeles: University of California Press, 1970), p. 305.

66. République Algérienne Démocratique et Populaire, *Constitution du 27 juin 1976* (1976), Articles 2 and 3.

67. Ibid., Articles 10, 11, and 12.

68. Elections for the APCs were first held in 1967 and then every four years

after that. The first elections for the APWs took place in 1969 and every five years thereafter. République Algérienne Démocratique et Populaire, *Constitution du 27 juin 1976* (1976), Articles 2 and 3.

69. Ruedy, *Modern Algeria*, p. 208.

70. Benjamin Stora, *Algeria 1830–2000: A Short History* (Ithaca and London: Cornell University Press, 2001), p. 145.

71. Khider was murdered on 4 January 1967 in Madrid, Krim on 20 October 1970 in Frankfurt.

72. Front de Libération Nationale, *Réorganisation de l'UGTA: Projet analytique de développement du synidcalisme en Algérie* (1968), p. 7.

73. Article 76 of the 1963 constitution solemnly asserted that "Arabisation must take place as quickly as possible throughout the territory of the Republic," while Article 3 of the 1976 constitution declared that "the state undertakes to broaden [généraliser] the use" of Arabic.

74. Arabic language tuition was made compulsory for pupils of all ages in 1962.

75. Bennoune, *The Making of Contemporary Algeria*, pp. 222 and 223.

76. Le Chef du Gouvernment, Président du Conseil des ministres, *Ordonnance no. 76-35 du 16 avril 1976 portant organisation de l'éducation et de la formation* (1976), Article 2.

77. *The Times*, "Algeria Gaols Frenchmen for Espionage," 19 November 1970, Issue 58027, p. 6, col. E.

78. *The Times*, "Algeria and France Fall Out Over Oil," 13 January 1971, Issue 58071, p. 4, col. G.

79. *The Times*, "France Ends Oil Talks With Algeria but Continues Trade Links," 16 April 1971, Issue 58148, p. 6, col. A.

80. *The Times*, "French Note Ends Close Ties With Algeria," 17 April 1971, Issue 58149, p. 5, col. E.

81. *The Times*, "Algeria Stops Flow of Workers to France," 20 September 1973, Issue 58892, p. 6, col. F.

82. SONATRACH stands for Société Nationale pour la Recherche, la Production, le Transport, la Transformation et la Commercialisation des Hydrocarbures.

83. Stone, *The Agony of Algeria*, p. 58.

84. By 1985 around 64 percent of secondary students were taught in Arabic.

85. The term "Berber Spring" referenced the anti-Soviet uprising in Prague in 1968.

86. Martin Evans and John Phillips, *Algeria: Anger of the Dispossessed* (New Haven, Connecticut, and London: Yale University Press, 2007), p. 129.

87. Ibid., p. 130, and Michael Willis, *The Islamist Challenge in Algeria* (New York: New York University Press, 1996), p. 82.

88. Willis, *The Islamist Challenge*.

89. John Entelis, *Algeria: The Revolution Institutionalized* (London and Sydney: Croom Helm, 1986), p. 85.

90. The Charter was adopted following a national referendum on 27 June 1976 and became the country's new constitution after a second referendum in November 1976.

91. Le Président de la République, *Le code de famille* (1984).

92. Front de Libération Nationale, La Charte D'Alger, Part II, Chapter 1, Article 18.

93. Indeed, the Algiers Charter declared that "Islam, far from being opposed to socialism . . . goes in the direction of socialism." Ibid., Part III, Chapter 2, Annex.

5

Economic Crisis and
the Descent into Violence

BY THE END OF BOUMEDIENNE'S presidency, the Algerian economy was much altered from when he had inherited it. The damage caused to the country's infrastructure and means of production by the war of liberation and postindependence scramble for power had been repaired; the pieds noirs' technicians, managers, and other professionals, who had fled in the closing months of the conflict had been replaced; and the chaos of the Ben Bella years had been overcome. But by far the most remarkable change was the massive expansion of the country's heavy industry sector. From virtually nothing, Boumedienne had built a network of state-owned industries, paid for by the revenues the country earned from selling oil and gas abroad.

But this development came at considerable cost. Throughout the 1970s, the emerging industrial sector absorbed billions of dinars at the expense of other parts of the economy. Agriculture in particular suffered from a chronic lack of investment as state funding was directed toward building, equipping, and staffing the new industrial complexes. By the time of Boumedienne's death, the enormous imbalance that had been allowed to develop between the different sectors of the economy was starting to have serious economic, social, and political consequences. The foreign debt the country had incurred to help finance the industrialization program continued to grow and became increasingly difficult to service. And the economy's overwhelming dependence on oil and gas for its export earnings left it extremely vulnerable to fluctuations in the global markets.

Shortly after becoming president, Benjedid launched his first five-year plan to restructure the economy and deal with some of the problems created by Boumedienne's single-minded pursuit of industrialization. The worsening economic situation of the 1980s, along with the Benjedid regime's response to it, had a profound impact on the nation-building process. First, it undermined the definition of the nation that had been promoted by the Ben Bella, Boumedienne, and Benjedid regimes. Socialism was renounced both in word and deed as the government restructured the economy and in the process sacrificed Algeria's jealously guarded economic sovereignty. These actions constituted a repudiation of the definition of the nation outlined by successive governments since independence.

Second, the developing economic crisis and the government's response to it caused the Benjedid regime to loosen its grip on the political system and social space. For the first time since independence, mass unemployment was rife. Standards of living declined while state welfare services and subsidies of essential foodstuffs disappeared. The social unrest that ensued prompted Benjedid to introduce a raft of reforms democratizing Algeria's political system. The introduction of multiparty democracy created a political opening for various Islamist, Berber, and other secular groups to challenge the regime's definition of the nation and its ability to promote it. This loss of control heightened the ongoing struggle between the traditional, secular elite and the Islamists and Berberists. And the struggle was made all the more bitter by the country's tradition of adopting a fixed, nonpluralist definition of the nation and severely restricting popular discourse on national identity. In the early 1990s, this struggle developed into armed conflict as Algeria slipped into civil war for the second time in its brief history as an independent state.

This chapter's analysis of the conflict between the secular elite, Islamists, and Berber minority is divided into three main sections. The first focuses on the country's economic development from independence until the early 1990s. In so doing, it identifies the structural weaknesses that contributed to the economic crisis of the 1980s. This leads, in the second section, to an examination of the social problems caused by this crisis, the Benjedid regime's response to them, and the Islamist and Berber movements' rise to political prominence. The final section then concentrates on the civil war of the 1990s.

The Economy Collapses

Benjedid's candidacy to replace Boumedienne was markedly different from that of his two main rivals, Abdelaziz Bouteflika and Mohamed Salah Yahiaoui. Both Bouteflika and Yahiaoui emphasized the various reforms they would introduce and changes they would make once they were president. Benjedid on the other hand, stressed the need for stability through continuity, the importance of preserving and enhancing Boumedienne's legacy rather than abandoning it. His cautious conservatism was warmly received by the military, which was anxious to consolidate and venerate Boumedienne's achievements and avoid any instability that could result from the implementation of radical reforms. The army's support was decisive. On 31 January 1979, the FLN gave in to the military's demands and nominated Benjedid as its only candidate for the presidency.

Yet Benjedid's indebtedness to the military did not prevent him from quickly rejecting Boumedienne's economic programs once he was in power. Despite the impressive achievements of these programs in transforming Algeria's agrarian economy into a semi-industrial one, serious macro- and microeconomic weaknesses had begun to emerge by 1980. The origins of these problems lay in the country's economic inheritance and the Ben Bella and Boumedienne regimes' development plans.

By the time the Political Bureau confirmed its triumph over the GPRA, Algeria's economy was in a sorry state. In the towns and cities, where one in three Algerians lived, factories, businesses, and industrial plants struggled to continue operating. Buildings were damaged, vital machinery broken, technicians and managers dead or living abroad, supplies of vital raw materials disrupted, road and rail links severed, investment scared away, and customers either unable or unwilling to buy. Even the new plants and factories built as part of the Constantine Plan struggled to maintain production. And the situation was little better in the countryside where the local economy had all but been destroyed. During the course of the war, hundreds of thousands of peasants had been killed by the French armed forces, FLN, and various other guerrilla groups. And to escape this violence, around one million people had fled to the coastal cities, Tunisia, Morocco, and France.[1]

The damage these deaths and departures caused to the rural economy was compounded by the French army's treatment of those who remained. Its policy of regroupement led to the separation of thousands of peasants from the land they owned or worked and on which they depended to feed their families. Whole forests and woods were destroyed by the French air force, which dropped napalm and defoliants on them to drive any FLN fighters hiding there into the open. And the army buried tens of thousands of land-mines in what had hitherto been productive fields.

Economic planning under Ben Bella was both haphazard and deeply politicized. In November 1962, shortly after the Political Bureau had consolidated its grip on power, he outlined his grand vision for the Algerian economy. He stated that it would comprise three sectors: the public, the semipublic, and the private.[2] The public sector was made up of the various state-owned-and-operated industries and businesses. During the course of Ben Bella's presidency, this sector steadily grew in size as he nationalized many pieds noirs–owned and foreign-owned enterprises. The private sector, on the other hand, shrank slightly as many individually owned concerns were given over to the public and semipublic sectors. But the sector that grew quickest was the semipublic, which consisted of the worker-managed or autogestion enterprises.

Ben Bella's autogestion policy was reactive, developed in response to events that had already unfolded, namely, the occupation of pieds noirs' properties by Muslim Algerians. The formulation and legal codification of the autogestion program began in October 1962. On the 22nd and 23rd of that month, Ben Bella issued two decrees officially sanctioning the self-appointed, worker-management committees set up to operate the farms and factories deserted by their European owners and establishing the National Bureau of Vacant Goods (Bureau National des Biens Vacants, BNBV).[3]

Guidelines for operating the worker-managed enterprises and the state's role in overseeing their activities were outlined in a series of decrees issued by Ben Bella on 18, 22, and 28 March 1963. The first of what became known as the March Decrees specified what constituted a vacant property, namely, any farm, factory, or other business that had ceased regular production and any house that had been unoccupied for two months. The second decree asserted that any such businesses were to be operated and managed by a committee made up of and chosen by its permanent workers. The third decree established the National Office of Agricultural Reform (Office National de la Réforme Agraire, ONRA) and stated that all profits generated by each worker-managed enterprise must be shared among the workforce, apart from an unspecified percentage that was to be given to the state for investment in its national employment fund.[4]

As well as being reactive and implemented in an ad hoc fashion, Ben Bella's autogestion policy was motivated by his own partisan political concerns. At the same time that he was developing the policy, he was also engaged in a power struggle with Mohamed Khider for control of the FLN and the UGTA leadership for control of their trade union. The spontaneous occupation of pieds noirs' properties was the most significant popular movement to have emerged in Algeria since independence.[5] As such, Ben Bella was determined to assume leadership of it in order to boost his own standing among the people and, in the process, consolidate his power base and gain an advantage over his political rivals. Political rather than economic considerations, therefore, drove the government's autogestion policy.

As a consequence, many of the problems within the agricultural sector during the colonial era remained unresolved. The old pieds noirs' estates, which were now managed by their workers, still received the bulk of the state's investment in agriculture to the continued detriment of private holdings, which produced most of the country's food. Even so, the productivity of these farms was limited by their inability to modernize. Ben Bella's personal commitment to the autogestion farms and estates meant that insufficient funds were available to train those who worked their own lands in modern farming techniques or provide them with the seeds, fertilizers, and machinery they needed. And no action was taken to either improve the quality of the land they worked or consolidate the various holdings that were individually too small to make a profit into larger concerns.

Despite occupying the best lands and employing modern farming methods, the autogestion enterprises failed to maximize their productivity. One of the main reasons for this was the elaborate bureaucracy that was put in place to interface between the farms and the state. Its main purpose was to ensure that overall control of these enterprises rested with the central state authorities rather than the workers. This was achieved through the sweeping powers granted to the state-appointed directors of each worker-management committee.[6] Ostensibly, the directors' primary function was to ensure that the work carried out by each enterprise complemented the government's macroeconomic plan. In practice, the considerable powers given them ensured that they, rather than the committees, had the final say in each enterprise.

Government control of the worker-managed enterprises was enhanced through the ONRA and its various subsidiaries. It was ONRA's responsibility to oversee the work done by the autogestion farms, direct state investment, and provide them with any technical assistance they might need. It was the task of the National Algerian Office for the Sale of Cereals (Office National Algérien de Commercialisation des Céréales, ONAC) to market the goods produced for export by the worker-managed farms, while the Office for Agricultural Reform (Office de la Réforme Agraire, ORA) marketed the goods they produced for domestic consumption. Through these agencies, the government had total control over investment in the autogestion farms, their access to essential supplies, and the sale of their produce. Real authority, therefore, lay not with the workers but the government. Yet again, economic principles and planning were forced to give way to political imperatives as Ben Bella sought to consolidate his influence over the semipublic sector.

Ben Bella's removal from office did not bring an end to the government's attempts to extend its influence over the economy or make itself the country's most important economic actor. Between 1965 and 1975 Boumedienne nationalized all remaining foreign-owned companies in the insurance, banking, mining, and energy sectors and most of the industrial enterprises in the autogestion sector. Unlike that of his predecessor, Boumedienne's nationalization program was not driven by personal political interests and rivalries but as part of a clearly developed economic strategy. As a result, it was pursued more thoroughly and systematically.

During his time in office, Boumedienne built a network of state-owned financial and management institutions to incorporate and develop the nationalized industries. The largest and best funded of these institutions were all in the heavy industry sector and included SONATRACH, the National Chemical Company (Société Nationale des Industries Chimiques, SNIC), the National Steel Company (Société Nationale de Sidérurgie; SNS), and the National Construction Company (Enterprise Socialiste pour le Développement National de la Construction, ESDNC). Each of these institutions was responsible for overseeing, expanding, and marketing the products of the industries that fell within the sector of the economy over which they were given authority.

The nationalization of foreign-owned businesses was a key component of Boumedienne's economic grand strategy drafted by his minister of industry, Abdessalam Belaid.[7] Belaid's thinking was strongly influenced by the theory "industrialising industries," which was being developed at around the same time by a group of French economists. The most celebrated of these was Gérard Destanne de Bernis, who analyzed colonies' economies before and immediately after they gained independence. He argued that as a result of their domination these territories were deprived of the investment, infrastructure, and trained personnel they needed to develop. Moreover, their economies were export oriented, and organized to service those of the colonizing powers. Key, usually unprocessed, products were harvested, gathered, or mined, and shipped to the metropole where they were refined and sold back to the colonies as processed goods. The colonial powers had little incentive to change this pattern of economic interaction. Not only were they reluctant to jeopardize the steady flow of important raw materials and products from their overseas territories, but they refused to allow the development of any colonial competitors to their own industries. This zero-sum logic made the metropoles even less willing to invest in education and those parts of the infrastructure not vital to their own interests, thereby further limiting the territories' ability to develop their economies.

Upon gaining independence, these territories had to quickly reorganize their economies to eliminate the structural weaknesses they had inherited and to make themselves less dependent on their former colonial masters. To achieve this, de Bernis argued, they must invest heavily in certain key sectors of the economy such as the steel, chemical, and machine tool industries. To establish and maintain these industries, the newly independent countries would have to develop other technologies and capabilities. They would have to provide their new industries with raw materials, buildings, machinery, and trained personnel, as well as the means to transport and sell their produce. Once established, these industries would not only drive the development of the whole economy, they would also stimulate positive social changes.[8]

The Boumedienne regime's commitment to this theory highlights an important continuity between the colonial and postcolonial eras. Through their embrace of it, Boumedienne and Belaid exposed their shared understanding of how economic development was achieved and what made for an advanced economy. For them, heavy industries held the key, as they performed a dual role that was at once both practical and symbolic.

Practically, the goods these industries produced, the jobs they created, the economic growth they stimulated, and the wealth they generated helped drive the economy forward and raise standards of living. Symbolically, they represented Algeria's ongoing transformation into a modern society possessed of a dynamic and diverse economy and foretold the progress that was still to come.

Yet this understanding was based on the development experiences of European countries, and in particular those of France and the USSR. Boumedienne and Belaid wanted Algeria to achieve similar levels of development, and they aimed to bring this about by following and implementing de Bernis's recommendations. Like them, de Bernis aimed to re-create the levels of development achieved by France and other European and North American countries. Such countries provided the benchmark against which Algeria was compared and ultimately found wanting. By adopting de Bernis's theory, Boumedienne and Belaid accepted a set of ideas, recommendations, and assumptions that were French in origin, which privileged French experiences, and which sought to re-create those experiences in other parts of the world. Rather than confirm and reinforce the demise of French values and planning concepts in Algeria, therefore, the Boumedienne regime helped ensure their continued primacy. French political rule of Algeria may have ended, but its development priorities and the ideas and beliefs that gave rise to them remained prevalent.

Belaid's economic grand strategy began in 1967 with the launch of the first of his three investment plans. Lasting three years, it laid much of the groundwork for the rapid expansion of Algeria's heavy industry. During its course, many of the remaining foreign-owned companies in the oil, gas, metallurgy, construction, fertilizer, mining, banking, and insurance sectors were nationalized. It also oversaw the rapid development of the network of state-owned financial and management institutions and an increase in the level of state investment in the public sector. A majority of this funding, around 55 percent, was given over to industry.[9]

This three-year plan was immediately followed by the first of Belaid's four-year plans. Under this new initiative, state funding for the public sector was tripled from 9.5 billion dinars to 28 billion dinars. Yet again, most of this money, around 57 percent of it, was spent building up Algeria's industrial capabilities.[10] This massive increase in state investment helped drive the plan's ambitious industrialization program. The government declared that such a program was "necessary for the requirements of a modern national economic system," and that it was the state's responsibility "to create the necessary conditions for the construction of heavy industry."[11] This program was continued under Belaid's second four-year plan, which was launched in 1974. Under this plan, public sector spending was quadrupled from 28 to 120 billion dinars. In addition to this huge increase, state invest-

ment in industry rose again to 62 percent of the public sector budget.[12] For
the final year of Boumedienne's presidency, his government adopted an
annual investment plan that maintained public sector and industry spending
levels at what they had been in 1977.

Of the total amount the regime invested in industry between 1967 and
1978, the lion's share went to SONATRACH and the hydrocarbon sector.
From the outset, both Boumedienne and Belaid were clear that this sector
was to be Algeria's industrializing industry, the engine that powered the
whole economy. Their decision was based on the continued strength of this
sector.[13] Since independence it had been the only one to have made a profit
year on year. This success resulted partly from the early involvement of foreign oil and gas companies, most notably the Compagnie Français des
Pétroles, Esso, Mobil, and Getty Oil. Their financial and technical support
enabled the sector to develop rapidly. The sector also benefited from the
strength of international demand for oil and gas throughout the 1970s, and
OPEC's quadrupling of oil prices in 1974.

Between 1967 and 1978, Belaid's economic strategy seemed to work.
The revenue generated by the hydrocarbon sector financed Boumedienne's
ambitious spending program and the rapid expansion of the country's industrial base. Oil production rose to around 50 million metric tons per year; production levels in the other, nonhydrocarbon sectors increased by an average
of 300 percent; unemployment fell from 29 percent of the workforce to 21
percent; average wages increased by around 20 percent; and the country's
Gross Domestic Product (GDP) grew between 6 and 7 percent each year.

However, these successes masked a variety of problems. Even though
the economy achieved an impressive rate of growth, it failed to fulfill its
potential. The main impediment was the centralized state bureaucracy,
which was too unwieldy to cope with the speed at which the economy was
developing. The same problem afflicted the regime's investment in the
country's infrastructure as it consistently proved incapable of erecting
enough sufficient buildings. By the late 1970s, houses, hospitals, clinics,
schools, and colleges were all in short supply. As the pressure mounted on
the state-owned financial and management institutions to meet their increasingly unrealistic investment goals, they turned more and more to foreign
companies for help. Not only did this contradict the regime's aim of making
Algeria's economy self-sufficient, it pushed up costs, drained the treasury's
coffers of its foreign currency reserves, and led the government to borrow
heavily from international banks.[14]

Increased international intervention made the Algerian economy ever
more dependent on foreign expertise, which in turn exacerbated the peren-
nial problem of low productivity. Despite the significant increase in industrial output, most of the new factories and plants struggled to fulfill their

production potential. This was partly due to the length of time it took to make these enterprises fully operational. But it was also the result of a chronic skills shortage within the Algerian workforce. In accordance with the theory of industrializing industries, the regime had built plants equipped with the latest technologies. Unfortunately, it overestimated how quickly Algerian technicians could fully master them. Their failure to do so limited the effectiveness of these technologies and increased the amount of time it took each enterprise to pay off the extra costs incurred by buying the most sophisticated machines and production systems.

Low productivity also reduced the economies of scale by making each unit more expensive to produce. Despite the rapid expansion of Algeria's industrial base and growth of its population,[15] the domestic market remained too small to absorb all of the goods produced by the new industries. And because of the inflated production costs and a lack of marketing experience and knowledge, Algerian industries could not compete with European and North American firms, leaving them unable to penetrate other overseas markets. Simultaneously, the Boumedienne regime's privileging of the public sector undermined the competitiveness of private sector businesses. Unable to match the state's investment in its public sector rivals, privately owned companies struggled to compete in the domestic market and remained poorly integrated into the national economy.

The private sector was not the only part of the economy to suffer as a result of the Boumedienne regime's investment priorities. Agriculture also suffered. By the end of the three-year plan, there was mounting evidence that the agricultural sector could no longer produce sufficient food to satisfy domestic demand. In 1962 the country had been self-sufficient in the food it produced and consumed. Seven years later, it was only 70 percent self-sufficient and that figure continued to fall year on year throughout the 1970s. The country's increasing inability to feed itself ran counter to the Boumedienne regime's aim of making it economically self-sufficient. It also created an additional and growing financial burden for the government as it had to pay to import ever more food.

On 8 November 1971, the Boumedienne regime responded by passing the Charter of the Agrarian Revolution. The Charter's main aims were to revitalize the agricultural sector and boost its productivity, stem the flow of peasants to the overcrowded cities, and increase rural support for the regime. To achieve this, it pledged to improve living standards in the countryside by redistributing hundreds of thousands of hectares of land to landless peasants, building thousands of new houses and settlements, and stimulating the rural economy. The Charter adopted an ambitious timetable that was divided into three phases. During the first phase, which lasted from January 1972 until June 1973, around 700,000 hectares of state and privately owned land were given to 50,000 peasants. During the second phase from July 1973 to June 1975, a further 650,000 hectares of land were distributed among 60,000 peasants. During the final phase, which began in July 1975, the country's sheep and goat herders were organized into cooperatives.

In return for this land, the new owners had to agree to work it themselves, diversify what they farmed, become more responsive to the demands and needs of the country, and try to produce a surplus for sale abroad. They also had to accept that they could not sell their land and had to work as part of a cooperative, in order to create economies of scale and facilitate the sharing of machinery and equipment. By the time Boumedienne died, 90,000 peasants had been given over a million hectares of land. And around 5,200 cooperatives had been established, and 700 new settlements built.

Yet, despite these accomplishments, the Charter failed to revolutionize Algerian agriculture. Throughout the 1970s, the country became less and less self-sufficient—so much so that, by 1980, Algeria's farmers were producing just a third of the food consumed by their compatriots. As a result, the government was forced to spend an increasing amount of its foreign currency reserves on importing food. The Charter also failed to reduce the number of peasants migrating from the countryside to the towns and cities. Throughout the 1970s, around 100,000 people left the countryside for urban centers each year.[16]

One of the main reasons for the Charter's lack of success was its failure to fundamentally restructure the agricultural sector. The Charter had aimed to boost productivity by redistributing land and creating a raft of new cooperatives. Despite all that they were given as part of the redistribution, the cooperatives still farmed far less land than the private estates, which together owned around 4,500,000 hectares, and the autogestion enterprises, which possessed over 2,000,000 hectares. As the smallest part of the agricultural sector, the Charter cooperatives struggled to make much of an impact on the sector's productivity levels. This task was made even more challenging by the small size of many of the farms. Over 50 percent comprised no more than five hectares each. Given that the minimum amount of land required to support a family was 10 hectares,[17] these microfarms were never able to produce a surplus. Their failure to do so was evidenced by the continued importance of the private estates to Algeria's food production. In spite of all the measures the Charter introduced and even though they received virtually no help from the government, privately owned farms still produced over 90 percent of the country's meat, 50 percent of its cereals, and 40 percent of its vegetables.

But perhaps the most important cause of the Charter's failure was the steady decline in state investment in the sector. Just as state funding for industry rose from one investment plan to another, it fell for agriculture.

Under the three-year plan, 17 percent of the public sector budget was set aside for agriculture. This was decreased to 15 percent under the first four-year plan and 13 percent under the second four-year plan. And even these shrinking investment pledges were never met. During the three-year plan, actual spending on agriculture amounted to only 16.5 percent of the total budget. This fell to 13 percent during the first four-year plan and just 5 percent during the second four-year plan.

Without adequate funding, the new cooperatives and autogestion farms could not afford to buy the essential goods and machinery they needed or pay their workers decent wages. Continual underinvestment in the sector, coupled with the government's policy of fixing food prices as low as possible for the benefit of city dwellers, created a large and ever-widening salary gap between industrial and agricultural workers. This discrepancy helped fuel rural-urban migration as thousands of peasants moved to the cities in search of better-paying jobs and caused the countryside to lose many of its youngest and best-trained workers. The aging and unskilled workforce that was left behind was unable to master the few modern farming practices and machines that had been introduced, making it incapable of raising productivity to the levels demanded by the government.

The agricultural sector's ability to increase its productivity was undermined further by the regime's reckless land-use policy. Even though only 3 percent of Algeria's territory was cultivable, it allowed houses, factories, and roads to be built on prime farmland.[18] By the end of the 1970s, around 141,650 hectares had been lost in this way. The regime also failed to do enough to safeguard the agricultural land that remained from erosion and desertification. As a consequence of this neglect and the exponential growth of Algeria's population, the ratio of arable land to each inhabitant grew steadily worse. In 1963 there had been 0.75 hectares of farmland per person, but by 1979 this had declined to just 0.40 hectares per citizen.[19]

The agricultural sector's failure to become more productive and increase its contribution to Algeria's GDP helped perpetuate another serious structural weakness—the economy's overreliance on the hydrocarbon sector for its export earnings.[20] Despite the rapid increase in industrial output, by the end of Boumedienne's time in office SONATRACH was still generating over 90 percent of Algeria's foreign currency revenue. Not only did this emphasize the limitations of Belaid's industrializing industries strategy since even after a decade of massive and sustained investment in nonhydrocarbon industries the weight of economic responsibility still rested with the oil and gas sector, it also left the entire economy dependent on a single, traditionally volatile market.

By the late 1970s, many of the flaws in Belaid's strategy and weaknesses within the economy had started to emerge. The first serious efforts to understand and address these problems were made in the months immediately after Benjedid became president. In December 1979, the new regime sponsored a conference to consider how to make the oil and gas industries more efficient and profitable. After days of deliberation, the assembled delegates advised the government to encourage greater foreign and private investment in the hydrocarbon sector and collaboration with SONATRACH. Their recommendations of increased privatization and the need for a new national hydrocarbon strategy formed the basis of the Benjedid regime's economic policy.

After a series of extraordinary meetings of the FLN's Central Committee, Benjedid launched his own five-year development plan in the summer of 1980. The plan's main objective was to rebalance and reinvigorate the economy by making the industrial enterprises more productive, developing the sectors neglected by the Boumedienne regime, improving the country's infrastructure, and encouraging ordinary Algerians to open personal savings accounts. To raise industrial output, the government organized loans to private entrepreneurs, liberalized the importation of goods, and systematically broke up the state-owned financial and management institutions. By the spring of 1983, the nineteen state industries had been split into 120 smaller companies. SONATRACH, the first to be broken up, was divided into four and then thirteen new companies,[21] while the ESDNC and SNS were broken down into twenty-five and seventeen enterprises respectively.[22] To underline this change in industrial policy, Benjedid sacked Belaid and Boumedienne's minister of energy, Sid Ahmed Ghozali, and appointed Abdelhamid Brahimi as the new the minister of economic planning.

To counteract the neglect suffered by the agricultural sector, the Benjedid regime restructured its funding commitments. Under the five-year plan, it reduced its investment in industry by 13 percent while increasing its spending on agriculture by 6 percent. It also facilitated the expansion of the private agricultural sector by introducing new legislation making it easier to buy and sell land. Under this law, which was passed in 1983, 687,966 hectares of farmland were sold by the state to private purchasers. As a result, the amount of privately owned land increased from 55 percent of the total to 62 percent.

The break-up of the state industries by the Benjedid regime and its promotion of private ownership did not mean, however, that it supported the complete liberalization of the Algerian economy or that it was ready to surrender its position as the country's most important economic actor. On the contrary, these measures were intended to enhance its control of the economy by making the state-owned companies more efficient and responsive to society's needs. By improving the public sector's productivity and making it better able to satisfy the demands of the domestic market, the regime aimed to make both it and the economy in general more self-sufficient and less dependent on central government handouts, foreign expertise, and expensive imported goods. It was this logic that inspired the break up of the large state industries. The regime believed that by replacing them with smaller companies, all of which continued to be owned and operated by the state, they would become more agile and flexible. And the companies and sectors the regime did allow to be privatized were strictly limited. Indeed, even after these reforms, the private sector was still much smaller than its public equivalent. Far from challenging the socialist element of its definition of the nation, the Benjedid regime's first five-year economic plan reaffirmed its commitment to it.

Economically, the Benjedid regime's five-year plan met with partial success. Despite the reduction in the level of state investment, industrial output increased by nearly 10 percent per annum. The hydrocarbon sector benefited from continued strong international demand and the doubling of oil prices in 1980. Yet, overall, the plan failed to completely rectify all the problems it had been introduced to address or to dramatically improve the performance of the economy as a whole. Algeria's farms and agricultural estates, especially those in the public and autogestion sectors, struggled to raise their productivity, forcing the government to increase its imports of food. The plan's social infrastructure program failed to keep pace with the exponential growth of Algeria's population and the movement of people from the countryside to the coastal cities.[23] Not only did this growth exert enormous pressure on the country's housing stocks, especially in the urban centers, which remained extremely low, it also led to a rise in unemployment. Between 1980 and 1982, around 280,000 new jobs were created, mostly in the industrial and service sectors. Unfortunately, about 200,000 young adults were joining the labor market each year. Throughout the duration of the plan, the economy was unable to create sufficient jobs to absorb either these new arrivals or the one million people who had been unemployed since the 1970s. Finally, the plan failed to relieve the economic burden being borne by the hydrocarbon sector. By the end of the plan, the oil and gas industries still generated around 95 percent of the country's foreign currency earnings. This dependency was to have serious economic, social, and political consequences.

Shortly after being reelected as president on 12 January 1984,[24] Benjedid launched his second five-year plan. This new initiative called for greater efficiency and austerity to improve productivity and offset the lower earnings forecast for the hydrocarbon sector as a result of falling international demand. The drop in oil prices in 1983, combined with the escalating cost of importing food and consumer goods, increased the government's sense of urgency about the need to improve the country's economic performance. This concern was heightened further by the renewed growth of Algeria's national debt. From 1980 to 1983 the regime had successfully reduced it by diverting money away from the public sector to finance the repayments.[25] But between 1983 and 1985, the debt jumped from $12.9 billion to $16.3 billion because of the loss of revenue caused by the 1983 dip in oil prices. Unfortunately for Algeria, this slump was the start of a major readjustment of the market.

Since the early 1980s, the global oil market had experienced a high degree of instability. Prices had fluctuated as the market compensated for the overinflation of the previous decade. But between 1985 and 1986, this volatility became far more serious as prices plummeted by around 60 percent from $30 a barrel to less than $10. The main causes for this dramatic fall were the increase in the amount of oil available and the onset of recession in the world's major economies. In 1985, the Saudi Arabian government decided to expand its share of the global market by raising its production levels and flooding the market with extra oil. At the same time, the dollar lost 40 percent of its value against the European currencies. This crash, combined with the lingering effects of the huge oil price rise in 1979, plunged the US and European economies into recession, reducing their demand for oil. In Algeria, this led to a 55 percent loss of revenue as the value of its oil and gas exports dropped from $47 billion to $21 billion.[26] The collapse of the dollar proved to be a double blow as it pushed up the cost of its imports from Europe.[27]

The government's response was both swift and drastic. Shortly after the crisis struck, it quickly set about trying to reduce its expenditure and divest itself of some of its more onerous economic responsibilities. Over the course of the next three years the regime slashed its import budget by just under a quarter,[28] while cutting its investment in the public sector by around a third. Yet despite these measures, it was unable to close the balance of payments gap.[29] And it could not prevent the country's foreign debt from growing ever larger.[30] The economic difficulties that resulted from the regime's failure to fully manage its expenditure and control the national debt were exacerbated by its debt repayment policy. Benjedid made it a point of national honor that his government pay the debt installments in full and on time, no matter the broader economic and social consequences. As the debt grew and consumed an ever greater proportion of the country's foreign revenue,[31] the regime cut its investment in the public sector and welfare services even further.

Hamstrung by the lack of investment and the other macroeconomic problems, all sectors of the economy struggled to cope with the developing crisis. In 1987 GDP growth turned negative,[32] prompting a surge in inflation and rise in the level of unemployment.[33] As basic foodstuffs became increasingly scarce and prices for what was available skyrocketed, the regime finally turned to the IMF for assistance. With its encouragement, Benjedid set about liberalizing the economy in late 1987. Starting with the agricultural sector, the regime dissolved the socialist, state-run farms and replaced them with new privately operated concerns. Although the state initially retained ownership of the land, everything on it—animals, machinery, and buildings—was given to those farming it. They were also given the right to sell and bequeath their land once they had worked it for five years.

In the spring of 1988, the regime turned its attention to the industrial sector. The state-owned financial and management institutions were transformed into Public Economic Enterprises (Enterprises Publiques Économiques, EPE). Each EPE was owned by one of the newly created independent Participation Funds (Fonds de Participation, FD) and managed by a corporate-style board of directors. These boards were given the power to wind up their respective EPEs (except those defined as vital to national security, such as oil, gas, and steel) if they were not economically viable after three years.

The rules governing the banking, insurance, and financial sectors were also liberalized. In the summer of 1988 legislation was passed giving banks the freedom to invest in any business or enterprise they chose, not just those in the sector to which they had previously been bound. This was followed in 1990 with new laws lifting some of the restrictions on foreign investment in the Algerian economy, opening the import-export trade to private interests, and deregulating the country's wage structure. To help finance these reforms, the regime received a standby assistance loan from the IMF and an economic reform support loan from the World Bank in 1989 and a financial sector adjustment loan from the World Bank in 1991.[34]

The reforms introduced as part of the second five-year plan and the increased intervention of the IMF and World Bank challenged the socialist dimension of the definition of the nation promoted by the Benjedid regime. The more the Algerian economy was liberalized, the harder it became for the regime to claim that it was still organized and run according to socialist principles. And although the state remained one of the country's main employers, in spite of the reforms Benjedid introduced,[35] it ceased to exert the same control over the economy that it once did. And the IMF's and World Bank's involvement challenged another of the regime's solemn and oft-repeated pledges: that it would not surrender an inch of sovereignty over Algeria's economy. This declaration sounded increasingly false as IMF and World Bank influence over the economy increased.

The erosion of the socialist element of the definition of the nation, promoted since 1962 by the Ben Bella, Boumedienne, and Benjedid regimes, was confirmed with the promulgation of a new national constitution on 23 February 1989. While Islam was once again confirmed as the state religion and Arabic was preserved as the national language,[36] no mention was made of the government's commitment to socialism, its determination to transform Algeria into a socialist state, the Algerian people's socialist character, or the intrinsically socialist nature of Islam. The complete absence of any such declarations amounted to an official rejection of socialism as a defining characteristic of the nation and the most fundamental reappraisal of the nation's identity by any government since independence.

Discontent and Democratization

The developing economic crisis and the regime's response to it had a devastating impact on ordinary Algerians. Month after month the number of forced redundancies rose as the EPEs, starved of investment and exposed to the rigors of the market, slashed their bloated workforces. For the hundreds of thousands of young Algerians entering the job market each year, there was little hope of finding gainful employment. And while many of those who kept their jobs or succeeded in finding work could consider themselves fortunate, they had to accept falling salaries as employers exploited the new legislation deregulating the country's wage structure, while the rapid and uncontrolled rise in inflation devalued the money they did earn.

The hardships endured by a growing number of Algerians were exacerbated by the austerity measures introduced under the second five-year plan. State investment in key social infrastructure projects was drastically reduced or stopped completely. The shortage of adequate housing in particular became critical as funding for existing construction schemes was cut. Welfare services, too, were stripped to the bone as food subsidies were reduced and new, more stringent means-testing measures were introduced. But not everyone suffered. A new cadre of speculators and entrepreneurs emerged who grew rich exploiting the opportunities created by liberalization. Many of them benefited from the links they had to members of the government and state bureaucracy, fueling suspicions that the elite were profiting from the crisis at the expense of ordinary Algerians. Popular resentment toward the elite increased throughout the mid- and late 1980s as evidence mounted of widespread corruption in the upper political echelons.

This dishonesty, coupled with its failure to safeguard living standards, undermined the regime's legitimacy and its socialist credentials. Since independence, successive governments had curried favor with the people by meeting (at least some of) their material needs. They had given Algerians jobs and houses, schools and hospitals, and, in so doing, claimed that they were building socialism in Algeria. In return for these services, Algerians agreed (or most did, at any rate) to accept certain limits to their political rights. But with the worsening economic crisis, Benjedid was forced to renege on his side of the postcolonial social contract. Not only did this call Algeria's socialist character into question but it led to angry demonstrations by Algerians who were no longer receiving what they were due.

Frustrated by the government's inability to deal with the economic crisis and the widespread corruption within the ruling elite, thousands of Algerians took to the streets repeatedly throughout the late 1980s to express their anger. In April 1985, shortly after oil prices had begun to plummet, riots broke out in the Algiers' casbah. These were followed, in November 1986, with a series of demonstrations and wildcat strikes in Algiers, Oran, and Skikda. Similar protests were held in Constantine, where they quickly developed into a protest against the regime's language policies. There was further worker and student unrest during 1987 and 1988 throughout the country. And with each year that passed, the number of towns and cities in which such protests were held increased.

In September 1988, a new wave of industrial action gripped the country. On 4 October, striking workers and university students were joined by school pupils who walked out of their classes amid rumors that a general strike was shortly to be called. The following day, thousands of youths blazed a trail of destruction through central Algiers as they attacked and damaged buildings belonging to the government, FLN, and the affluent. Over the next couple of days the country was paralyzed as the violence spread to other urban centers. The number of groups involved also increased as the workers, university students, and school pupils were joined by Berber nationalists and Islamic fundamentalists. Overwhelmed by the scale of the demonstrations, the government responded on 6 October by declaring a state of emergency and instructing the security forces to restore order by whatever means necessary. Fearful of the anarchy into which the country seemed to be slipping, the police, gendarmerie, and army gave no quarter to the protestors.[37] Although they successfully reclaimed the streets for the government, they did so at enormous human and political cost.

The brutality of the security forces' response led to a huge outcry from the general public. Much of this anger was directed at the SM units that had been responsible for many of the deaths and were suspected (correctly, as it turned out) of torturing some of those arrested. The events of what became known as Black October heralded a sea change in popular attitudes toward the army. The general affection in which it had been held since 1962, as the vanquisher of the French and keeper of the sacred spirit of the war of liberation, gave way to suspicion and hostility. Rather than the people's protector, it was now viewed as its oppressor.

The popular outrage generated by the military's actions had two important political consequences. In an effort to appease public sentiment, Benjedid was forced to promise to reform Algeria's political system and security apparatus. These reforms, which proved to be the most radical since independence, helped undermine the government's control of the country's political and social space and paved the way for the emergence of the Islamists and Berberists as powerful political forces. Benjedid also had to distance himself from the military. He sought to do so by sacking the head of the SM, General Medjdoub Lakhal Ayat, and pledging to reassert civilian control over the army. However, in so doing, Benjedid alienated many of its officers. They felt betrayed and let down by the government whose orders they had been carrying out. This rift grew wider over the next few years to the serious detriment of both Benjedid personally and the democratic process that he was shortly to introduce.

Benjedid's overhaul of Algeria's political system began almost immediately. Throughout mid- and late October 1988, he hastily organized a referendum on a series of changes he wanted to make to the national constitution. The most radical of these was the proposal to make the government and the prime minister directly accountable to the National Assembly. On 3 November the country's voters went to the polls and overwhelmingly endorsed his recommendations. To maintain the momentum that this result created and underline his determination to shake up the existing political order, Benjedid appointed Colonel Kasdi Merbah as his new prime minister two days later.[38] As a known admirer of Boumedienne, Merbah's selection was intended to help placate the army. But it did not signify a change of heart by Benjedid. His determination to transform Algerian politics was reaffirmed at the sixth FLN congress, which took place on 28 and 29 November. In a speech to assembled delegates, Benjedid intimated that he would end its status as Algeria's only legal political party. His words were given extra weight by his recent dismissal of the FLN's deputy secretary-general and stalwart of the old order, Mohamed Chérif Massaadia.

Despite these threats, Benjedid's grip on the party, which had been enhanced by Massaadia's departure, was sufficiently strong to ensure that he once again secured its nomination for the forthcoming presidential election. After standing as the only candidate, Benjedid was duly elected for his third term on 22 December 1988 by 81 percent of those who voted.[39] The mandate this victory gave him allowed him to press ahead with his reform package. Its keystone was the new constitution that was submitted to the Algerian voters for their approval on 23 February 1989. Once again they gave Benjedid a glowing endorsement as 72 percent of them voted in favor of adopting it.[40] In addition to marking the regime's official rejection of the socialist element of its definition of the nation, the constitution was significant for the provisions it made to liberalize the political system and encourage greater public participation in it. At the heart of its attempts to do so was Article 42 under which Algerians were for the first time permitted to establish "associations of a political nature."[41]

No sooner had the new constitution been adopted than a raft of political organizations were founded and began clamoring for official recognition as parties. Some of the groups that were established called for the introduction of sharia law, while others demanded greater political and cultural rights for Berbers, even though the constitution forbade the formation of any association that was explicitly religious, regional, or linguistic in character. By late autumn of 1989, the regime had bowed to this pressure and recognized several groups as political parties including the FIS and the FFS.[42]

The FIS was the latest in a long line of groups calling for Islam to play a more prominent role in shaping Algerian politics and society. The origins of this movement stretched back to the AUMA, which had opposed the Sufi brotherhoods and resisted French colonial rule. Once independence had been achieved, some of the AUMA's former members became disillusioned with the Ben Bella regime, its commitment to socialism, and the type of society it seemed determined to create. In January 1964, these individuals helped found a new group called Al Qiyam (The Values). Just like the AUMA when it was first founded, Al Qiyam did not directly challenge the regime politically. Instead, it focused on religious, cultural, and social issues such as encouraging people and the state to observe Islamic practices and dress.

Yet, also like the AUMA, such issues called into question existing government policy. The group quickly became more overtly political, declaring in its journal *Humanisme Musulman* in 1965 that "all political parties, all regimes and all leaders that do not base themselves on Islam are . . . illegal and dangerous."[43] Such sentiments reflected the influence of anti-Western thinkers and writers on Al Qiyam's leadership. Hachemi Tijani, the group's secretary-general, embraced the works of scholars like Jamal al-Din al-Afghani and Sayyid Qutb, who denied the compatibility of Islam with European ideas and technologies. They argued instead that Muslim societies could only become truly Islamic and recapture their past glories by completely rejecting Western cultures and influences. The adoption of these ideas by Al Qiyam members marked an important difference between their group and the AUMA.

Under Boumedienne, the government adopted a new strategy to contain the growing Islamic opposition to the state. This approach entailed both repressing Al Qiyam and other activists and adopting issues close to the Islamic movement's heart. In this way, Boumedienne successfully stymied opposition to his regime while boosting its Islamic credentials and sapping Al Qiyam's support base. Over time, as the regime reaffirmed its commitment to socialism and successfully countered the challenge posed by the Islamic movement, the government stepped up its repression of Al Qiyam members and supporters. Finally, the group was outlawed by ministerial decree on 17 March 1970.

Rather than totally destroy the movement, the Boumedienne regime's repression of Al Qiyam drove it underground. Other associations and organizations to emerge in the late 1960s were Dawa wa Tabligh and Takfir wa

Hijra. Made up of former members and sympathizers of Al Qiyam, such groups continued to challenge, albeit weakly, the regime's embrace of socialism and to denounce its lack of religiosity. The mid- to late 1960s also saw the emergence of a new cadre of scholars who, along with their adherents, came to dominate the Islamic movement for the next thirty years.

One of these thinkers was Malek Bennabi. In the years immediately following independence, Bennabi gained a following among the student body at the University of Algiers. Although never a member, he was strongly influenced by the AUMA. But he did not accept everything the AUMA did or support all that its leaders recommended. Bennabi had been particularly opposed to the AUMA's increased involvement in the political process and its cooperation with the assimilationists whom he denounced. Yet his thinking, and that of his followers, remained firmly rooted in the AUMA tradition. The caution with which they approached the works of Sayyid Qutb and general rejection of his ideas led to them being described as Djazarists or Algerianists.[44] The Djazarists and the Qutbists came to form the two main trends within the Algerian Islamic movement.

Another Islamic scholar to emerge in the early 1970s was Abdallah Djaballah. In the autumn of 1974 he helped found, along with Hussein Mashuma, Abdelkader Boukhakham, and Kamel Bezaz, the Islamic Renaissance Movement (Mouvement de la Nahda Islamique, MNI). Like the group surrounding Bennabi, the MNI was mostly made up of students, this time from Ain el Bey University in Constantine. Unlike Bennabi and his supporters, however, the MNI was more sympathetic to Qutb and the Egyptian Muslim Brotherhood.

So, too, was Mahfoud Nahnah, another emerging thinker, writer, and activist leader. Like many in the Islamic movement, he was appalled by what he considered the Ben Bella and Boumedienne regimes' lack of religious observance. He was especially dismayed by the 1976 National Charter and constitution, which committed the country to socialism and claimed that Islam and Algerians were inherently socialist. In defiance Nahnah carried out petty acts of sabotage for which he served four of a fifteen-year prison sentence. Soon after his release he helped found the Association for Guidance and Reform, a charitable organization committed to promoting religiosity and improving Algerians' knowledge and understanding of Islam.

Despite their shared hatred of Boumedienne and determination to transform Algeria into a truly Islamic society, the members of the Islamic movement remained deeply divided. The split between the Djazarists and Qutbists proved to be intractable, and the divisions these arguments created were deepened by the personal and political rivalries that existed between the various leaders as they each sought to expand their followings at one another's expense. As a result, intergroup cooperation became difficult to organize, undermining the movement's ability to coordinate its actions against the regime and the effectiveness of its protests. Confronted by small pockets of opposition and resistance, the regime was easily able to contain them and dismiss their importance.

Yet despite the fissures and fractures that permeated the Islamic movement, its leaders were not totally incapable of putting aside their differences. Indeed, in the early and mid-1980s, a number of mass demonstrations were held demanding, among other things, the acceleration of the Arabization program, the outlawing of alcohol and mixed-sex education, and the expansion of religious education. In November 1988 this cooperation even extended to the establishment of an umbrella organization, the League of the Islamic Call (Rabitat al-Dawa) under which all the main actors and associations were united.

In addition to emphasizing the benefits of joint action, the rallies of the 1980s also highlighted the growing strength of the Islamic movement. After its initial tolerance of Islamic activists, the Benjedid regime resurrected Boumedienne's dual approach to dealing with them. While it came down hard on the captured MIA fighters and student militants, it also promoted Islamic issues and enacted legislation, such as the Family Code, which were supported by many in the movement. Yet such measures failed to halt the growth in support for Islamic groups. As the economic situation worsened, more and more Algerians turned to them for help, guidance, and leadership.

Despite the official measures enacted against them, the different Islamic groups and associations busily set about raising their profiles among the Algerian population from the early 1980s onward. In addition to the very visible initiatives they organized and participated in, such as the rallies and demonstrations, the groups also exploited the regime's weakening grip on the country's social space. As the decade progressed, they gradually gained control of thousands of mosques and prayer rooms in towns and cities across Algeria. Furthermore, they established networks of social amenities such as clinics, medical centers, and funeral homes that the state was no longer either willing or able to provide.

Although many leading Islamic intellectuals and activists joined Rabitat al-Dawa, they continued to argue and fight among themselves. The old rivalries and divisions between the Djazarists and Qutbists endured and were brought into stark relief with the creation of the FIS in February 1989. The fifteen senior members of the Islamic community who founded the FIS were quickly joined by other prominent thinkers, commentators, and activists. But others, most notably Abdallah Djaballah and Mahfoud Nahnah, refused to join. Instead, they established their own parties. On 6 December 1990 Nahnah founded the Movement for an Islamic Society (Al-

Harakat li-Mujtama` Islami, HAMAS), while, later that month, Djaballah had the MNI legally recognized.

Islamic groups were not the only ones to petition the government for recognition as political parties. So, too, did a variety of secular associations. One of these was the FFS, which had been founded by Hocine Aït Ahmed in September 1963 to resist Ben Bella and the Political Bureau. Despite its checkered past and attempts to overthrow the government, it was granted party status on 20 November 1989. One month later, on 15 December, Aït Ahmed returned to Algeria for the first time in nearly twenty-five years. His aim was to capitalize on the raised profile the party had achieved in Kabylia and the rest of the country through its efforts to orchestrate Berber protests against the government over the past decade to develop the FFS as a national force within Algerian politics. As a show of strength and unity, he helped arrange a mass rally in Algiers on 31 May 1990. Attended by around 100,000 people, it was of a similar size to that held by the FIS a month before on 20 April.

Unlike the FIS, however, the FFS remained a regional party. The FFS's commitment to safeguarding and extending the Berber community's rights and liberties, and the methods it sometimes employed, unnerved and alienated many Algerian Arabs. The FFS was also unable to match the FIS's organizational capabilities. It had no equivalent to the FIS's network of mosques, schools, and religious centers. And, as a consequence, it could not match its ability to mobilize its supporters or disseminate its views.

The FFS also had to take care to safeguard its own support. One of its main competitors was the Rally for Culture and Democracy (Rassemblement pour la Culture et la Démocratie, RCD) founded by Dr. Saïd Sadi in December 1989. A former acolyte of Aït Ahmed, Sadi established the RCD after he and his former mentor fell out in the late 1980s. Yet the rancor between the two men, which continued to grow throughout the 1990s, did not prevent their respective parties from adopting similar agendas. Both groups demanded that Algeria remain a secular state and called for greater cultural and linguistic rights for Berbers. As a consequence, the two parties drew their support from the same section of society and competed for the loyalty of the same group of voters. Given that it was better established and its past efforts to improve the lot of the Berber community, the FFS continued to be the dominant party in Kabylia. But the RCD did attract the support of specific groups within Berber society, most notably young, educated city dwellers.

Although secure within the Berber heartlands, both the FFS and RCD struggled to win support in the remainder of the country. Their commitment to the Berber cause was certainly one factor that contributed to this. Another was the fierce competition they faced from other parties such as the

Socialist Vanguard Party (Parti de l'Avant-Garde Socialiste, PAGS) and the Movement for Democracy in Algeria (Mouvement pour la Démocratie en Algérie, MDA). The PAGS was founded in 1966 by El Hachemi Chérif as the successor to the Algerian Communist Party, which was outlawed shortly after independence. Perhaps unsurprisingly given its heritage, the PAGS was committed to the consolidation of socialism in Algeria and consistently criticized the Ben Bella, Boumedienne, and Benjedid regimes for not doing enough in that regard. Operating clandestinely until it was legally recognized in December 1989, its members infiltrated the UGTA and other trade union movements with the aim of promoting the party line.

The slackening of the Benjedid regime's grip on the country's political system continued apace throughout the winter of 1989. The members of the new political opposition issued repeated demands that fresh parliamentary elections be held as soon as possible. While Benjedid balked at this proposal, he did agree to hold local and regional elections in June the following year. Confident that the FLN would win a majority of the votes cast, Benjedid approved electoral legislation that favored the bigger parties at the expense of the smaller ones. On 12 June 1990 Algerians went to the polls again for the third time in just over a year and a half. Partly because of voter fatigue, and partly as a result of the boycott called by the FFS and other secular parties, turnout was at it lowest since independence, with around two-thirds of the country's voters taking part.

Despite the comparatively low turnout, the election was largely free and fair. To the delight of many in the Islamic movement and consternation of an equal number in the regime, the FIS won 55 percent of the total votes cast. This result gave it control of 853 of Algeria's 1,539 municipalities and 32 of its 48 wilaya councils. By comparison, the FLN received 28 percent of the vote and retained control of just 487 municipalities and 14 wilaya councils. The scale of the FIS's achievement was augmented by the electoral rules that Benjedid had implemented to help the FLN. In light of the financial and organizational means at the FLN's disposal, which it had accrued during the long years it had remained the country's sole political party, the FIS's victory delivered a stinging rebuke to the political leadership. To Benjedid's surprise, Algerians seized the opportunity presented by the election to admonish him and his government and to demand the wholesale reform of the postindependence political order.

The result of the June election not only gave the FIS its first taste of power, but greatly enhanced its ability to shape the debate on Algerian culture and national identity, on what it meant to be Algerian. In February 1989, the group's executive, the *majlis al-shura,* issued a paper entitled "Characteristics of the Islamic Salvation Front," outlining their six core objectives. These included (1) working to unify the global Muslim community or *umma*; (2) promoting Islam, both at home and abroad, as a solution to existing political, economic, and social problems and as an alternative to secular ideologies; (3) adopting a moderate approach to politics based on the Quran's Golden Mean; (4) combating individual selfishness and egotism; (5) encouraging initiative; and (6) protecting the sacred message of Allah received through Muhammad. In the districts and areas over which it gained authority, the FIS quickly set about trying to realize its aims. Cafés and shops selling alcohol had their licenses revoked or were forced to close. The wearing of shorts and other revealing clothes was forbidden. Rai music was outlawed and mixed-sex schools were systematically shut.

Yet the FIS's leaders were unable to enact all the laws they wanted because of existing legislation. They surmised, not unreasonably, that the only way they could mold Algeria the way they wanted was by gaining control of the national government. So over the weeks and months following the local and regional elections, they stepped up their efforts to make Benjedid call a National Assembly election. He was already under enormous pressure to do so because of these earlier results. In fact, it was only with the greatest difficulty that he was able to retain any control over the reform process he had initiated.

On 2 August 1990 Iraqi forces poured across the border into neighboring Kuwait. Five months later, on 17 January 1991, a coalition force led by the United States launched Operation Desert Storm to liberate Kuwait. The FIS seized on the deployment of US and European troops to the Gulf to condemn the Algerian government for not doing enough to help Iraq defend itself and to whip up anti-Western sentiments, which it used to galvanize its own supporters. Alarmed at the effect this barrage of criticism was having on public opinion and the growth in support for the FIS, the National Assembly passed new legislation in April 1991 redrawing constituency boundaries, prohibiting husbands from voting for their wives, and outlawing electioneering in mosques. This law was intended to help the FLN by creating a network of electoral districts that would maximize the number of seats the FLN was predicted to win and undermine the FIS's ability to mobilize its followers.

In protest, the FIS called for a general strike to be held on 25 May. The FIS's leadership hoped that in addition to forcing the government's hand, the strike would demonstrate the party's power and popularity shortly before the parliamentary election that Benjedid had announced would take place on 27 June. Even though the strike was not universally observed, the limited and poorly organized demonstrations that did occur alarmed the army. Increasingly fearful about what it viewed as the breakdown in law and order, it put pressure on Benjedid to crack down on the FIS. So on 4 June, he declared a state of emergency. The clashes that followed between the army and FIS activists led to the deaths of over fifty people and the imprisonment of several hundred more.

On 5 June Prime Minister Mouloud Hamrouche resigned and was replaced by Sid Ahmed Ghozali. In an attempt to placate both the military and the FIS, Ghozali postponed the National Assembly election and promised to review the recently passed electoral law. Unfortunately, Ghozali's compromise satisfied no one. Frustrated by this new delay, the FIS threatened to declare jihad against the government. On 30 June, the army responded by arresting thousands of FIS members and sympathizers, including Madani and Belhadj. With its president and vice president behind bars, the party's majlis al-shura appointed Abdelkader Hachani as its interim leader. Widely respected within the FIS and broader Islamic movement, his appeals for calm worked, and clashes between party activists and the security forces declined.

Throughout the summer and autumn of 1991, Ghozali held frantic negotiations with members of the government, the armed forces, the National Assembly, and the opposition parties in an attempt to keep the democratic process on track. In October, a modified electoral law was passed that satisfied both the FLN-controlled Assembly and the other political parties. In addition to increasing the number of electoral districts to 430, it also reduced the voting age to 25. Despite these compromises, Hachani refused to accept the new law as it ruled that Madani and Belhadj would be ineligible to stand as candidates because they were in prison. Eventually, however, on 14 December, he relented and put all his energies into encouraging the party faithful to vote in the election scheduled for 26 December.

Yet again, the FIS gave the Algerian establishment a bloody nose. In the first round of voting it won 47 percent of the vote and outright majorities in 188 of the country's 231 electoral districts.[45] Second behind the FIS was the FFS, which gained 7.5 percent of the vote and overall majorities in twenty-five constituencies. Despite receiving a far higher percentage of the vote than the FFS, the FLN could only manage third place, winning 25 percent of the vote and just fifteen seats. Of the remaining parties that took part, none won any seats. HAMAS received 5.3 percent of the vote, the RCD 3 percent, and the MNI 2 percent. The three other seats that were won outright were all taken by independent candidates who together got 4.5 percent of the vote. And even though over four hundred allegations of electoral misconduct and fraud were filed with the Constitutional Court by disgruntled parties, candidates, and voters, most observers—both in Algeria and abroad—recognized the election as largely free and fair.

The second round of the election, which would decide who would occupy the remaining 199 seats in the National Assembly, was scheduled to take place on 16 January 1992. But within the government frantic discussions were taking place over whether or not it should be allowed to take place. Throughout late December and early January, Chadli was besieged by a group of his cabinet colleagues demanding that he call a halt to the electoral process. Led by Ghozali and Majors-General Khaled Nezzar and Larby Belkheir, who were serving as the ministers of defense and interior, respectively, they argued that Benjedid had a duty to intervene to stop the FIS's almost certain victory and prevent it from gaining power. When Benjedid stalled, amid rumors that he was secretly meeting Hachani to discuss the handover of power, his opponents took matters into their own hands. In so doing, they helped plunge Algeria into civil war.

The Military Intervenes and the Islamists Respond

On 11 January 1992, Benjedid spoke to the nation in a televised address. Over the past few years, Algerians had grown accustomed to such broadcasts and his appeals for calm, patience, and courage. Yet few were prepared for what he had to say. He began predictably enough with assurances of his government's tireless commitment and promises of better times ahead. But part way in, he broke from his script to announce with the utmost solemnity that he was resigning as president in order to safeguard "the unity of the people and the security of the country."

The unexpectedness and self-sacrificing tone of Benjedid's declaration hinted at a remarkable truth—that his decision to step down had not been of his own making. A few days before the broadcast was shown, Major-General Nezzar had presented Benjedid with a stark choice: resign or be overthrown. Nezzar's ultimatum was no idle threat. He represented a cabal of government ministers, FLN leaders, and prominent businessmen. But more importantly, he had the backing of those who controlled Algeria's most powerful institution—the army.[46] Despite being an old soldier himself and having been supported by the military following Boumedienne's death, Benjedid was now viewed as a threat to the army's political interests, the unity of the country, and the traditions and values of the war of liberation because of his continued support for the democratic process.

To draw a veil of legitimacy over their actions, Nezzar and his coconspirators were careful to engineer a constitutional crisis. Days before they forced Benjedid to resign, they made him dissolve the National Assembly. In so doing, they removed the speaker of the Assembly from office. As Benjedid's legal successor in the constitutional line of authority, his dismissal ensured that once Benjedid resigned there would be no clear candidate to assume control of the government. This leadership crisis was made absolute following the chairman of the Constitutional Council's refusal to act as interim leader.[47] Under the cloak of confusion that they had created, Nezzar and the other leaders of the coup invested power in the Higher Security Council (Haut Comité de Sécurité, HCS), which had hitherto advised the president on matters of security and national defense.

Made up of six members, the HCS included the main leaders of the coup—Ghozali, Nezzar, Belkheir, Guenaïza, Hamdani Benkhelil, the minister of justice, and Lakhdar Brahimi, the minister of foreign affairs. The day after it assumed power, it postponed the next round of voting, annulled the results of the first ballot, and established a new committee—the High State Council (Haut Comité d'Etat, HCE)—to govern Algeria. The HCE had five members—Nezzar, Mohamed Ali Haroun, Ali Kafi, Tedjini Haddam, and Mohamed Boudiaf (one of the Nine Historics), who was appointed as its chair. It took power on 14 January 1992 and was to act as a collective president until December 1993, the date Benjedid's presidency would have come to an end.

Over the weeks and months following Benjedid's resignation, the HCE worked tirelessly to wipe the FIS off the face of Algeria's political map and from people's memories. Central to its strategy was the outlawing of the party, the arrest and detention of its leaders and members,[48] and the closure of its mosques, meeting rooms, charities, and businesses. As a result of these actions, the party's organizational structure was shattered, and those members who remained at liberty were forced either to renounce their allegiance or to operate clandestinely. And the arrest of many of its leaders and the scattering of those who escaped prison created schisms that undermined the party's cohesion and therefore its ability to operate as an effective opposition force.

One of the main challenges to confront the FIS throughout much of the 1990s was to preserve its leadership of the Islamist movement and retain its political relevancy. At the heart of this challenge lay three key dilemmas: (1) who was in charge and had the right to speak in the name of the FIS; (2) how should the organization respond to the rapidly growing Islamist *maquis*; and (3) which group or faction within it, if any, should it support? For a number of years, these questions remained unresolved.

By early March 1992, five of the FIS's most senior figures, including its leader and his deputy, were either in prison or under house arrest. Rather than risk capture, several of those who remained at liberty fled the country in search of sanctuary abroad. Two of those who left were Anwar Haddam and Sheikh Abdelbaki Sahraoui, who went to Chicago and Paris, respectively.[49] They were joined in exile by Rabah Kébir,[50] who, after escaping from house arrest, fled to Germany in September 1992. Shortly after making their escapes, Haddam and Kébir each declared himself spokesman for the FIS.

Haddam set up, with himself as its head, a body called the FIS Parliamentary Delegation, and Kébir assumed the title of official representative of the FIS abroad.

Perhaps unsurprisingly, given that each man had acted unilaterally, they came to represent competing, rather than complementary, centers of authority. And they were not the only ones to claim leadership of the FIS. So, too, did Abderrazak Redjam, Mohammed Saïd, and Ikhlef Cherrati.[51] Choosing to remain in Algeria, they worked together to establish the dissident newspaper *Minbar El-Djoumma* and the underground radio station Idaat El-Wafa. As a former member of the FIS's Provisional Executive Bureau (Bureau Executif Provisoire, BEP), Redjam continued to release official statements on the organization's behalf. But in spite of his background and his efforts to maintain contact with rank and file members, both Haddam and Kébir were reluctant to recognize either Redjam's or Saïd's or Cherrati's authority.

In late 1992, Madani finally intervened. In a note smuggled out of the prison at Blida, where both he and Belhadj were being held, he recognized Kébir as the "sole authorized spokesman of the FIS abroad."[52] In an effort to enforce this ruling and reassert his own authority over what remained of the FIS within Algeria, he ordered Redjam to stop releasing statements in the organization's name. Yet this failed to bring an end to the infighting. Haddam, Redjam, Saïd, Cherrati, and Sahraoui all refused to recognize Kébir's authority and continued largely as they had done before. And accusations were leveled against Madani, by Haddam in particular, that he was only supporting Kébir because he was a friend of his sons who were also based in Germany. Far from resolving the leadership crisis that had gripped the FIS since the start of the HCE's crackdown on the organization, Madani's intercession only added a new level of complexity and bitterness to it.

The rivalry that remained continued to be fueled by disagreements over the FIS's relationship with the various Islamist insurgent groups that were set up throughout the early 1990s. Initially, both Kébir and Haddam tried to distance themselves and the FIS from the recently reformed MIA. They reasoned that they were far more likely to receive help and support from European and North American governments if they presented themselves as democrats and the FIS as the injured party than they would if they openly backed an armed group calling for *jihad*. In contrast, those individuals still in Algeria (Redjam, Saïd, and Cherrati) were more supportive of the MIA, praising the group and its activities in the pages of *Minbar El-Djoumma* and over the airwaves of Idaat El-Wafa.

The contrasting positions adopted by these individuals reflected the different political realities they each faced. Neither Haddam nor Kébir could afford to ignore the sensibilities of the US and German authorities as their power and influence within the FIS rested in part on their relations with them. They had little choice, therefore, but to declare their opposition to the use of violence. Similarly, Redjam, Saïd, and Cherrati could not ignore the MIA or the angry young men thirsty for vengeance, as to do so would have meant marginalizing themselves. Indeed, even if they did not openly advocate armed resistance, they could scarcely criticize those who did. The differences between these stances highlighted the crucial dilemmas confronting the FIS: should it remain true to its pledge to achieve power by peaceful means and jeopardize its leadership of the Islamist movement or throw the full weight of its support behind the MIA and risk alienating the international community even more than it had done already?

Throughout late 1992 and early 1993 the FIS's relationship with the MIA and the extent of its support for the armed insurrection became intertwined with the ongoing leadership struggle. All of those who wanted to increase their influence in the group tried to shape its strategy to suit their own respective aims. Kébir, therefore, was adamant that the FIS must continue to seek power by nonviolent means. Any official renewals of the FIS's commitment to such a strategy inevitably strengthened his hand while simultaneously weakening those of Redjam and Saïd. They, in contrast, argued that the FIS should adopt a more openly bellicose line given that their power base was made up of young militants and MIA fighters.

Although this ongoing contest destabilized the FIS, the mixed signals given out by those involved in it enabled the organization to go some way to appeasing both the insurgents at home and the prodemocracy forces abroad. Throughout this period, the lack of a coherent or overriding strategy meant that the FIS was, to a limited extent, able to be all things to all people. Yet, clearly, the longer the Algerian government refused to back down, the harder it was for it to maintain this position. Furthermore, it also relied on neither factions achieving preeminence over the other and, perhaps more importantly, the organizations enjoying cordial, if not good, relations with the leader of the insurgency.

Certainly for as long as the MIA remained the dominant insurgent group this seemed possible. Although its leader, Abdelkader Chébouti, was never a member of the FIS and owed no allegiance to either the group or Madani personally, he worked closely with Redjam, Saïd, and Cherrati. And in January 1993 he was honored by Belhadj, who declared that if he had been free, he would have joined "Brother Chébouti" in his fight against the HCE.[53] But in July 1992, a new faction emerged called the Armed Islamic Group (Groupe Islamique Armé, GIA). Founded by Mansour Meliana, it was a loose confederacy of three small bands of fighters. Meliana was a former comrade of Chébouti, but their friendship had turned into bitter rivalry when Chébouti beat Meliana to the position of MIA leader.

The GIA was conceived and created, therefore, in opposition to the

MIA. And this remained the case even after Meliana's arrest on 28 July 1992. Following his demise, the three bands that made up the GIA gravitated back into the MIA fold. But from October to December 1992, they, along with two other MIA factions that had previously remained loyal to Chébouti, fell under the influence of an ambitious young commander called Abdelhak Layada. On his insistence, these five bands broke from the MIA in January 1993 to become the reformed GIA. Upon doing so, Layada declared that neither he nor any of the fighters now under his command would follow Chébouti's orders.

Yet Layada's ambitions did not stop at having an armed group of his own to command. On the contrary, he wanted nothing less than leadership of the entire insurgency. Like the wartime heads of the FLN, he aimed to unite the various armed factions, by whatever means necessary, under the GIA banner. These aims placed the GIA on a collision course with both the MIA and the FIS. As long as Chébouti remained in command, the MIA would resist all attempts to subsume it as part of the GIA. And despite their many disagreements, Madani, Belhadj, Kébir, Haddam, Redjam, Saïd, and Cherrati remained united in their belief that the FIS should continue to lead and speak on behalf of the Islamist movement.

The GIA's opposition to the FIS was reinforced by Layada's rejection of democracy. Heavily influenced by the radical cleric Omar El-Eulmi,[54] Layada argued that it had never been his "intention to participate in elections or enter parliament" as "the right to legislate belongs solely to God."[55] Instead, he insisted that the transformation of Algeria into an Islamic republic could only be achieved by violent means. His views became the avowed position of the GIA, which adopted as its official mantra the slogan "no dialogue, no truce, no reconciliation." Like the FLN during the war of liberation, the GIA swore that it would never enter into negotiations with the government or stop until it achieved its final goal.

The GIA's dismissal of democracy and all those who engaged in it as sacrilegious, was completely at odds with the FIS's continued (albeit weakening) commitment to win power through the ballot box. And any hopes that relations between the two organizations might improve following Layada's arrest by the Moroccan security services in July 1993 quickly evaporated following Sid Ahmed Mourad's assumption of the GIA's leadership. As a former follower of Meliani, his hostility toward the FIS was particularly strong. As well as sharing his old patron's hatred of Chébouti and all those who sided with him, he fully supported Layada's views on democracy and the need to wage total war against the government and anyone who stood in the GIA's way of uniting the Islamist movement under its leadership.

In the face of such intransigence and mindful of the GIA's desire to usurp its position as leader of the Islamist movement, the FIS responded by organizing its own armed units. Throughout the latter half of 1993 and the early months of 1994, it set about helping the MIA step up its recruitment of fighters. This process was facilitated by the government's steady release of thousands of FIS militants and activists from its prison camps in the Sahara.[56] These young men, whose bitterness and commitment to the Islamist cause had invariably grown during their time in captivity, were often only too willing to take up arms against the state. To increase the number of armed fighters it could call on still further, the FIS opened negotiations with the leaders of other insurgent factions, most notably Ahmed Ben Aicha and Madani Merzak of the Movement for the Islamic State (Mouvement pour l'État Islamique, MEI),[57] about the possibility of their adding their units to those of the MIA as part of a new group called the Islamic Salvation Army (Armée Islamique du Salut, AIS).

On 18 July 1994, the AIS was formally established with Ben Aicha and Merzak as two of its commanders.[58] Its creation signaled the start of a new phase in the rebellion and a shift in the FIS's relations with the insurgents. While the MIA's and the MEI's loyalty to the FIS was largely beyond doubt (as evidenced by their willingness to join the AIS), relations between these groups had been almost entirely informal. The AIS, in contrast, was far more clearly an extension of the FIS. From the outset, Ben Aicha and Merzak both accepted Madani's and Belhadj's authority over them. And the primacy of the political leadership over the military commanders was reinforced by the choice of name for the new group. Just as the ALN derived its name from the FLN, so the AIS derived its from the FIS.

Yet the creation of the AIS highlighted just how frightened the FIS's leaders were of the GIA. Its hardline stance, commitment to action, and determination to take the fight to the enemy, gave the GIA a dynamism that appealed to the angry young men of the Islamist movement. In contrast, the FIS appeared staid and timid and increasingly out of touch with what these youths felt and wanted. As a result, thousands of them, including many who had been members of the FIS, flocked to the GIA's colors. Throughout the course of 1993, its ranks swelled dramatically as it captured the initiative and came close to seizing the leadership of the Islamist movement from the FIS.

But perhaps most worryingly for Madani and Belhadj were the high profile defections. The loss of senior members of the organization to the GIA was especially damaging as it helped reinforce the impression that the FIS's ship was sinking. Two of the most important people to leave the group were Abderrazak Redjam and Mohammed Saïd. On 13 May 1994, they sat side by side with Saïd Mekhlouf and Cherif Gousmi (who had taken over as supreme commander of the GIA)[59] at a conference and pledged the FIS's allegiance to the GIA's high command. They also swore on the FIS's behalf "to abide by the Book, the *sunna* and the *salafiyya* tradition"; that there would be "no dialogue, no ceasefire, no reconciliation . . . with the apostate regime"; that "*jihad* . . . [was] an Islamic imperative until judgement day";

that "the GIA . . . [was] the only legitimate organizational framework for *jihad* in Algeria"; and that "all holy fighters must join the GIA."[60] What made Redjam's and Saïd's defections all the more galling to Madani, Belhadj, and Kébir was their attempt to take the entire FIS with them.

In response to these departures, the FIS released a statement through its Executive Authority Abroad (Instance Exécutive du FIS à l'Étranger) refuting the oaths taken by Redjam and Saïd, and dismissing their authority to speak on behalf of the organization.[61] The creation of the AIS, therefore, was intended, at least in part, to halt the flow of FIS members to the GIA. By presenting the group as more dynamic, Madani, Belhadj, and Kébir aimed to increase the group's appeal to the disaffected and vengeful young men who formed the core of its support. And in so doing, they hoped to reassert the FIS's leadership of the Islamist movement.

The establishment of an armed wing brought the FIS other benefits as well. For a start, it helped the group withstand the various threats issued against it by the GIA. Relations between the two organizations had never been good, but on 4 January 1996 they took a definite turn for the worse when Djamal Zitouni, the new leader of the GIA, declared open war on the AIS and FIS. But as well as protecting the FIS from such threats, the AIS ensured the FIS's continued relevancy. With thousands of armed fighters under its command, neither the GIA nor the government could totally ignore the FIS and its agenda. Indeed, the very existence of these fighters strengthened the FIS's negotiating position with the Zéroual and Bouteflika regimes.

While the creation of the AIS gave the FIS's leaders another tool with which to pursue their objectives, it did not signal the end of their efforts to find a political solution to the ongoing crisis. Quite the contrary; they continued to negotiate with the government and put political pressure on it to secure Madani's and Belhadj's release from prison, the relegalization of the party, and the resurrection of the democratic process. Yet these negotiations only really began once Liamine Zéroual took over as president. During the six months that Boudiaf was chairman of the HCE, the FIS's path to mainstream politics was completely barred. In this instance, his stance was in total harmony with that of the military's high command.

But on 29 June 1992, Boudiaf was assassinated. His successor was Ali Kafi who, in a statement released shortly after he had taken office, intimated that the door to the FIS's return might soon be opened. Indeed, his pledge to involve all "existing forces of the nation" in a "search for a way out of the crisis," was interpreted by many as a cautious invitation to the FIS.[62] But any hopes this gave rise to among the FIS's leadership and supporters were quickly extinguished. It soon became apparent that only those parties not in the process of being outlawed were to be allowed to take part in the talks Kafi was proposing. Under pressure from the military to hold the line originally taken by Boudiaf, Kafi continued to exclude the FIS.

Yet the HCE's tentative opening of negotiations with the country's main political parties did have one silver lining for the FIS. With the exception of Saïd Sadi of the RCD, the leaders of these parties demanded that, in return for their cooperation, the HCE restart the democratic process, respect the outcome of the first round of voting, and immediately lift the ban on the FIS. Arguably, their ongoing commitment to democracy helped the FIS retain some of its political relevancy. By working together, these parties achieved a degree of influence that, while not great in the political circumstances that prevailed in Algeria at that time, was more than what they would have enjoyed had they each acted alone or in competition with one another. And as the most politically disadvantaged member of this informal coalition, given that it was the only one to have been declared illegal, the FIS gained more than most.

Faced with a united front, the HCE was immediately thrown into a dilemma—how to return Algeria's politics to a more normal footing without giving in to the demands presented to it? At the heart of this conundrum lay the FIS. The HCE and the military refused to countenance its relegalization. But their refusal to do so placed a major obstacle in the path to any negotiations with the political parties and ensured the continued enmity of the FIS's numerous supporters. And in its quest to stabilize the political situation and legitimize itself, the HCE could not afford to thumb its nose at any of these groups. Winning over or, at the very least, placating the FIS's followers was vital to its strategy of breaking the organization and stemming the rising tide of support for the insurgency.

The HCE's solution was an ill-advised compromise. Although it continued to rule out any lifting of the ban on the FIS, it did set about releasing thousands of its members and activists from the prison camps in the Sahara. Furthermore, it saw to it that Madani and Belhadj received much lighter sentences at their trials in July 1992 than they, and most other people, were expecting.[63] In so doing, the HCE hoped to curry favor with the FIS's supporters and the leaders of the political parties and perhaps even persuade them to soften their stance on the relegalization of the FIS. But as it turned out, the HCE failed to achieve any of these objectives. Far from reducing the flow of recruits to the MIA and GIA, its prisoner release program actually increased it. And any gratitude it was hoping to receive in return for the more lenient sentences it gave Madani and Belhadj never came due to the deep-felt anger of most FIS members and supporters at being denied the chance to take power.

This anger, and the frustration and sense of injustice that gave rise to it, fueled the growth of the Islamist maquis. Those who joined it were determined to make the HCE pay for its actions and achieve by force what the FIS had been unable to accomplish by democratic means—the transformation of Algeria into an Islamic republic. Their resolve, combined with that of the military's high command to break the Islamist movement as a political force once and for all, made the onset of violence almost inevitable.

The first clashes occurred before the National Assembly election had actually taken place. On 28 November 1991, sixty MIA fighters, many of them veterans of the armed struggle against the Soviets in Afghanistan, attacked the police station at Guemmar close to the Tunisian border. As well as making off with nearly fifty assault rifles, two thousand rounds of ammunition, and a number of rocket launchers, the raiders killed three policemen. The army responded by flooding the area with troops and launching a massive manhunt. As a result of this operation, twenty-five of the raiders were killed and a further twelve were taken prisoner. But despite this success, the military's subsequent actions ensured that, far from being an isolated occurrence, this attack became the first of many.

With the start of the New Year, the MIA prepared to launch fresh attacks against the government and its agents. On 10 February 1992 (nearly a month after Benjedid had announced his resignation), its gunmen shot and killed eight policemen in two separate incidents. Small scale operations such as these made up the bulk of the maquis's activities for much of the next two years. But in the summer of 1992, Islamist militants were blamed for what remains one of the most audacious assassinations of the entire conflict—the murder of Boudiaf himself.

On 29 June 1992, Second Lieutenant Boumaarafi Lembarek rushed onto the stage at the House of Culture in Annaba, where Boudiaf was delivering a speech to a group of businessmen, and shot him several times at close range, wounding him fatally. Shortly after he was arrested, Lembarek stated that he had acted "on his own initiative" for reasons of "religious conviction."[64] His confession was immediately seized on by members of the HCE and the military's high command as irrefutable proof of the FIS's involvement. It was, they claimed, Madani and Belhadj who put Lembarek up to the attack and it was on their behalf that he carried it out.

Yet this lone gunman theory was quickly rejected by the special commission set up to investigate the murder.[65] In its first report, published exactly one month after the attack had taken place, it concluded that Lembarek had not acted alone and that the security services were guilty of negligence and gross incompetence. These findings made the HCE's acquittal of the ten other members of Boudiaf's bodyguard it had arrested along with Lembarek all the more surprising and suspicious. Then in September 1992, the commission made a thinly veiled attack on the HCE itself by recommending that it conduct a full internal inquiry to find out who in the government had prior knowledge of the assassination attempt. Perhaps unsurprisingly, the HCE refused to comply. Finally on 9 December 1992, amid much speculation that its four members had been coerced by the HCE and military, the commission retracted its earlier statement and announced that Lembarek had acted by himself.

In spite of this late retreat, the commission's findings cast serious doubt over the version of events put forward by the government. And even though nothing has ever been formally proved, suspicions remain that the military was involved in the assassination plot. Such accusations are supported by extensive circumstantial evidence, the most important piece being that, by the time of his death, Boudiaf had made some powerful enemies within the army's high command. For a start, he was rumored to be using his good offices with King Hassan II of Morocco, which he had built up during his long exile there, to resolve the ongoing dispute between Algeria and Morocco over the Western Sahara by acquiescing to the Moroccans' demands. Any such settlement was totally unacceptable to the army because of the huge loss of face it would force them to accept.

But of even greater cause for concern was Boudiaf's pledge to use "all necessary means" to put an end to the "practices that corrupt our country and tarnish its reputation."[66] True to his word, he had placed Major General Moustepha Belloucif and Lieutenant Colonel Fekir Mohamed El-Hebri—both of whom had held senior posts in the ministry of defense during the Benjedid presidency—under investigation. And in so doing, he had created an enormous amount of disquiet within the upper echelons of the military and state bureaucracy. Indeed, these investigations were recognized as establishing a dangerous precedent, whereby senior officers and government officials might actually be prosecuted for engaging in corruption. And leaving office provided no guarantee against pursuit by criminal investigators.

Finally, the HCE failed to provide any satisfactory or convincing answers to several key questions, including why Lembarek's unit—the Special Intervention Group (Groupe d'Intervention Spéciale, GIS)—had been given responsibility for arranging Boudiaf's security when it had never performed such a duty before? How had the FIS or MIA found out about the speech, and how had they recruited Lembarek? And what lessons had been learned from the two earlier attempts on Boudiaf's life, which had also taken place in the Annaba area? Without doubt, the Islamist movement was glad to see the back of Boudiaf. He had, after all, agreed to head up an illegitimate government that had stolen power from the FIS and set about persecuting its leaders and members with a great deal of vigor. But Lembarek's confession notwithstanding, there was no real evidence tying the MIA or any other insurgent group to the assassination. Not for the last time, Islamist fighters were blamed for a crime they almost certainly did not commit.

But even if the MIA and GIA were not involved in Boudiaf's assassination, they did, between them, kill thousands of people. Between February and September 1992 around four hundred people were killed by the insurgents. Most, but by no means all, were agents of the state—policemen, gendarmes, and soldiers. And as the year progressed, the attacks became more spectacular. On 26 August 1992, MIA militants bombed Houari Boumedienne Airport on the outskirts of Algiers, killing eleven people and injuring a further 128. Then on 14 December 1992, Islamist gunmen ambushed a police patrol car close to the Apreval mosque in Kouba, killing five of its occupants and seriously wounding the sixth. This was the single most deadly attack against the security forces of the year.[67]

And the pattern of violence continued throughout the spring and summer of 1993 as MIA and GIA gunmen brought terror to the streets of Algiers and other towns and cities. On 13 February, an unsuccessful attempt was made on the life of General Nezzar. The following month Djilali Labès, a former minister of higher education, and Ladi Flici, a member of the recently created National Consultative Council (Conseil Consultatif National, CCN), were murdered on consecutive days.[68] After initially targeting individuals connected to the regime, the GIA expanded its pool of potential victims to include any prominent Algerians engaged in what it considered to be un-Islamic activities. As a result, the respected writer and social commentator Tahar Djaout was assassinated on 26 May, followed by the internationally renowned scientist Mahoud Boucebci on 15 June. Then on 21 August former prime minister Kasdi Merbah was killed. Exactly one month later on 21 September, the GIA kidnapped and killed two French oil workers.

October was to be another bloody month. During its course, Djilali Belkhenchir, the prominent academic working in the field of child health care, was murdered by the GIA along with three foreign contractors employed by SONATRACH and two Russian military advisers. And on 24 October, its gunmen snatched three members of the French embassy—Jean-Claude Thévenot, his wife Michèle, and Alain Fressier. Yet they were luckier than most. Six days later they were rescued from the prayer room in which they were being held captive by members of the security forces. But their survival did not signify any softening of the GIA's stance or an increased desire on its part to reduce the amount of blood being shed. On the contrary, the GIA never intended to kill these workers but instead use them as messengers. Before their captors departed prior to the arrival of the security forces, one of the abductees was handed a note ordering all foreigners to "leave the country" within one month and warning that anyone who failed to do so would "be responsible for his own sudden death."[69]

As far as the GIA was concerned, such threats served a dual purpose. For a start, they helped rid the country of nonbelievers, of men and women who, by virtue of not being Muslims, were inherently un-Islamic. But perhaps more importantly they helped isolate the government and exacerbate its economic problems by scaring away foreign investors. Any further decline in standards of living played straight into the GIA's hands by increasing popular frustration with the government. The effectiveness of the GIA's threats can be measured, at least in part, by the seriousness with which they were taken by those foreigners residing in Algeria. Within days of the contents of the note being made public, around three thousand of the seventy thousand foreign nationals living in the country had left.[70]

The Nation-Building Process Under the Haute Comité d'Etat

From the outset, Boudiaf was adamant that issues of identity lay at the heart of Algeria's troubles. In a speech marking his first one hundred days as chairman of the HCE, he argued that the country was "suffering from three crises—a moral crisis, a spiritual crisis, and an identity crisis." These catastrophes were the result of Algerians being continually torn "between socialism and capitalism . . . East and West . . . the French and Arabic languages . . . Arabism and Berberism . . . tradition and modernity." Such competing pressures were not only tearing the country apart, they were also preventing Algerians from being true to themselves. Boudiaf's final plea, therefore, was for Algerians to "stop imitating," to "break out from all complexes and be [them]selves."[71]

Boudiaf's analysis brought into sharp relief a question that has endured since the early decades of the twentieth century—what does it mean to be Algerian? Until the mid-1980s, Algeria's leaders had been quite clear as to what they thought the answer was: to be Algerian was to be a Muslim Arab socialist. But certain sections of society, most notably the Islamists and Berbers, rejected this understanding. For the Islamists, Algerians were Muslims first and foremost. They were not, nor could they ever be, socialists, as socialism was totally incompatible with Islam. The Berbers similarly rejected the definition of the nation promoted by Ben Bella, Boumedienne, and Benjedid, albeit for very different reasons. What they wanted was a more pluralist definition that was less exclusionary of ethnic minorities and incorporated other cultural characteristics.

Yet both these definitions were themselves rejected by the HCE. That of the Islamists was thought too much of a challenge to the country's secular values as well as the traditions of the war of liberation. And that of the Berbers was believed to threaten the very unity of the country. Instead, the HCE reaffirmed the definition outlined in the 1989 constitution, which identified Algerians as Muslim Arabs. Also like earlier regimes, it attempted to ensure that its definition achieved preeminence by controlling the discourse on national identity.

To gain this control, the HCE set about asserting its authority over the political system. But given that it had to contend with a growing and increasingly dynamic insurgency, this task inevitably took on a military dimension. To help the security forces in their fight against the terrorists and insurgents, the HCE passed a series of laws enhancing their powers. One of its first measures was to declare a state of emergency on 9 February 1992.[72] Under its provisions, the minister of the interior, police, gendarmerie, and army were empowered to control the movement of people, vehicles, foodstuffs, and essential goods; establish regulated residential zones; make homeless or place under house arrest anyone disrupting public order or hindering public services; force people to carry out work if striking illegally; and order the searches of people and property at any time of the day or night.[73]

Following the attack on Houari Boumedienne Airport, the HCE pushed through a series of even more draconian laws. On 26 September 1992 it passed legislation creating a new counterterrorist unit under the leadership of Major General Mohamed Lamari and three special courts to try those charged with committing terrorist offenses. Not only were the identities of the military and civilian judges who sat on the panels that presided over these courts kept secret, but those who appeared before them had no right to appeal the sentences they received even if they were condemned to death. The HCE also introduced other changes to the country's terror laws. On 30 September 1992 it lowered the age of criminal responsibility for acts of terrorism from eighteen to sixteen, increased the length of time a suspect could be held without charge from two to twelve days, and made the possession and distribution of subversive texts and materials illegal. Then, on 5 December 1992, it introduced nighttime curfews in the wilayas of Aïn Defla, Algiers, Bouira, Boumerdès, Médéa, and Tipasa, which were then extended to Chlef, Djelfa, and M'Sila on 29 May 1993.[74]

The curfews put in place by the HCE were integral to its efforts to reassert government authority over the country's social space. By preventing ordinary people from being out and about during the hours of darkness, the HCE and military were able to occupy and dominate the public spaces of Algeria's major towns and cities for a portion of each day. Practically, these measures were supposed to bolster the army's counterinsurgency and counterterrorist campaigns by restricting people's movement during those periods of the day when it was easiest to act unobserved. Clearly, given the continued rise in the number and size and the attacks carried out by the MIA and GIA, these precautions were not wholly effective. But symbolically they made the point that, under the current regime, access to the country's public places was not a right but a privilege that was granted and regulated by the government.

As part of these efforts, the HCE also set about smashing the vast network of Islamist civil society groups. Made up of thousands of mosques, religious schools, charities, and businesses, this network had played a major role in helping the FIS achieve victory in the local, regional, and National Assembly elections. The mosques and the prayer rooms had provided the FIS with public forums in which to criticize the government and promote its own political agenda. They had also served as community centers where FIS activists had provided a range of social and welfare services. In so doing, the party built up its support base as it helped people cope with the worsening economic situation. And the network as a whole gave the FIS nationwide reach, something no other party, save for the discredited FLN, had.

By breaking up this network, the HCE aimed to undermine the FIS's influence among the general population while simultaneously increasing its own. On 29 November 1992 it took its first step toward achieving this by passing legislation ordering the closure of various businesses, charities, and cultural organizations run by FIS members and sympathizers. One of the most important bodies forced to shut down was the Islamic Labor Union (Syndicat Islamique du Travail, SIT), which it accused of being the "true nucleus of the armed organization of the dissolved party."[75] Then on 22 December 1992, it passed a law requiring all mosques and prayer rooms to apply for a state license. Under this legislation, any place of worship that refused to do so or whose application was rejected was to be immediately closed. Grounds for denying a mosque a license included allowing imams who did not hold state-approved qualifications to preach. Through these measures, the HCE was better able to control who said what in the country's mosques and prayer rooms.

The HCE's determination to restrict the population's ability to speak freely in public also led it to censor the media. During the final months and years of Benjedid's presidency, Algeria's journalists had been largely free to report what they liked. But their ability to continue doing so was severely curtailed following the HCE's declaration of a state of emergency. Under its terms, the government had the right to seize and destroy any publication, stop any television or radio broadcast, close down any media outlet, and arrest any journalist who, it felt, spoke out of turn. Armed with such sweeping powers, the HCE could ensure that nothing critical of the government or military was ever published or that any competing definitions of the Algerian nation were presented to the general public.

The climate of fear and self-censorship created by the HCE was fortified by the campaign of terror mounted against the country's journalists by the GIA. It decreed that they, along with academics, teachers, writers, and artists, exerted an unholy influence on Algeria that must be stopped. From the summer of 1993 onward, therefore, it began murdering reporters, targeting in particular those who wrote in French or who criticized the insurgents. Between May 1993 and June 1994, fourteen journalists were assassinated by the GIA, and dozens more had lucky escapes. One of those to survive was Omar Belhoucet, the editor of the newspaper *El Watan*. He was attacked on 17 May 1993 by two gunmen who opened fire on his car shortly after he had dropped his children off at school. In light of such attacks, more than five hundred journalists fled abroad. Many of those who remained in Algiers grouped together in secure compounds like the Club des Pins in the west of the city.[76] In spite of their mutual animosity, the HCE and GIA were united in their distrust and hatred of the media and efforts to prevent it from functioning freely.

The HCE's censorship of the media helped it regain control of the country's political system. Over the weeks and months following Benjedid's resignation, it set about reversing the gains made by the FIS and establishing strict limits on who could participate in the political process. On 4 March 1992, the Algiers Judicial Council declared the FIS illegal, a ruling that was upheld by the country's Supreme Court the following month after the party lodged an appeal. The court's decision was significant as it paved the way for the dissolution of the FIS as a legal political party and governing authority. Not only were its leaders arrested and members imprisoned, but the councils it controlled were given over to special executive panels whose unelected members were handpicked by the HCE. As a result, by mid-December 1992, the FIS had lost control of 125 local and over 200 municipal councils.

Yet ending the democratic process and dismantling the FIS formed only part of the HCS's and HCE's efforts to gain control of the political system. Boudiaf also set about trying to legitimize the HCE and restore popular confidence in the political leadership by bringing other institutions and bodies into the government and increasing the number and diversity of the people involved in drafting and passing legislation. On 22 April 1992, he orchestrated the creation of the CCN. Made up of sixty people representing a variety of political and civil organizations, interest groups, and stakeholders, it was intended to replace the National Assembly and act as a sounding board for the HCE's policies and programs. However, its lack of autonomy and legislative powers generated popular suspicions that it possessed little meaningful power and only provided a rubber stamp for the HCE's policies.

Boudiaf responded to this skepticism and suspicion by founding a new political body called the National Patriotic Rally (Rassemblement Patriotique National, RPN). Envisaged as a secular version of the FIS, Boudiaf hoped to unite the country's nonsectarian and nonregionalist parties under its aegis. The main purpose of the RPN was to draw popular support away from the FIS and to gain the allegiance of the mass of Algerians who had voted for the FIS in the last election but were not committed Islamists. By the end of May 1992, around a dozen parties had joined the RPN coalition.

To encourage further cooperation, in May 1993 Ali Kafi announced that the HCE was planning to enter negotiations with selected opposition parties, hold a referendum on constitutional changes it wanted to introduce, and create a transitional body to oversee the return to democratic elections once the HCE's mandate expired in December of that year. Although the referendum was never held, because of the worsening security situation, the HCE did open negotiations with the FFS and FLN over who or what should replace it at the end of the year. The HCE hoped that these talks would increase its legitimacy and help it control the future development of the political process. And in some ways they did. By opening a dialogue with the HCE, both the FFS and FLN acknowledged it as Algeria's government. But in the face of their continued insistence that the FIS be relegalized, the HCE turned its attention to the smaller secular parties and entered into talks with them. To oversee and conduct these negotiations it created the National Dialogue Committee (Comité National de Dialogue, CND) in October 1993.

Boudiaf's efforts to resuscitate the political process included trying to restore the public's faith in its leaders. Motivated by deep personal conviction, he made tackling high-level corruption in the government, state bureaucracy, and army a priority. Not only was this course of action extremely popular with the vast majority of ordinary Algerians, it also deprived the FIS of an important part of its agenda. During the local, regional, and parliamentary elections, the FIS had successfully used the widespread corruption within the upper echelons of the state as a stick with which to beat the Benjedid regime and gain the support of many Algerians. Following Boudiaf's death, however, Ali Kafi retreated from this hardline stance, going so far as to dismiss the minister of justice in November 1992 for being too proactive in his pursuit of corrupt officials. Kafi's position disappointed many ordinary people and handed the initiative on this particular issue back to the opposition parties.

By the end of 1993 dialogue between the CND and the various opposition parties had broken down completely. The main point of contention remained the status and future of the FIS. As a result of this impasse, no decision was reached as to who would replace the HCE once its term expired on 31 December. To give the CND more time to hammer out a solution, the HCE extended its mandate by a month. Yet even with this extra breathing space the CND and opposition parties remained deadlocked. Finally, on 30 January 1994, the military's patience snapped and it appointed Liamine Zéroual as the country's new president.

Zéroual's selection was driven as much by his reputation for honesty and being a man of the people as it was by his military credentials. As a young man he had joined the FLN and fought the French during the war of liberation. He had remained in the army after the war and rose through the ranks to become a general in 1988. As an Arabic speaker, he enjoyed the respect of many in the Arabophone community and was not tainted by what had happened in the early 1990s as he had resigned from the army in 1989. He was seen by many in the military as a one of their own, a natural ally whose popularity would help unite the country.

After being sworn in, Zéroual immediately had to contend with the deteriorating security situation. The HCE's military operations against the Islamist insurgents and nation-building efforts had failed to restore law and order in the country. Its attempts to regain control of the political system and social space had been undermined by its lack of legitimacy while the ongoing violence forced it to renege on its promises to restore democracy. The year 1994 was to be one of the conflict's bloodiest. The assassination of high-profile targets by the insurgents continued unabated. On 5 March Ahmed Asselah, the principal of the School of Fine Arts, was killed by Islamist gunmen. Two weeks later, GIA militants stormed and occupied the center of Blida. They were eventually repulsed by the security forces but dozens of people were injured in the process. Then, on 8 May, two French priests were shot and killed in the Algiers casbah. Three weeks after that, on 31 May, Salah Djebaïli, the rector of the University of Bab Ezzouar, was assassinated.

June was especially bloody. On the first of the month, Abdelkader Hattab, a regional GIA leader, was killed along with nine of his men by fighters of a rival group. On 18 June Youcef Fathallah, head of the Algerian Human Rights League, was assassinated. And, eleven days later, two bombs exploded at an RCD rally in Algiers, killing two and injuring sixty-four. On 7 July seven Italian sailors had their throats slit at the port of Djendjen, while on 3 August five members of the French embassy were killed by a car bomb. Then, on 29 September, the popular raï singer, Cheb Hasni, was shot and killed close to his family home in Oran. Finally, on 3 December 1994, Said Mekbel, a prominent journalist working for *Le Matin* newspaper, was gunned down while eating lunch in a restaurant in Algiers.

But arguably the most spectacular action of the year came on Christmas Eve, when four GIA militants seized Air France flight 8969 shortly before it took off for Charles de Gaulle Airport. Over the next twenty-four hours, they executed three passengers—an Algerian policeman, a Vietnamese diplomat, and a member of the French embassy in Algiers—when their demands were not met. After more fruitless negotiations, the Algerian authorities agreed to let the plane fly to France. But rather than go to Paris, it touched down at Marignane Airport near Marseilles at around 3:00 a.m. on 26 December. A little over two hours later, the aircraft was stormed by French Special Forces. All four of the hijackers were killed during the assault. It was not to be the last time that the violence in Algeria spilled over into France. In retaliation, the GIA murdered five Catholic missionaries of the Pères Blancs order in Tizi Ouzou on 28 December.

On 30 January 1995, the GIA exploded a huge car bomb near the center of Algiers, killing forty-two people and injuring a further 256. A little under a month later, on 21 February, it orchestrated a prisoner mutiny in the Serkadji jail in Algiers. Rather than negotiate, the government ordered that the prison be retaken by force. The following day hundreds of police and soldiers stormed the complex. During the pitched battles that followed, ninety-six inmates were killed. This took the total death toll up to one hundred as, once the fighting had died down, the bodies of four prison guards were found, their throats slit. In just over six weeks, nearly four hundred people had been either killed or injured in Algiers alone.

But there was to be no let up in the violence. Indeed, the GIA stepped up its campaign as it attempted to disrupt preparations for the presidential election scheduled to take place on 16 November and make real Djamal Zitouni's threat to open up a new front in France. Zitouni had made public his determination to take the fight to France in two statements released on 30 and 31 October 1994, shortly after he had taken over as the GIA's leader. The seizure of the Air France flight represented the first action along this new front. And it was followed up with two attacks in the summer of 1995. On 11 July, GIA gunmen shot and killed Sheikh Abdelbaki Sahraoui while he was attending his mosque in Paris. From the outset, he had been a vocal critic of the GIA's use of terror tactics and murder of innocent civilians. He had also acted as a willing intermediary between the French authorities and the FIS's leaders. Such actions earned him the bitter enmity of the GIA's high command, and it had threatened to kill him several times before.

Exactly two weeks later, the GIA raised the stakes by detonating a bomb at the Metro-RER station of Saint-Michel on the Porte de Clignancort-Porte d'Orléans line, killing eight people and injuring a further one hundred. In stark contrast to the FIS, the GIA's leaders did not want to establish or maintain diplomatic links with any European government. Instead, they remained focused on waging total war against the Zéroual regime and any foreign power that helped it. Their determination to attack France was strengthened by its colonial past. They reasoned that colonial rule was responsible for much that was impious in Algeria, such as the French language, Christianity, feminism, and secularism.

In addition to the attacks it launched in France, the GIA continued its campaign back home. On 17 August it exploded two car bombs close to the Club des Pins residential compound, killing two people and injuring seven. Two weeks later it attacked a government building in the Bab el-Oued district of the capital, killing nine and wounding just under one hundred more. Less than a month after that, on 28 September, Aboubakr Belkaïd, a former government minister, was murdered while driving to a meeting of veterans of the Federation of France of the National Liberation Front.

Such attacks, and the GIA's extension of its campaign to France, told of the ongoing dynamism and continued vigor of the insurgency. Yet not everything was as it seemed. The GIA's failure to prevent or severely disrupt the presidential election in November damaged its prestige. And, perhaps more seriously, once the voting was over, the security forces no longer had to concern themselves with guarding polling booths and could instead refocus their efforts on pursuing and destroying the insurgents. In contrast, Zéroual, after winning his second term in office, emerged even stronger than before. Not only had he successfully staged an election, which was reasonably free and fair, but he had also won it by an enormous margin, giving him the popular mandate he needed.

In the face of this setback, and under sustained pressure from the army, the GIA was forced to retreat. From late 1995 onward, it shifted its attention to the Mitidja plain, the fertile crescent of land that separates Algiers in the north from the Atlas Mountains to the south. The Mitidja was of enormous strategic importance to the GIA. It provided the main communication link between the group's bases and training camps in the mountains and its recruitment centers, funding sources, and assassination targets in Algiers. Protecting this link, therefore, became one of the GIA's top priorities. For if the security forces ever succeeded in gaining control of the Mitidja, they would cut the GIA in two and, in the process, severely compromise its operational effectiveness.

To make up for the difficulties it was encountering, the GIA extended its list of potential targets. Throughout January and February 1996, it issued a series of statements identifying conscripts, the families of police and army officers, and anyone working in the oil and gas industries as its enemies deserving of death. Zitouni also stepped up his efforts to gain control of the entire insurgency and purge the GIA's ranks of anyone he suspected of being sympathetic toward the FIS. This led him, on 4 January 1996, to declare war on the AIS on the grounds that it was now under the control of the security services.

The split between the GIA and AIS that Zitouni's actions helped cement played straight into the security forces' hands. So, too, did his attempted purge of the GIA's ranks. The vicious internecine fighting his actions sparked tore the GIA apart for a number of weeks, eventually leading to his own murder by members of a rival faction. He was replaced as supreme commander by Antar Zouabri. Well known for his cruelty and deep hatred of the West, he issued a communiqué on 13 June 1997 dividing Algeria's population into two groups—those who supported the GIA and those who did not. Anyone in the latter group was considered an enemy and an apostate and was marked for death.[77]

During the final months of 1996, as the country edged toward the referendum of 28 November,[78] the GIA stepped up its attacks against civilians. On 10 November, it blew up a car laden with explosives close to a bus stop in an Algiers suburb, killing fifteen. Two days later, its operatives cut the throats of thirty-two people. Exactly a fortnight after that, it detonated another car bomb near the center of Blida, killing five and injuring a further fifteen. And on the day of the referendum itself, it murdered twenty-six people in a number of separate attacks. Then, on 3 December, it exploded a bomb at the Paris RER station of Port Royal on the Aéroport/Mitry-Claye-Saint-Rémy-lès-Chevreuse line, killing three people and wounding another one hundred.

The start of the new year did not bring with it any let-up in the violence. On 15 January, fourteen people died and fifty more were injured when the GIA exploded a bomb in the center of Boufarik, a small town some 30 kilometers southwest of Algiers. It followed up this attack by slitting the throats of twenty-two people eight days later. Then, on 31 January, it decapitated thirty-one residents of the town of Médéa, around 70 kilometers south of Algiers. Eighteen days after that, it murdered nineteen people in the town of Babi Ali. Finally, on 21 April, its militants slaughtered ninety-three civilians, at least half of them women and children, living on the outskirts of Algiers.

These latest attacks provided grisly proof of the GIA's determination to drown Algeria in blood as it carried out one massacre after another. As part of its efforts to safeguard its lines of communication, the people it most often targeted were the unfortunate inhabitants of the towns and villages lying between Algiers, Médéa, and Larba, an area that quickly became known as the Triangle of Death. The seeming nihilism of the violence unleashed by the GIA shocked and appalled domestic and international observers in equal measure.

Many of the worst attacks took place under the cover of night. After surrounding a settlement and cutting all roads and telephone wires leading from it, GIA militants armed with automatic weapons, swords, knives, and axes, went from house to house killing any men, women, and children they found. Sometimes they tortured their victims beforehand; on other occasions, they mutilated their corpses. Such operations often lasted hours, only ending with the breaking of dawn. The indiscriminate nature of the killing, and the abuse meted out to the victims (either before or after death), was intended to maximize the terror caused in nearby settlements and to reinforce the GIA's stark warning: support us totally and without reservation or suffer the consequences.

This was the fate that befell the town of Raïs. During the night of 29 August, armed men killed around three hundred of its residents in an attack that lasted several hours. And less than a week later, the same thing happened at Béni-Messous. Lying a short distance beyond Algiers' city limits, it was invaded by dozens of militants who murdered fifty of the town's inhabitants. And then, on 22 September, the settlement of Bentalha was attacked. During a killing spree that lasted six hours and was carried out by one hundred armed men, over four hundred of its citizens died. In each instance, the security forces did not intervene once the attack had begun. Their failure to do so was surprising given the length of time each massacre lasted and the proximity of several police, gendarme, and army bases to the three towns.

One of the few rays of hope to shine forth during these dark days was the AIS's decision to call a cease-fire. On 21 September, the day before the Bentalha outrage, its high command ordered that all fighters should put down their weapons—at least for the time being. This decision represented no small triumph for the military, and was the outcome of several weeks of secret negotiations. But while it marked the withdrawal of one major actor from the armed struggle, it did not signal an end to the violence. Indeed, to demonstrate to the country that it was still around—as if anyone needed any reminding—the GIA ensured that 1997 ended as 1998 began—amid much bloodshed.

In late December, its fighters carried out a series of fresh massacres in the villages and settlements dotted throughout the mountains just south of Relizane; over four hundred people died. And then on 11 January 1998, hundreds more were killed at Sidi Hammad, lying on the outskirts of the capital. These fresh atrocities brought renewed calls from the international community for something to be done. And so it seemed to be. In April 1998, two mayors from Relizane were arrested along with ten other people on charges that they had taken part in the December massacre. In the weeks that followed, it emerged that they were members of a progovernment militia that was responsible for at least some of the deaths that had occurred. Shortly after news of this official involvement broke, the cases against the two mayors were quickly dropped. Not much, it seemed, had changed after all. And this impression was reinforced in September 1998 when a new insurgent group—the Salafist Group for Preaching and Combat (Groupe Salafiste pour la Prédication et le Combat, GSPC)—announced its determination to transform Algeria into an Islamic republic.

The Nation-Building Process Under Liamine Zéroual

In the face of this ongoing violence Zéroual embarked on a process of nation building. The definition of the nation he outlined was virtually the same as that promoted by Benjedid and the HCE and was enshrined in the new constitution he introduced in November 1996.[79] Just as before, the twin themes of Islam and Arabism lay at its heart.[80] But in addition, it identified Berberism as a "fundamental component" of the Algerian nation.[81] This acknowledgement represented a notable triumph for Berbers. For the first time ever, they and their culture were given explicit recognition in the constitution, the country's most important legal and political document. Yet this victory was not as complete as they hoped it might be. For a start, the acknowledgment was relegated to the preamble and at no point was Tamazight given equal status with Arabic. But, perhaps more importantly, what little recognition was given was not backed up with legislation.

To ensure its definition achieved preponderance, the Zéroual regime worked to regain control of the country's political system and social space. His attempts to do so were strongly influenced by the split that had emerged within the armed forces, governing elite, and main political parties between those who wanted to enter into dialogue with the Islamists and those who wanted to destroy them. The split between the conciliators and eradicators, as the two camps became known, emerged during the final months of 1993. The first camp was led by the FFS and FLN and was the favored approach of a majority of ordinary Algerians. The second camp was led by senior army officers and government ministers such as Major General Mohamed Lamari, Prime Minister Redha Malek, and Minister of the Interior Selim Saadi. It also had the support of left-wing and Berber groups like the UGTA and RCD.

Like the HCE before it, the Zéroual regime's main aim was to rehabilitate the political process in a way that was acceptable to the military, safeguarded Algeria's territorial integrity, and enabled it to control the discourse on Algerian national identity. However, Zéroual's approach to gaining control of the political system differed in one significant respect from that of the HCE—he was prepared to negotiate with the FIS. Rather than simply exclude the FIS in the hope that by doing so it would be rendered irrelevant, Zéroual sought to draw it into the political process in accordance with predetermined, strictly delineated guidelines. His willingness to do so meant that he was naturally sympathetic to the conciliators' arguments. But he also recognized the importance of the military dimension as well as the need to keep the armed forces on board.

As a result of the unstable security situation, Zéroual was obliged to adopt a more sophisticated approach to controlling the political arena than his predecessors. It simply was not possible for him to crudely dominate it by outlawing and excluding all opposition. Instead, he had to achieve hegemony by generating consent, by gaining the support of the various stakeholders—Islamists, Berberists, secular parties, the military, and the people. As a consequence, his nation-building promotion assumed even greater importance as it became vital to generating the support he needed and to shaping Algeria's political, economic, and social structures and practices.

Zéroual's commitment to appeasing these stakeholders was demonstrated as soon as he took office. Throughout February 1994 he entered into secret talks with Madani and Belhadj but stopped after Malek and Saadi complained. Before resuming these negotiations in August, he was careful to get the military on board and assert his own authority by dismissing Malek and Saadi. Although these fresh talks ended in failure, Zéroual persuaded Madani and Belhadj to remain true to the principle of multiparty democracy and managed to get five other opposition parties to the negotiating table. And he followed this initiative by announcing on 31 October 1994 that presidential elections would be held sometime the following year.

Yet, despite his efforts to enter into dialogue with the opposition parties, Zéroual was not prepared to allow them to dictate the pace and direction of the reform process. On 13 January 1995, a coalition of opposition parties including the FLN, FFS, MNI, and FIS published a joint communiqué called the Rome Platform outlining what political changes they would like to see introduced.[82] Although many of the Platform's recommendations were similar to those outlined by Zéroual, he immediately denounced it. The regime's response to the Rome Platform was driven as much by its determination to retain control over shaping the country's political process as it was the military's hostility to the FIS. Even though Zéroual was personally committed to democracy and pluralism, he refused to support the Platform because he felt that to do so would hand the initiative to the opposition parties and give them a degree of control over the political process that he was not willing to accept.

Despite this setback, Zéroual reopened negotiations with Madani and Belhadj in the summer of 1995. When these came to nothing, he got the military's backing to launch a new three-stage plan. The first stage required Madani to call on the insurgents to lay down their weapons and denounce violence. Once this had been done, Zéroual promised to release him and all the other imprisoned FIS leaders. Then, during the second stage, Zéroual promised to pardon all insurgents who surrendered during the amnesty period that would be called. Finally, during the third stage, he promised to recognize the FIS as a legal party if it changed its name and agreed to abide by the secular principles established in the 1989 constitution. Although Madani personally accepted the terms of this new initiative, the other members of the FIS's majlis al-shura rejected them.[83]

The strength of popular support for Zéroual was made apparent by the result of the presidential election of 16 November 1995. In what was one of the country's freest and fairest elections, Zéroual won by a landslide with 61 percent of the vote. His nearest challenger was Mahfoud Nahnah who received 25 percent of the votes cast.[84] Zéroual exploited the momentum this victory created to convince the military of the need to rewrite the country's constitution. The Zéroual regime's determination to control the political discourse on Algeria's national identity was made clear by the stipulations of Article 42. While it guaranteed Algerians' right to create political parties, it insisted that this right could not be used to violate the "fundamental values and components of the national identity, the national unity, the security and integrity of the national territory, the independence of the country and the People's sovereignty as well as the democratic and republican nature of the State."[85] To ensure that such violations could not occur, the constitution decreed that political parties could not represent specific "religious, linguistic, racial . . . or regional" groups.[86]

Zéroual's ability to control the political system was enhanced still further by the electoral successes of the National Democratic Rally (Rassemblement National Démocratique, RND). Founded on 6 January 1997 by Abdelhak Benhamouda, it was staunchly progovernment. And it remained so even after Benhamouda's assassination three weeks later, as his replacement—Abdelkader Bensalah—was a close political ally of Zéroual. In the National Assembly election of 5 June 1997, the RND won 38 percent of the vote, giving it 156 seats in the lower house of the new Assembly. In contrast, the Movement for a Peaceful Society (Mouvement pour la Société de la Paix, MSP), which finished second, received just 16.7 percent, giving it sixty-nine seats.[87]

The RND's grip on power was strengthened still further following its victories in the APW and APC elections held on 23 October 1997. Denounced by all the other political parties as deeply flawed, the RND won 52 percent and 55 percent of the vote, respectively. These results made the RND the dominant party at the national, regional, and local levels of government. Furthermore, they helped ensure that it was strongly represented in the National Assembly's upper house, the Council of the Nation (Conseil de la Nation, CN).

The division of the National Assembly into two chambers was one of the reforms introduced by the 1996 constitution. Under its terms, each house was granted a different set of responsibilities, meaning that neither could act independently of the other. Indeed, the right to propose new legislation belonged solely to the lower chamber. But nothing could become law unless it was approved by three-quarters of the CN's members and the president. If a party wanted to gain control of the National Assembly, therefore, it needed to be the dominant force in both houses; no easy feat in light of how the CN's 144 members were selected. One-third of them were appointed directly by the president, and the remaining two thirds were elected by the APWs and APCs. The ballot by which these assemblies decided the allocation of the ninety-six seats at their disposal took place on 25 December 1997. But since the RND was the dominant party in both, it was able to ensure it received eighty of those seats. In so doing, it seized control of the National Assembly's legislative agenda.

Notes

1. Mahfoud Bennoune, *The Making of Contemporary Algeria, 1830–1987* (Cambridge: Cambridge University Press, 1988), pp. 89–90.
2. As reported in *The Times*, "Algeria Plans for Nationalization," 20 November 1962, Issue 55553, p. 10, col. G.
3. The main purpose of the BNBV was to rehouse the thousands of displaced people in properties abandoned by the settlers.
4. République Algérienne Démocratique et Populaire, *Décrets de mars* (March 1963).
5. John Ruedy, *Modern Algeria: The Origins and Development of a Nation*, 2nd ed. (Bloomington: Indiana University Press, 2005), p. 198.
6. Every enterprise was governed by its own committee.
7. Belaid held the post from 1965 until 1978.
8. Gérard Destanne de Bernis, "Industries industrialisantes et les options algériennes," *Revue Tiers-Monde* (July/September 1971), p. 547.
9. During that period, industry was scheduled to receive 49 percent of all state investment. Richard Lawless, "Algeria: The Contradictions of Rapid Industrialisation," in *North Africa: Contemporary Politics and Economic Development*, ed. Richard Lawless and Allan Findlay (London: Croom Helm, 1984), p. 165.
10. Ibid. Industry was supposed to receive 45 percent of all funding but it got 57 percent.
11. Ministère d'Information et de la Culture, "Le choix industriel de l'Algérie," Dossier Documentaire 16 (Novembre 1971), p. 22.
12. Under this plan's initial spending commitments, 44 percent of the public sector budget was set aside for industry. Richard Lawless, "Algeria: The Contradictions of Rapid Industrialisation," in *North Africa: Contemporary Politics and Economic Development,* ed. Richard Lawless and Allan Findlay (London: Croom Helm, 1984), p. 165.
13. In 1967 it made the state 880 million dinars. This rose to 1,320 million dinars in 1969, 1,659 million in 1971, and 3,200 million in 1972. Cited in Benjamin Stora, *Algeria 1830–2000: A Short History* (Ithaca and London: Cornell University Press, 2001), p. 153.
14. In 1972 Algeria's foreign debt stood at $2.5 billion. By 1979 it had risen to $23.5 billion.
15. Algeria's population grew from 12,500,000 in 1966 to 17,500,000 a decade later.
16. Stora, *Algeria 1830–2000*, p. 157.
17. Salah E. Zaimeche and Keith Sutton, "Persistent Strong Population Growth, Environmental Degradation, and Declining Food Self-Sufficiency in a Rentier Oil State: Algeria," *The Journal of North African Studies* 3, no. 1 (spring 1998): p. 69.
18. Ibid.
19. Ibid.
20. In 1962 agriculture contributed 32 percent of Algeria's GDP. This had fallen to 12 percent by 1970.

21. SONATRACH was split into four enterprises in May 1980. These were then divided into thirteen companies in 1982.

22. Ruedy, *Modern Algeria*, pp. 234–35.

23. Between 1960 and 1990, Algeria's population grew at an average annual rate of 2.7 percent.

24. Benjedid received 95 percent of all votes cast after standing unopposed.

25. In 1980 Algeria's national debt stood at $16.3 billion. It fell to $15.9 in 1981, $13.9 billion in 1982, and $12.9 billion in 1983.

26. George Joffé, "The Role of Violence within the Algerian Economy," *The Journal of North Africa Studies* 7, no. 1 (spring 2002): p. 38.

27. By 1985, around 65 percent of Algeria's imports came from Europe.

28. In 1985, Algeria imported $8.8 billion worth of goods. By 1988, its imports were valued at $6.7 billion.

29. In 1985, Algeria's budget deficit stood at $4.2 billion, in 1986 $186 million, in 1987 $2.4 billion, and in 1989 $945 million.

30. In 1985, Algeria's foreign debt stood at $16.3 billion. It rose to $19.6 billion in 1986, to $23.3 billion in 1987, and to $23.4 billion in 1988. Werner Ruf, "The Flight of Rent: The Rise and Fall of a National Economy," *The Journal of North Africa Studies* 2, no. 1 (summer 1997): p. 8.

31. In 1986, debt repayments absorbed half of Algeria's export earnings. By 1988, it was consuming 87 percent.

32. GDP shrank by 1.5 percent that year.

33. By the end of 1988 unemployment stood at 30 percent.

34. World Bank, Algeria-Structural Adjustment Loan (1995), report available at www-wds.worldbank.org/servlet/WDSContentServer/WDSP/IB/1997/09/05/000009265_3971229182718/Rendered/PDF/multi0page.pdf, p. 1 (accessed 9 July 2006).

35. By 1991 around 50 percent of Algeria's workforce was employed by the state.

36. République Algérienne Démocratique et Populaire, *Constitution du 23 février 1989* (1989), Articles 2 and 3.

37. It took the security forces four days to impose law and order. By the time they had done so, hundreds of people, mostly young men, had been killed and thousands more arrested and imprisoned. The government placed the official death toll at 155. Islamic, Berber, and human rights groups claim that the real figure is far higher and lies somewhere between 250 and 550.

38. Merbah held this office until 9 September 1989.

39. Turnout for this referendum was 90 percent.

40. Turnout for this election was 80 percent.

41. République Algérienne Démocratique et Populaire, *Constitution du 23 février 1989* (1989), Article 42.

42. The FIS was created on 14 February 1989 and recognized as a political party on 14 September 1989. The FFS was acknowledged on 20 November 1989.

43. Cited in Hugh Roberts, *The Battlefield Algeria 1988–2002: Studies in a Broken Polity* (London and New York: Verso, 2003), p. 9.

44. Michael Willis, *The Islamist Challenge in Algeria* (New York: New York University Press, 1996), p. 59.

45. Turnout for this election was the lowest yet at 60 percent of the electorate.

46. One of the cabal's members was General Abdelmalek Guenaïza, chief of the General Staff.

47. The chairman of this council was Abdelmalek Benhabilès.

48. Abdelkader Hachani, the FIS's interim leader, was arrested on 22 January

1992. And six days later so, too, was Rabah Kébir, the party's most prominent spokesman.

49. Haddam had stood as an FIS candidate in the National Assembly election. Sheikh Sahraoui was one of the founder members of the FIS.

50. Kébir was a member of the FIS's governing majlis al-shura. He had also held its Political Affairs portfolio.

51. Both Redjam and Saïd had been members of the FIS's majlis al-shura. Cherrati was a former assistant and adviser to Othman Aissani, one of the FIS's multiple vice presidents.

52. Cited in Willis, *The Islamist Challenge*, p. 276.

53. Ibid., p. 277.

54. El-Eulmi acted as the GIA's spiritual guide until he was killed by Algerian security forces in April 1993.

55. Cited in Willis, *The Islamist Challenge*, p. 282.

56. By the spring of 1993, around eight thousand of the ten thousand people held captive had been released.

57. The MEI was established in February 1992 by Saïd Mekhlouf. Mekhlouf later defected to the GIA.

58. Chébouti himself was killed by Algerian security forces in the autumn of 1993.

59. To date the GIA has had six supreme commanders: Abdelhak Layada (January 1993–July 1993); Sid Ahmed Mourad aka Djafaar al-Afghani (July 1993–February 1994); Cherif Gousmi aka Ahmed Abu Abdallah (February 1994–September 1994); Djamal Zitouni (October 1994–July 1996); Antar Zouabri (July 1996–February 2002); and Rachid Oukali aka Abou Tourab (April 2002–present).

60. Joint communiqué cited in Mohammed M. Hafez, "Armed Islamist Movements and Political Violence in Algeria," *The Middle East Journal* 54, no. 4 (autumn 2000): p. 577.

61. Established in Tirana in September 1993 under the leadership of Kébir, the Executive was the group's official representative overseas.

62. Cited in Willis, *The Islamist Challenge*, p. 307.

63. Madani and Belhadj had been awaiting trial since their arrest on 30 June 1991. Each was sentenced to twelve years in prison.

64. Cited in Ruedy, *Modern Algeria*, p. 260.

65. The commission's determination to uncover the truth may have been because it was headed by Ahmed Bouchaib, a friend of Boudiaf.

66. Cited in Martin Stone, *The Agony of Algeria* (New York: Columbia University Press, 1997), p. 109.

67. Stora, *Algeria 1830–2000*, p. 211.

68. Labès was killed on 16 March and Flici on the 17th.

69. Cited in Willis, *The Islamist Challenge*, p. 284.

70. Ibid., pp. 283 and 284.

71. Cited in Martin Evans and John Phillips, *Algeria: Anger of the Dispossessed* (New Haven and London: Yale University Press, 2007), p. 175.

72. Two days before the year-long declaration expired, it was renewed for an indefinite length of time.

73. UN Human Rights Committee, Examination of Reports Submitted by States Parties under Article 40 of the Covenant (18 August 1998), available at www.unhchr.ch/tbs.doc.nsf/(symbol)/CCPR.C79.Add.95.En?Opendocument, pp. 91–140 (accessed 4 July 2003).

74. In all wilayas the curfew lasted from 10:00 p.m. to 6:00 a.m.

75. Cited in Willis, *The Islamist Challenge*, p. 293.

76. Evans and Phillips, *Algeria: Anger of the Dispossessed*, p. 191.

77. Ibid., p. 223.

78. The referendum was to decide whether the country should adopt a new constitution.

79. It was approved by 86 percent of the country's voters in a nationwide referendum.

80. Article 2 of the 1996 constitution asserted that "Islam is the religion of the state," while Article 3 declared that "Arabic is the national, official language." République Algérienne Démocratique et Populaire, *Constitution du 28 novembre 1996* (1996), Articles 2 and 3.

81. Ibid., Préambule.

82. The Platform was the product of two summits held by these parties in Rome between 21 and 22 November 1994 and on 13 January 1995. The event was arranged and hosted by the Catholic community of San Edigio.

83. The other members of FIS's ruling council were Belhadj, Hachani, Ali Djeddi, and Abdelkader Boukhamkham.

84. Turnout was high, despite the threats made by some of the insurgent groups, with 75 percent of the electorate taking part.

85. République Algérienne Démocratique et Populaire, *Constitution du 28 novembre 1996* (1996), Article 42.

86. Ibid., Article 42.

87. The MSP used to be known as HAWAS. Both it and the MNI changed their names in order to comply with the legal stipulations of the 1996 constitution that outlawed all parties representing exclusively regional, ethnic, linguistic, and religious constituencies. The MNI changed its name to the Renaissance Movement (Mouvement de la Nahda, MN).

6

National Identity and the Ongoing Struggle

BY THE SUMMER OF 1998, it seemed as if the worst of the storm had passed. The massacres of the previous year, in which so much innocent blood had been spilled, were becoming ever more infrequent. The GIA, often the perpetrator of these crimes, was in turmoil as Zouabri continued to liquidate anyone he suspected of treachery or who disagreed with him. The AIS was still holding true to its cease-fire and, in due course, would lay down its arms for good.[1] And the security forces, by fair means and foul, had gained the measure of the rebels. In fact, the whole insurgency looked to be in terminal decline. The trickle of deserters from the GIA's ranks seeking readmission to mainstream society had become a steady flow as the maquis shrank to just a few hundred fighters.[2]

Central to the Zéroual regime's success, was the counterinsurgency campaign waged by the security forces. This ongoing armed response served a variety of military, political, and social purposes. First and foremost, it prevented the insurgents from overthrowing the government. After all, the GIA's challenge was primarily an armed one. Unlike either the FIS or the FLN during the war of liberation, the GIA did not really seek political support for its campaign either at home or abroad. On the contrary, it knowingly spurned international acceptance by targeting foreign nationals living and working in Algeria and carrying out attacks in France.

And by defending the Zéroual regime, the security forces acted as a key enabler. The protection they provided gave it time and space to rehabilitate the country's political system and economy and to pursue its nation-building program. These initiatives were vitally important to the country's long-term stability, as they addressed some of the factors that had led to the onset of the violence in the first place. Yet the price of this progress was extremely high for both the Algerian public and Zéroual personally. After six years of fighting, the total number of civilians killed ran into the tens of thousands, while many more had simply disappeared or languished in prison cells. Civil and political rights had been reduced to an absolute minimum, while members of the elite continued to act with impunity. And, perhaps worst of all, the military had made a mockery of the democratic process. Ordinary people now had little choice but to accept a political order that was built on lies and violence and was rooted in illegitimacy.

Zéroual also had to count the cost. His refusal to simply do as he was told and insistence on negotiating with the FIS and other political parties made him some powerful enemies among the eradicators. As summer turned into autumn, they began to plan for his removal. And all the while the country was still plagued with violence. Although the GIA was undoubtedly much weakened, it remained true to its dictum of "no dialogue, no truce, no reconciliation," and continued to kill and maim. When Zéroual's successor, Abdelaziz Bouteflika, eventually took office, he too was confronted by an armed challenge to his authority.

And he responded just like his predecessors—by trying to strengthen the internal connections between his regime and the people through a process of nation building. But yet again, the definition of the nation his regime promoted continued to be rejected by Islamists and Berberists alike. The former remained adamant that Islam was the most important characteristic of the nation, that Algerians were, first and foremost, Muslims. The government's refusal to acknowledge this and transform the country into an Islamic state only helped sustain their anger and keep the fires of the insurgency burning. And many in the Berber community remained similarly frustrated. Despite all their protests and the occasional promise made by this or that government, they had still not been given the same cultural and linguistic rights as the Arabs.

The primary goal of this chapter, therefore, is to examine the program of nation building pursued by President Bouteflika from April 1999 until early 2008. The chapter will begin by charting the inexorable decline of the insurgency over this period, paying particular attention to the effectiveness of the security forces' counterinsurgency campaign. In so doing, it will be better equipped to explain how the military has retained so much of its political influence. The armed forces' abiding position as kingmaker is integral to Algeria's ongoing story and forms part of the political context in which Bouteflika has had to operate and pursue his nation-building program. Finally, the chapter will draw together the main analytical threads of this and all the other chapters as it offers some concluding comments.

Down But Not Out: The Insurgents Endure

On 11 September 1998 Zéroual shocked the nation by announcing his resignation. With over a year left before his term officially ended, his decision to stand down was as unexpected as it was constitutionally unnecessary. But like Benjedid before him, who had made a similar announcement exactly six years and ten months earlier, Zéroual's hand had been forced. His negotiations with the leaders of the FIS, AIS, and GIA had angered the military hardliners. They were not content simply to contain and defeat the insurgents; they wanted to destroy the entire Islamist movement. By entering into talks with these groups, Zéroual granted them official recognition and, more importantly, presented them with an opportunity to withdraw from the fray still intact.

But allowing the Islamists to live to fight another day was not Zéroual's only indiscretion. Of equal concern to the eradicators were his concerted efforts to build up his own power base. From the beginning he had been something of a disappointment to them with his continued unwillingness to do as he was told. But despite his determination to pursue his own agenda, he had still needed the military high command's political support. They, after all, had put him in power. With his own party and a popular mandate to govern, however, Zéroual's dependence on them had lessened. So much so, that the eradicators were worried that he might soon be able to ignore them entirely.

To prevent any further decline in their political influence, the eradicators, led by General Mohamed Lamari, Chief of Staff, set about hounding Zéroual from office. And after forcing him to step down, they began purging the government of his supporters. The most notable scalp they claimed (aside from that of Zéroual himself) belonged to Prime Minister Ahmed Ouyahia. He was eventually driven to resign on 14 December 1999. The following day, Smaïl Hamdani was appointed as his successor and given the task of making ready for the presidential election scheduled to take place the following February.

But this date was soon pushed back to 15 April 1999 after several parties complained that it did not give them enough time to meet the country's stringent electoral laws. One of the main challenges they faced was collecting the 75,000 signatures they each needed to be allowed to field a candidate. And of the forty-eight individuals who declared their intention to stand, only twelve managed to meet this particular requirement. Of those who did, five were ruled ineligible on technical grounds by the country's Constitutional Council. The seven who remained in the race were Hocine Aït Ahmed; Abdelaziz Bouteflika; Abdallah Djaballah; Mouloud Hamrouche; Ahmed Taleb al-Ibrahim; Youssef Khateb; and Mokdad Sifi.

In spite of its extensive behind-the-scenes machinations, the military's high command swore it would remain impartial and respect the democratic process. But it was an open secret that it wanted Bouteflika to win. He also enjoyed the support of several other influential political parties and civil society groups, including the RND, FLN, and UGTA. Their backing gave him a huge advantage over his rivals. The financial and human resources they put at his command and his privileged access to the state-controlled media enabled him to mount a campaign that dwarfed those of his rivals. So great was this disparity that several of the other candidates began to question the fairness of the whole election.

Their fears seemed to be confirmed shortly before the first round of voting took place. To ensure that there was adequate policing on Election Day, members of the police and armed forces voted forty-eight hours earlier at special polling stations to which no observers were allowed access. As well as this lack of oversight, it quickly became apparent that the military's high command had ordered the junior ranks to vote for Bouteflika, which they did en masse. In light of these irregularities, the other six candidates called on Zéroual to bring a halt to proceedings before he stepped down. When he declined to do so, they all pulled out, leading to widespread calls, both at home and abroad, for the election to be rerun.

But Hamdani, under pressure from the military, insisted that it go ahead. In protest, each of the candidates who had withdrawn encouraged his followers and supporters to boycott the election. And thousands more followed suit either because they saw little point in voting or through fear of what the GIA and GSPC might do to them if they did. Whatever their motivations, though, sufficient people refused to take part to ensure one of the lowest voter turnouts in the country's postindependence history.[3] And perhaps equally significant, not all those who did participate voted for Bouteflika. Even though he was the only candidate standing, he received just 74 percent of all votes cast. The remaining 26 percent of ballots were spoiled.

Despite these protests and the considerable unease the election generated abroad, the result was allowed to stand. And on 27 April 1999, Bouteflika was inaugurated as Algeria's new president. His triumph made clear the military's continued political influence. It had been Lamari and his cohorts who had led the charge against Zéroual. And it had been they who had made Bouteflika's victory certain (even though he probably would have won without their interference). But in so doing, they cast a pall of doubt over the progress made by Zéroual and his government. The high command's actions stretched the veneer of legitimacy he had helped create for the regime extremely thin.

Arguably, it was in the military sphere that the most dramatic progress had been made. The AIS had called a halt to its campaign, the GIA had been forced to beat a retreat, and the Islamist maquis had shrunk to only a fraction of its former size. The danger it now posed to the state was much diminished from what it had been before. But while this was undoubtedly good news for the regime, dozens (and often hundreds) of civilians continued to be killed or maimed each month. Indeed, around 2,500 people died during the course of 1999 alone. And despite the various setbacks they had encountered, both the GIA's and the GSPC's leaders remained hungry for the fight.

The start of the new millennium witnessed an upsurge in the level of violence as the GIA and GSPC stepped up their terror campaigns, and members of the Berber community fought running battles with the police in a series of massive riots. Although triggered by entirely different factors, these events were linked both in what they were trying to achieve and in how they impacted on the government. For a start, the GIA's, GSPC's, and Berberists' actions were all driven by their dissatisfaction with the definition of the nation promoted by Algeria's leaders since independence. The insurgents' primary goal was to transform the country into an Islamic republic, and the Berberists wanted their culture and language to be afforded the same status as those of the Arab population. The cumulative effect of both groups' actions was to force Bouteflika to engage in his own program of nation building.

The GIA's and GSPC's redoubling of their efforts was prompted by the National Assembly's promulgation of the Law of Civil Concord (LCC) on 13 July 1999. Under its terms, any individual guilty of committing certain types of crime—including rape and murder—would be granted a more lenient sentence as long as they surrendered to the authorities and expressed a genuine desire to be reintegrated into society. Article 1 of the LCC stated that anyone who gave themselves up would, depending on what they had done, be treated in one of three ways—pardoned completely, put on probation for between three and twelve years, or imprisoned for not more than ten years. Only those individuals guilty of taking part in massacres or of detonating explosive devices in public places were barred from taking advantage of this scheme. They would still be tried under existing legislation and could, if found guilty, be sentenced to death.

The statutory changes introduced by the LCC were not permanent, however, and came to an end on 13 January 2000. But while they lasted, five thousand militants already convicted of various crimes benefited from them by having their sentences quashed. And a further 5,500 insurgents sought to do likewise and surrendered to the authorities. In addition to the LCC, Bouteflika granted a presidential pardon to all AIS fighters on 10 January 2000 as a reward for the groups laying down its arms. As a result of these amnesties, the insurgency was dealt a body blow as thousands of fighters turned themselves in. And this defeat was made all the worse for those fighters who refused to give up, by the legitimacy it bestowed on Bouteflika. Within less than a year, he had seemingly gone a long way to fulfilling two of his main election pledges—returning peace to Algeria and rebuilding national unity.

But it was not a total triumph for the government. For a start, some of the families of those who had been murdered or raped by insurgents were outraged that convicted criminals were being let off so lightly. So, too, were the friends and relations of those who had been killed by the army or the police. The LCC made no mention of the security forces' culpability and, instead, blamed the violence solely on the Islamists. The families of the 5,000–10,000 people who had disappeared while in police custody found this a particularly bitter pill to swallow as they were still no closer to finding out what had happened to their loved ones. And perhaps predictably, the LCC and AIS amnesty provoked a backlash from the GIA and GSPC as they strove to convince the world that they were not beaten yet.

The determination of Zouabri and Hattab was matched by many of the militants left under their command who felt slighted at not being offered the same terms as the fighters of the AIS. Parts of the military were also disappointed with the LCC albeit for very different reasons. They felt it gave far too much away to the rebels and that the president needed to take a tougher line. To mark their frustration and remedy the softness they saw creeping into government policy, they launched a major assault against the insurgents as soon as the LCC deadline passed.

As a result of this offensive and the LCC, the insurgents were forced onto the back foot throughout the spring and summer of 2000. Their main priority was simply survival, as they set about shoring up their position and planning what to do next. But as the army offensive began to tail off and the dust settled on the LCC, the GIA and GSPC renewed their campaigns against the regime and their other enemies. From early autumn onward, the level of violence rose rapidly as the country was gripped by a new wave of assassinations, massacres, and armed clashes between the insurgents and security forces. In October alone over two hundred people were killed nationwide. And for the year as a whole, five thousand people died in violent circumstances—twice the number that had been killed in 1999.[4]

A significant number of these deaths occurred in Kabylia where Berber youths fought a series of running battles with the police and gendarmerie. The whole area had been in a state of high tension for the past eighteen months, ever since the murder of the popular folk singer Lounès Matoub. He was gunned down in mysterious circumstances on 25 June 1998 while driving into Tizi Ouzou. The government quickly blamed the attack on Islamist insurgents, pointing to the fact that the GIA had held him captive for two weeks in 1994.[5] Yet such arguments failed to convince many in the Berber community, including Matoub's wife. Why, they asked, had the GIA decided to kill him now when it had declined to do so before? And why did the authorities not conduct an autopsy as they should have done? The absence of any satisfactory answers to these questions led many to suspect the security forces, especially in light of the sustained campaign of intimidation mounted against Matoub by the government in the years leading up to his death.

The timing of his death was indeed fortuitous for the government. Since the late 1980s he had been a fierce critic of the policy of Arabization, viewing it as part of a deliberate campaign to obliterate Kabyle traditions and culture. Central to this policy was the installation of Arabic as the language of public discourse. The achievement of this moved a step closer on 5 January 2000, when the law requiring all state institutions and government bodies to conduct their business in Arabic finally came into force. Had he been alive, Matoub would almost certainly have protested against the enactment of this legislation, just as he had objected to the promulgation of similar laws.

Although this piece of legislation was a legacy from the Benjedid regime, Bouteflika could have delayed its implementation just as Boudiaf had done when he was chairman of the HCE. If nothing else, such an action would have been well received by the Berber community and helped convince it that he was sympathetic to their concerns. As it was, Bouteflika's decision not to delay was taken by many Berbers as evidence of his hostility to their demands. And all Berbers were united in their opposition to the law itself. Its enactment signaled the final triumph of Arabic as it became the language through which government and education at all levels were conducted.

Over the next couple of years, the Berber community's relations with the regime deteriorated even further. On 18 April 2001, Massinissa Guermah, a young man from Beni Douala not far from Tizi Ouzou, was shot and killed by gendarmes after being taken into custody. His death, the offensive statement issued by the gendarmerie explaining it, and the arrest of three youths at Bejaïa four days later triggered widespread rioting that quickly spread to other towns and villages throughout Kabylia. In an effort to restore calm, Bouteflika delivered a speech calling for national unity on 26 April. But his failure to acknowledge or even mention the linguistic and cultural concerns of the Berber community served to strengthen the hostility it felt toward him and added fuel to the protests and demonstrations that were still taking place.

The response of the security forces to these disturbances was typically brutal. Throughout late April, over one hundred protestors were killed and around five thousand more injured in clashes with the police, gendarmerie, and army. The funerals for those who died were attended by hundreds or, in some cases, thousands of mourners and often turned into new demonstrations against the government. In an attempt to break the cycle of violence and defuse the situation, Bouteflika announced on 1 May that he was launching an official inquiry into the events of the past few weeks. Yet the grudging manner in which he made this pledge and his veiled accusations that the Berber community was allowing itself to be manipulated by outside forces did little to assuage its fears or soothe its anger.

Many Berbers were also deeply suspicious of the investigation itself. They were convinced that its primary purpose was to silence them and cover up any wrongdoing by the security forces. As it turned out, the board of inquiry found that some gendarmes and police officers had acted unlawfully and that command structures had broken down. But while it was conducting its investigations, the Berber community took matters into its own hands. Throughout the summer of 2001 traditional tribal councils sprang up throughout Kabylia. Their purpose was to facilitate the dissemination of information throughout the community and enable its various parts to coordinate their actions better.

To help direct their efforts, and the Berber community as a whole, a new body called the Inter-Wilaya Coordination of Tribes, Districts, and Communes (Coordination Interwilaya des Archs, Daïras et Communes, IADC) was established in May 2001. Over the months following its creation, the IADC presented the regime with a series of detailed demands known collectively as the El Ksueur program.[6] As well as calling for the immediate release of all those imprisoned during the recent demonstrations and the prosecution of all members of the security forces implicated in the deaths of protestors, it demanded that the government look after all victims of state repression, recognize Tamazight as an official language, increase state investment in Kabylia, and allow greater public scrutiny of the security forces.

Confronted by this sustained opposition and the findings of the inquiry he had launched, Bouteflika adopted a more conciliatory approach in his dealings with the Berber community. In the autumn of 2001 he instructed his prime minister, Ali Benflis,[7] to open direct negotiations with representatives from it. As a result of these discussions, which took place in Algiers throughout December 2001 and into January 2002, Bouteflika agreed to address a number of the IADC's key demands. In March 2002, he announced that compensation would be paid to the victims of police brutality and that over twenty officers would be tried for murder. But, most significantly, he agreed to the legal recognition of Tamazight. On 8 April 2002, the National Assembly passed a constitutional amendment making Tamazight a "national language" and committing the state to work "for its promotion and development in all its linguistic variations . . . all over the national territory."[8]

Yet the IADC and wider Berber community were still not satisfied. Even though Tamazight was recognized as a national language, it was not made an official language like Arabic. As a result Tamazight speakers did not enjoy the same linguistic rights as their Arabic-speaking compatriots. With the support of both the FFS and RCD, the IADC called on the Berber community to boycott the National Assembly elections scheduled for 30 May 2002. As a result, voter turnout for that election was at one of its lowest levels since independence with just 46 percent of the electorate taking part.[9]

Talks between the regime and Berber leaders continued throughout 2003, but neither side was prepared to back down over the status of Tamazight. In the run up to the presidential election of 8 April 2004, talks between the two sides broke down again. The FFS and IADC repeated their call for Berbers not to participate in the election and promised to disrupt preparations for it in Kabylia. But the effectiveness of their actions was compromised by Saïd Sadi's decision to stand as a candidate. Partly as a consequence of this split in the Berber front, voter turnout for this election was higher than what it had been in May 2002, with 58 percent of the electorate taking part. Amid widespread accusations of vote rigging, Bouteflika, representing the RND and MSP, won 85 percent of the vote.[10] Sadi finished fourth, winning just 2 percent.[11]

Despite the damage this "Brezhnevian" victory—as *Le Matin* described it[12]—did to Bouteflika's reputation both at home and abroad, the RCD's breaking of ranks with the IADC and FFS weakened the Berber community's negotiating position. As a result, the talks that were held intermittently over the following two years proved to be inconclusive as the Berber lobby failed to get what it wanted. And, the split between the Berber parties endured following the RCD's decision to contest the National Assembly election of 17 May 2007 and the FFS's refusal to do so. With just 35 percent of the country's voters taking part, turnout for this election was the lowest ever.

With the standoff between the government and Berber community still ongoing, the country seems scarcely any closer to achieving national unity. For a start, many Berbers remain deeply suspicious of Bouteflika. No matter the concessions he offers—which are never quite enough and are always too late in coming—he has been a key political actor in Algeria since independence. A member of the Oujda Clan, he held ministerial positions under both Ben Bella and Boumedienne, and he had been one of the front-runners to become president in 1979 before the military plumbed for Benjedid instead. It remains extremely difficult, therefore, for Berbers to separate him from the policy of Arabization given his service in the governments that first devised and implemented it.

Bouteflika's attempts to achieve national reconciliation have also been hampered by the ongoing resistance of the GIA and GSPC. The attacks they carried out polarized society and perpetuated the political, economic, and social instability that has wracked the country for the past two decades. Indeed, through their systematic murder of moderates, they have played their part in destroying the middle ground, the political space so essential to the peaceful resolution of the conflict. And while the tactics they use appall most Algerians, some still support their primary objective of establishing an

Islamic Republic. As long as they exist and continue to operate, the insurgents remain a divisive influence in Algeria.

Yet their capacity to be so has declined. The flurry of attacks carried out by their operatives in late 2000 dwindled away with the start of the New Year. In the face of the army's repeated onslaughts, they were forced to retreat ever deeper into the country's vast hinterland. Short of men, money, weapons, and essential supplies, their ability to act was left much reduced. But it was not destroyed altogether.

On 12 October 2001, GIA militants murdered two shepherds and kidnapped a third near Tiaret, around 150 miles (240 kilometers) southwest of Algiers. Forty-eight hours later, twenty of their comrades ambushed a detachment of militiamen at Bir El-Alter close to the Tunisian border, killing eleven of them. Just under a month after that on 7 December, two policemen were gunned down in a cafe in Tizi Ouzou by a group of ten fighters. And over the next twenty-four hours, five more people were killed and four others wounded in two separate attacks carried out in and around the city. These deaths took the total toll for the final three months of 2001 to well over one hundred.

The new year started with yet more bloodshed as rival factions within the GSPC fought each other for control of the group. On 15 January 2002 a firefight broke out between the followers of Nabil Sahrawi and those of Abdul Razzaq Bara along the wooded slopes of the mountains some 25 miles (40 kilometers) northwest of Batna. With Sahrawi's position now more secure, the GSPC resumed its offensive against the state. On 22 January it kidnapped and killed a young conscript in Balhadaf and a motorist driving along the road to Hajout. Then on 11 February, GIA gunmen shot and killed six members of one family in Boukra, around 19 miles (30 kilometers) south of Algiers. This brought the total number of killings for the year up to 210. And it was still only early February.

On 5 March, thirteen members of the GSPC were killed and one hundred more arrested by the security forces on the southern outskirts of Algiers. Just over a fortnight later, on 21 March, six family members were murdered and their corpses mutilated by Islamist militants in the village of Souq al-Had, around 125 miles (200 kilometers) west of the capital. Then on 2 April, twenty-one soldiers were killed near Molai al-Arabi after being ambushed by GIA fighters. And exactly one month after that, thirty-one people were murdered in two separate massacres. One of these occurred in the Teyart district around 125 miles (200 kilometers) southwest of Algiers. Sixteen people had already been murdered there by militants seven days earlier.

As June turned into July, the frequency and scale of these attacks increased steadily. On 5 July, thirty people died and a further thirty-six were injured when a massive car bomb exploded on the outskirts of Algiers. Two days later, six shepherds had their throats cut while tending their sheep in woods a short distance outside the city. Then on 10 July, GIA militants murdered nine people and wounded another two, again in the Teyart district. Finally, on 28 July, fifteen members of the GIA were killed in a joint police-army operation. These deaths pushed the total death toll for the year up to one thousand.

A further 134 people—including eighty insurgents—were killed during the course of September. One of those to lose his life was Emad Abdelwahid Ahmad Alwan, a senior member of Al-Qaida (AQ). He was killed in an ambush on the outskirts of Batna some 200 miles (320 kilometers) southwest of Algiers. Alwan's death was a notable victory for the security forces and the government as he had been forging closer links with Algeria's insurgents. The GSPC's leaders, in particular, were keen to establish a formal union between the two groups. Indeed, in October 2003, Nabil Sahrawi (the GSPC's new leader) declared his full support for "Osama bin Laden's jihad against the heretic America."[13] By killing Alwan, therefore, the army struck a blow against these intentions and, perhaps more importantly, earned the regime the gratitude of the US government.

As autumn turned into winter, so the attacks continued. Arguably the most serious of these took place in mid-October. In the remote town of Baq'at al-Hajaj, in the so-called Triangle of Death, thirteen boys at the Al-Fiqh Quranic School were murdered. The government blamed insurgents for the attack, but many local residents doubted this explanation. After all, why would Islamists attack a center of religious education? There were no such doubts, however, as to who was responsible for the car-bomb attack in Batna that killed five soldiers and wounded another five.

Between March and May 2003, the army captured five hundred GSPC fighters and killed several hundred more in a series of huge sweeps in the east of the country. But, in June, the pressure was relieved slightly when a small band of GSPC fighters led by Amari Saifi kidnapped thirty-two European tourists as they traveled across the Sahara. To avoid capture, the militants made the unfortunate holidaymakers march from one oasis to another until they crossed the border into neighboring Mali. During the course of these treks, one person died and another escaped during a rescue attempt mounted by the Algerian security forces. But the remainder were not freed until 18 August 2003, and then only after the German, Swiss, and Austrian governments paid the GSPC a joint ransom of $5 million.[14]

Yet even in the short term, these much-needed funds failed to turn the tide of battle in the GSPC's favor. The army still pursued its fighters relentlessly through the eastern wilayas, killing 150 of them and forcing dozens more to hide in caves in the Babour Mountains. One of those who died was Hassan Hattab, the group's founder. Although he was rumored to have stepped down as leader earlier in the year, these reports were never confirmed. And whether they were true or not, he remained an influential figure within the GSPC and broader Islamist movement. Whatever his official title at the time of his death, therefore, the army claimed his killing as a victory.[15]

To put an end to the mounting speculation that the GSPC had collapsed following Hattab's death, his successor—Nabil Sahrawi—reiterated the group's determination to establish an Islamic republic through "blood, body parts, and lives."[16] But such threats sounded increasingly hollow after he was shot and killed by soldiers on 19 June 2004. And more seriously for the GSPC, his death unleashed a new wave of internecine violence. The two main pretenders to Sahrawi's throne were Khatab Mourad (who was also known as Abdelber Abou Omar) and Abdelhami Sadaoui. Throughout July and August 2004, their forces attacked one another repeatedly as each man attempted to stake his claim. And all the while the army continued to kill and capture dozens of GSPC fighters as it mounted yet another search and destroy operation, this time in the area surrounding Bejaia.

The summer of 2004 was indeed one of the darkest periods in the GSPC's history. Yet with the onset of autumn its situation began to improve. On 6 September 2004, Abdelmalek Droukdel (who was also known as Abou Mossab Abdelwadoud) became the group's new emir, bringing to an end the bitter and bloody leadership contest. In their determination to stop each other from succeeding Sahrawi, Mourad and Sadaoui had weakened each other to such an extent that neither of them could prevent Droukdel from seizing power. Under him, the GSPC returned to the offensive, mounting a series of attacks throughout 2005. As a result, the death toll for the year jumped to five hundred. But it was still a lot less than what it had been in the peak years of the mid-1990s.

On 2 January 2005, GSPC fighters ambushed an army patrol near Baskara, killing eighteen soldiers and wounding another nineteen. Less than three weeks later, on 21 January, its operatives detonated a bomb in the main cemetery in Ein al-Rummaneh, killing three people and injuring a further five. A couple of weeks after that, its militants shot and killed a soldier during a gun battle on the outskirts of Sidi Dawoud, some 30 miles (50 kilometers) east of the capital. Then, on 30 March, its men ambushed a military convoy as it skirted the Bumahni forest near Tizi Ouzou, killing four soldiers.

As spring turned into summer, the frequency of the GSPC's attacks increased. On 7 April, its fighters murdered thirteen people at a fake road-block set up across the main highway linking the village of al-Araba'a with that of Tablat. Then on 23 April, its operatives assassinated four members of the security forces near Ein al-Defl, to the west of Algiers. And the very next day, its militants exploded a bomb in Bir El-Alter, killing two civilians. On 15 May, its men ambushed an army patrol near Khanshala in the far east of the country, killing eleven soldiers. And at the end of the month, its fighters attacked another military convoy, killing two and injuring five.

On 4 June, the GSPC mounted one of its largest operations to date when

150 of its fighters assaulted a Mauritanian army outpost, killing fifteen soldiers. In a statement released shortly afterward, Droukdel said the attack was to avenge "our brothers . . . detained . . . in Mauritania."[17] And less than a week later, its operatives detonated a bomb under a truck carrying militiamen, killing thirteen of them and wounding another six. Then on 30 July, a band of GSPC fighters shot six soldiers on the western outskirts of Algiers, killing two of them and wounding the other four. And the day after that, its militants attacked an armored vehicle on the outskirts of the eastern city of Tejlabin wounding five people, including a civilian caught in the cross fire.

As summer turned into autumn, the violence continued. On 14 August, soldiers shot and killed ten GSPC fighters in Ein al-Delfi and Almedia on the western and eastern outskirts of the capital. Four days later, unidentified gunmen murdered three civilians in the settlement of Ain Romana. And five days after that, twelve GSPC militants were killed during clashes with troops in the area around Annaba. Then in mid-September, GSPC fighters killed four members of the security forces close to Skikda. And its operatives killed two more policemen and injured a further five when they exploded a bomb in Al-Maseela just south of the capital a few days later. On 1 October, GSPC militants murdered three civilians in two separate attacks. And at the end of the month, its gunmen killed three people and injured another seven in three incidents, all in the east of the country.

The rise in violence during the course of 2005 gave the government and public notice of the GSPC's continued existence, capabilities, and determination. But as the year drew to a close, the group's fortunes, and indeed those of the insurgency as a whole, took another turn for the worse. On 14 August, Bouteflika announced that a referendum would be held the following month on a proposed law called the Charter for Peace and National Reconciliation (CPNR). Similar to the LCC in both content and objective, it promised more lenient sentences to any members of the GIA or GSPC who surrendered to the authorities and expressed a genuine desire to be reintegrated into mainstream society. Only those individuals who had exploded bombs in public places or participated in massacres were barred from taking advantage of its terms.

The referendum was held on 29 September 2005 and turnout was high with a little over 80 percent of the electorate taking part. Of those who voted, 97 percent supported the CPNR's promulgation. With such massive public backing, the government duly enacted it, setting a deadline of 28 August 2006 for insurgents to give themselves up. And like the LCC before it, the CPNR met with considerable success. By the time the deadline expired, around three hundred fighters or one-third of the GSPC's estimated total membership had surrendered to the authorities. The problems this massive loss of manpower presented Droukdel were compounded by the death of Ahmad Zarabib in January 2006. One of Droukdel's most trusted lieutenants, Zarabib was shot and killed during a gun battle with government forces near Bejaia.

Once again, the GSPC found itself teetering on the brink of destruction. Weakened and vulnerable, it turned increasingly to Al-Qaida for help and support. Eventually Droukdel got his wish and, in September 2006, he announced a formal alliance between the two groups. As if to confirm this, the GSPC embarked on a coordinated bombing campaign over the weeks and months that followed. Algiers, in particular, was targeted. On 30 October, GSPC operatives planted two devices in an Algiers suburb that killed three people and wounded another twenty-four. And on 10 December it attacked a coachload of British and US workers in the capital. Finally, in January 2007, it changed its name to Al-Qaida in the Land of the Islamic Maghreb (AQLIM).

Throughout 2007, AQLIM continued its bombing campaign, carrying out its most spectacular attacks on 11 December. In quick succession two bombs—the first planted a short distance from the Palais de Justice just off the Rue Abane Ramdane, the second placed close to the headquarters of the United Nations' mission in Algeria—exploded with deadly effect. As a result of these blasts, over twenty people died and dozens more sustained injuries. But the shock waves from these blasts reverberated far beyond the confines of the city and even Algeria. One after another, governments and political leaders around the world joined President Bouteflika and UN Secretary-General Ban Ki-Moon in a chorus of condemnation of those responsible.

These attacks came at the end of another bloody year for Algeria. Right at its start, on 30 January 2007, AQLIM militants had attacked an army post not far from the city of Batna, killing five soldiers. On 13 February the group had bombed seven police stations in the villages of Si Mustafa, Meklaa, Draa Benkheda, Illoua Oumalou, and Souk El Had (which it had already attacked twice before), resulting in the deaths of six people and injury of thirteen more. On 8 April, its fighters had ambushed an army patrol in the Zaccar forest in the Ain Defla region, killing nine soldiers. And two days later they had bombed the prime minister's office and a police station in the capital. Then on 11 April, its operatives had detonated a series of bombs hidden around central Algiers, killing over thirty people and injuring a further two hundred.

The violence continued into the summer. Throughout early May, AQLIM fighters had clashed with soldiers throughout northcentral and northeastern Algeria as they tried to disrupt preparations for the National Assembly elections being held later that month. Then, in July, a suicide bomber had attacked a military barracks near Bouira killing nine soldiers. And on 8 September, thirty people had died and a further fifty had been injured when another suicide bomber attacked the naval base at Dellys, 50 miles (80 kilometers) along the coast from Algiers.

Countering the Insurgency

This latest wave of bombings seemed to give the clearest indication yet that the GSPC's link-up with AQ was breathing new life into the insurgency. Its spectacular and coordinated attacks on the prime minister's office and UN headquarters highlighted a shift in its thinking and an expansion of its capabilities. And in making them, AQLIM served the government notice of its determination to continue fighting. Yet no amount of posturing could disguise the fragility and limitations of this renaissance. The AQLIM was still no closer to transforming Algeria into an Islamic republic. Not since the halcyon days of the mid-1990s when the state stood on the brink of collapse had victory been within easy reach of the insurgents. And with each year that passed, it grew ever more distant. As a result, it was never more than one step away from total destruction.

The bind that AQLIM and the GIA found themselves in was due in no small measure to the actions of the security forces. After an initial period of confusion, during which they struggled to contain the rebellion, they devised and prosecuted an effective counterinsurgency strategy. In developing their response, the security forces followed a similar path to that of their French counterparts during the war of liberation. In the beginning, both the French and Algerian armies were ill equipped to meet the threat that confronted them. Yet they adapted quickly by upgrading their capabilities, establishing or expanding specialist units, developing their tactics, and devising new training programs. And they were not afraid to abuse political, civil, and human rights to achieve their ends. Indeed, both armies tortured, kidnapped, raped, illegally imprisoned, and disappeared scores of suspects in order to destroy and discredit their respective enemies.

One of the first actions taken by the Algerian army was the expansion of its counterinsurgency unit. In 1992 this force numbered just fifteen thousand men and was too small, too ill equipped, and too poorly trained to deal with the rapidly growing maquis. And apart from fighting the MIA some seven or eight years earlier, it had little recent experience of waging and sustaining a counterinsurgency campaign. Aware of the unit's limitations and quick to grasp the nature and extent of the threat posed by the MIA, GIA, and AIS, the military's high command set about expanding and improving it. So successful were they that by the end of 1995 it had grown to three times its original size and come to form the cutting edge of an army that now numbered half a million men.

Despite the rapidity of their expansion, the security forces still lacked sufficient resources to contain the insurgency in the early years. The main difficulty they encountered was conducting multiple operations simultaneously. As well as discharging their everyday duties, which continued regardless, these forces had to police and guard towns, cities, regions, and communities, while seeking out and destroying the rebels. And they had to do so while they were reforming themselves. Guarding in particular tied up enormous numbers of soldiers, gendarmes, and police officers, thereby greatly reducing the number of personnel available to attack the insurgents. And this problem was exacerbated by Algeria's great size. The sheer distance between settlements meant that the security forces either had to abandon some of them to the insurgents or spread themselves thinly over vast areas.

Many towns and villages therefore, but especially those in the hinterland, were not given adequate protection. Isolated and poorly defended, they made easy pickings for the insurgents. And as the conflict continued and security in the cities improved, they were attacked with increasing regularity. To help them defend themselves and reduce the burden on the security forces, each municipality was encouraged to raise its own militia. Made up of local civilians, these forces assumed some of the responsibility for protecting the settlements in their respective areas. Officially, there were two types of militia—the Legitimate Defense Groups (Groupes de Légitime Défense, GLD) and the Patriots (Les Patriotes). In practice, however, there was virtually no difference between them.

The first of these forces were created in late 1994 upon the orders of President Zéroual. As the decade progressed they grew rapidly both in size and number so that by the end of the decade there were a quarter of a million civilians under arms, helping guard hundreds of settlements the length and breadth of the country. As well as improving the security of these towns and villages, the militias freed up thousands of troops to carry out more aggressive search and destroy operations against the insurgents. And by drawing local residents into the defense of their homes and families, the government dissuaded at least some of them from joining the insurgency.

Yet such forces were of only limited use without effective coordination. Central to the military's counterinsurgency campaign, as it had been to the French army's war against the FLN, was intelligence. And it was in the collection of intelligence that the military demonstrated its willingness to abuse human rights. The torture of many suspects was carried out by members of the shadowy Department of Information and Security (Département du Renseignement et de la Sécurité, DRS). Set up in 1990 to replace the discredited SM, it was placed under the authority of the ministry of defense. At its head was the director—Mohammed Médiène. And beneath him were three section chiefs—General Saïdi Fodhil (External Security), General Kamel Abderrahmane (Army Security), and General Smaïn Lamari (Counterespionage).

Most interrogations were conducted by Lamari's section at the DRS bases in Ben-Aknoun, Blida, Constantine, Oran, and elsewhere. Any suspect who resisted or refused to talk was physically and psychologically abused until they did. And with no legal representation or access to the outside world, the only option left open to them was to cooperate. In many cases, even that was not enough to save their lives. Once they had told their interrogators all they wanted to know, many suspects were summarily executed or disappeared.

A few, however, were spared and turned into double agents by the DRS. These turncoats served two main functions—to supply intelligence on the band of fighters they joined and to sow discord among its members. By exploiting the jealousies and suspicions that already existed (often in bountiful supply), these agents, and through them the DRS, were able to compromise the effectiveness of these groups as fighting forces, expose them to capture or elimination, and even make them turn on themselves. Within a short space of time, the DRS proved itself adept at mounting such black operations, going so far as to engineer prison breakouts and establishing its own insurgent group in order to plant informants in the GIA, MIA, and AIS.[18]

Yet the military high command was not content simply to defeat the insurgents; it wanted to destroy the entire Islamist movement once and for all. It was this determination that led to the outlawing of the FIS, the systematic persecution of its members and supporters, and the outright refusal of the eradicators to negotiate with its leaders. But it also gave rise to more sinister activities as the security forces strove to damage the movement's reputation and turn the general public against it. Since the mid-1990s a growing body of evidence has emerged implicating certain army units in some of the massacres carried out along the mitidja plain.

Much of this evidence is circumstantial—the army's repeated failure to stop the slaughter of civilians even when it knew it was happening and had troops stationed close by, that some of the killers wore military uniforms or carried army-issue rifles, and that the insurgents could not have committed all the atrocities they have been accused of. While there is no conclusive proof that the army was involved in any these massacres, the fact that these rumors persist and are so widely accepted speaks volumes about popular attitudes toward the security forces. Indeed, the general disregard they have shown for the lives and well-being of ordinary people has won them few admirers among the civilian population.

And the same is true internationally. Groups like Human Rights Watch and Amnesty International have repeatedly criticized Algiers for not doing enough to safeguard political, civil, and human rights. Foreign governments too have called on the regime to practice good governance and show more respect for the rule of law. Yet that has not stopped them from providing it with increasing levels of political, military, and economic support. At first the US and EU governments simply wanted to avoid isolating Algiers. Based on their recent experiences with Libya, these governments reasoned that policies of cautious engagement were the way ahead. But as the 1990s progressed, this desire to maintain dialogue developed into willingness and, in some instances, eagerness to provide help.

Indeed, in the mid-1990s, Washington's main objective was nothing more adventurous than supporting President Zéroual in his ongoing struggle against the eradicators. But within a few short years, this had given way to the far more ambitious and controversial goal of building closer military ties between the two countries. To achieve this, Washington had to court the very group of officers who had worked and conspired against Zéroual. In spite of this irony and mounting evidence of the Algerian security forces' systematic abuse of human rights, Washington sent Admiral Thomas Lopez, the commanding officer of US Naval Forces Europe (NAVEUR), on an official visit to Algiers in 1998 to discuss ways of improving military cooperation.[19]

As a first step toward achieving this, the USS *Mitscher* was dispatched later that year to take part in a search and rescue exercise with vessels from the Algerian navy. This was followed in May 1999 with a far larger joint exercise involving several ships from the US Sixth Fleet. But despite this progress, US-Algerian cooperation remained limited as President Clinton refused to lift the embargo on the sale of US arms to Algiers. Washington's attitude changed, however, following the terrorist attacks on the World Trade Center and Pentagon on 11 September 2001.[20]

Over the weeks and months that followed, Bouteflika worked hard to present Algeria as a frontline state in the struggle against Islamic fundamentalism and his government's counterinsurgency campaign as an integral part of the global war on terror (GWOT). His attempts to woo Washington and Europe were helped enormously when Algerian soldiers shot and killed Emad Abdelwahid Ahmad Alwan—AQ's envoy to the GSPC—in September 2002. Bouteflika skillfully used Alwan's death as evidence of both Algeria's frontline position and its commitment to the GWOT. And his efforts were rewarded when Washington announced it was sending Assistant Secretary of State William, Burns on an official visit to Algeria later that year. Arriving in early December, Burns quickly endeared himself to his hosts by declaring that "Washington had much to learn from Algeria on ways to fight terrorism."[21] But more importantly, on 10 December, he announced the suspension of the ban on US arms sales to Algiers.

Shortly before Burns left for Algiers, official approval was finally granted to a new US counterinsurgency program called the Pan-Sahel Initiative (PSI). With a start-up budget of $7 million, the PSI was designed to help the states of the Sahel—Chad, Mali, Mauritania, and Niger—better secure their borders against Islamist insurgents operating out of Algeria. To enable them to do so, the US European Command (EUCOM) sent the 10th Special Forces Group (Airborne) to Timbuktu in Mali to establish and operate a training base for units from all four countries. And it also provided the troops of these units with vital equipment, including all-terrain vehicles, body armor, desert camouflage, and communication and navigation tools.

The value of the PSI was demonstrated during the spring of 2004. Alarmed by rumors that the GSPC was planning to kidnap competitors in the Paris-Dakar rally as they drove through Mali, EUCOM scrambled a reconnaissance plane to sweep the Sahara for any insurgent activity. During its sortie, the aircraft came across a group of fighters deep in the Algerian desert. As it turned out, it was the same band that had kidnapped the European tourists the previous summer. The information gathered by the plane was passed to Algerian, Chadian, Malian, and Nigerian ground forces that closed in around the group. In the firefights that ensued, around fifty insurgents were shot and killed. The remainder fled across the border into Mali, then Niger, and finally Chad, where they were captured by members of the Movement for Democracy and Justice (MDJ), a rebel group fighting the Chadian government. Eventually, in October 2004, the MDJ handed their prisoners over to the Algerian authorities.

Following this success, Washington increased the PSI's budget to $125 million. And then in June 2005 it launched a new program called the Trans-Sahara Counter Terrorism Initiative (TSCTI) with an annual budget of $100 million. More ambitious in scope, it aimed to prevent the radicalization of communities living along the edges of the Sahara and to stop the illegal flow of money, people, and weapons across the region's porous borders. And whereas the PSI focused on four countries, the TSCTI targeted nine— Algeria, Chad, Mali, Mauritania, Morocco, Niger, Nigeria, Senegal, and Tunisia. Responsibility for achieving these goals was divided between several US government departments and agencies. The Department of Defense was made responsible for planning and overseeing any military operations, the Department of State was put in charge of improving airport security, the Department of the Treasury was charged with stopping money laundering, USAID instructed to manage any development projects, and EUCOM ordered to provide training and logistics support.[22]

As under the PSI, this training was provided by the 10th Special Forces Group (Airborne) and latterly the National Guard's 20th Special Forces Group. To mark the official start of the TSCTI, a massive training exercise called Operation Flintlock was launched on 6 June 2005. Lasting twenty days and involving thousands of troops from each of the nine participating countries, the US, and other NATO member states, Flintlock was the largest US military exercise in Africa since the end of the World War II. As it began to wind down, Washington proclaimed it a great success. And while it remains unclear whether the exercise has improved the counterinsurgency capabilities of the participating countries, there is little doubt that it has raised the US profile in the region.

The US intervention has been welcomed by most of the region's governments even though, by agreeing to cooperate with Washington, they have exposed themselves to the wrath of AQLIM and its allies.[23] France, on the other hand, remains more circumspect. For much of the past 150 years it has been the dominant power in the region. And while it supports the US initiatives against the Islamist insurgents operating out of Algeria, it is reluctant to surrender any of its influence. Washington's courting of Algiers and its neighbors continues to generate a certain amount of disquiet in Paris. So much so that some of its recent actions and initiatives in Algeria have been motivated, at least in part, by a desire to ward off the US challenge.

Indeed, in a move designed to overshadow and draw attention away from William Burns's trip to Algeria, Jacques Chirac visited the country less than three months later. As the first French head of state to visit since independence, the event was rightly hailed as historic. Arriving in Algiers on 2 March 2003, he was greeted by a rapturous crowd some half a million strong. And the following day he delivered a speech to both chambers of the National Assembly to thunderous applause. The warmth of the welcome he was given highlighted the genuine affection many Algerians now had for France and the strength of their support for President Chirac's outspoken opposition to the impending invasion of Iraq.

Perhaps unsurprisingly, French interest in the Algerian conflict had always been strong. The geographical proximity of the two countries, their shared history, and the size of the Algerian community in France meant that it could never be otherwise. And it grew with the murder of every French citizen. But like Washington, Paris was uneasy about some of the methods employed by the Algerian security forces, especially as they led to increased demands within France that it should acknowledge and apologize for the French army's use of torture during the war of liberation. Yet any such doubts were pushed to one side following the GIA's seizure of Air France flight 8969 and its subsequent attacks against the Paris Metro system.

From the earliest days of independence, France has maintained military garrisons in several of its former colonies. And although it has no bases in Algeria, it still has around one thousand troops stationed in both Chad and Senegal, and a further four hundred in the Central African Republic.[24] But unlike the US, for whom military assistance is one of the main ways it helps the Algerian government, France has provided mostly political and economic support. It continues to be one of the main driving forces behind the Euro-Mediterranean Partnership (EMP) or Barcelona Process, which was launched in November 1995. Made up of the twenty-seven members of the European Union and twelve African and Middle Eastern states (including Algeria), it seeks to implement various proposals and objectives agreed at series of conferences held in Barcelona and elsewhere.

One of the EMP's primary goals is to combat the terrorist threat, and in 2005 all thirty-nine EMP members signed up to the Euro-Mediterranean

Code of Conduct on Countering Terrorism. Among other things, the signatories agreed to "implement in full all Security Council resolutions addressing the issue of terrorism . . .; strive to achieve the ratification and implementation of all thirteen UN Counter-Terrorism Conventions; . . . exchange information on . . . terrorists and their support networks . . .; refuse asylum to terrorists and deny them safe haven . . . ; [and] share expertise and best practices on countering terrorism."[25]

But as well as encouraging EMP members to coordinate their countert-errorism efforts, the Code also calls on them to work together "to identify the factors which contribute to the terrorist threat and share experiences and expertise on how to address them."[26] Arguably, it is in this area that the European Commission has made its greatest efforts in Algeria. As part of the EMP and the European Neighborhood Policy (ENP), the European Commission and European Investment Bank (EIB) have spent millions of euros trying to help President Bouteflika's government deal with some of the factors fueling the insurgency in Algeria. Between 1995 and 1999 these payments amounted to €164 million. And for the period of 2000 to 2006 they were doubled to €338.8 million.[27]

Most of the money provided by the European Commission and EIB has been spent trying to improve Algeria's crumbling infrastructure. Even before the violence began, its transport network, sewer systems, power stations, and water processing plants had struggled to cope with the demands being made of them. But once the insurgency got underway, the situation rapidly grew worse. From the earliest days of the conflict, MIA, GIA, and AIS fighters deliberately targeted the country's infrastructure, damaging and destroying roads, electricity cables, telephone lines, and oil installations. And the devastation they wrought served only to increase the pressure on those networks, systems, and services that remained.

No part of the country was spared. In rural areas, whole towns and villages were left without power, water, or working telephone lines for days and weeks on end. And in the cities and other large urban centers, public services and amenities were stretched to breaking point and beyond by the massive influx of migrants from the countryside. Impoverished by the collapse of the rural economy and terrified by the spiraling violence in the Triangle of Death, thousands fled to Algiers, Oran, Tizi Ouzou, and Annaba in search of work and refuge. What they found were teeming slums plagued by severe water shortages and power cuts that could last for hours at a time.

Perhaps the most serious problem in the cities was the chronic shortage of housing. In 1987, the national census recorded that an average of seven and a half people were living in each dwelling.[28] Throughout the early 1990s, this figure remained virtually unchanged as first the Benjedid regime and then the HCE struggled to build sufficient homes fast enough. Then in 1995, under pressure from the IMF to reduce public spending, President

Zéroual slashed his housing budget by 70 percent. Such a reduction made it all but impossible for his government to maintain the number of people living in each house at its existing level, let alone reduce it. To do that, it needed to build nearly a million new homes.[29]

The weight of responsibility for addressing these issues rested squarely on the government's shoulders. Yet in addition to this duty of care, improving the quality of ordinary Algerians' lives impacted on the success of its counterinsurgency campaign. The appeal of the FIS had rested, at least in part, on its provision of welfare services. And the ability of the Islamist maquis to attract recruits, even after the security forces had gained the upper hand, was partially due to the continued anger many young men felt toward the government for their poor standard of living. Forced to live in cramped apartments in crumbling tower blocks, they were susceptible to the insurgents' siren call. By improving public services and rebuilding the country's infrastructure, therefore, the government could remove some of the grievances driving young men to join the maquis.

But more pressing was its need to create jobs—lots of jobs. Between 1998 and 2005, official unemployment hovered at around 30 percent, although the real figure was almost certainly higher. Those most badly affected were sixteen- to twenty-five-year-olds. Within this age group, unemployment stood at 54 percent. And while the remainder could consider themselves fortunate to have jobs, many were poorly paid, underemployed or overqualified for the work they were doing. The frustrations this gave rise to were intensified by the absence of any hope that the situation might soon improve. And without an income, many young men lacked the means to support themselves, get married, or move out of the familial home.[30] The disappointment and resentment this inevitably generated drove some into the arms of the insurgents. As well as providing these young men with the means to strike back at the regime, these groups also offered a wage, a purpose, and a sense of belonging.[31]

The high level of unemployment was exacerbated by demographic pressures. Since independence, Algeria's population has grown at a phenomenal rate. Between 1960 and 1970 it increased by around 2.4 percent each year, between 1970 and 1980 3.1 percent, and between 1980 and 1990 2.9 percent. And the high growth rate persisted throughout the 1990s and into the new millennium. Each year between 1990 and 2000, the population increased by around 2.3 percent and between 2000 and 2005 by 2.1 percent. This sustained growth made the Algerian population bottom-heavy with a huge number of children and youths. With each year that passed, thousands of young adults entered the job market for the first time. To find work for them all, and for everyone else of employment age, the economy needed to generate around 250,000 new positions each year between 1990 and 2000. And since 2000, this figure has jumped to 360,000 posts because of continued demographic growth and further job losses during the previous decade.

From the very beginning, the rehabilitation of the economy has been of the utmost importance to the regime's counterinsurgency efforts. But since the late 1980s, when President Benjedid first invited the IMF and World Bank to intervene, Algeria's economic problems have been too great for successive governments to face alone. Arguably the most serious problem they have had to confront has been the country's foreign debt. Although Benjedid did manage to gain some control over it in the early 1980s, after that it increased steadily year on year. In 1983 it stood at $12.9 billion, in 1984 $14.9 billion, in 1986 $19.6 billion, in 1989 $26.1 billion, in 1991 $28.6 billion, and in 1994 $28.7 billion. But of perhaps greater significance was the increase in the amount of Algeria's export earnings that were required to service it. In 1989 the debt had consumed an onerous 68 percent of the country's foreign earnings. By 1994, this had risen to an unsustainable 91.8 percent.

Finding itself crushed by the sheer weight of what the country owed its foreign lenders, the HCE and Zéroual were forced to turn to the IMF and World Bank for assistance. Much of the government's economic planning from mid-1993 onward was dedicated to meeting the various criteria set down by these institutions for gaining their help. Even before the agreement of the SAPs in 1994, therefore, the IMF and World Bank already possessed significant influence over Algeria's economy. Not only did this underline the absolute demise of socialism and the socialist dimension of the definition of the nation promoted by the Ben Bella, Boumedienne, and Benjedid regimes, it also emphasized the increasing loss of economic sovereignty experienced by the country. Both these realities upset and angered the more traditional elements within the ruling elite and general population.

But before it set about wooing the IMF and World Bank, the HCE attempted to refinance the debt through short-term borrowing. So, in March 1992 it borrowed $1.5 billion from the French bank Crédit Lyonnais. This policy was given added vigor by Belaïd Abdessalam when he became prime minister on 8 July 1992.[32] He refused to devalue the dinar any further and introduced measures to protect the country's domestic markets from outside competition. Unfortunately, the strategy failed to address the EPEs' continued low productivity. And by the summer of 1993, the country was on the verge of defaulting on its debt repayments.

On 21 August 1993, Abdessalam was replaced as prime minister by Redha Malek who, despite continued opposition from certain members of the elite, reopened negotiations with the IMF almost immediately. And to help make sure that he did, the French government refused to reschedule a $5.6 billion debt Algeria owed it. In early April 1994, Malek and the IMF concluded a stabilization agreement. In accordance with its terms, Malek devalued the dinar by 40 percent and increased the price of basic foodstuffs and other essential items by as much as 100 percent. Then almost immediately after, he resigned. He was replaced as prime minister by Mokdad Sifi on 15 April 1994.[33]

Despite the deep unpopularity of Malek's reforms and the increased hardships they visited on the Algerian people, Sifi and Zéroual remained committed to them. The following month, the IMF made available a stand-by loan of $648 million, thereby paving the way for the government to start renegotiating Algeria's debts with its major creditors. In June 1994, it reached an agreement with the Paris Club to reschedule repayment of an existing $5 billion loan over a fifteen-year period. Then in July 1994, the French government offered it a new loan of over $1 billion. Further funds were made available by the IMF in April 1995 when it offered Algiers a loan of $1.8 billion. And over the next two months, both the London and Paris Clubs agreed to reschedule the repayment of the $3.2 billion and $7.5 billion owed them respectively.[34]

By the late summer of 1995, a degree of control had been exerted over the debt as repayments fell from over 100 percent of the country's export earnings to around 30 percent. In return for this international support, first Zéroual and then Bouteflika were obliged to press ahead with the liberalization of the economy. Between 1995 and 2002, they privatized a host of industries, including the state-owned telephone network, metallurgy plants, and cement factories; opened parts of the domestic market to foreign competition; eliminated the remaining price controls; and closed around one thousand public-owned enterprises. The only sectors of the economy not directly affected by these changes were the oil and gas industries, which continued to attract by far the largest share of all foreign investment in the country. Despite all the changes encouraged by the IMF and introduced by Zéroual and Bouteflika, SONATRACH has retained its monopoly.

These reforms and the ongoing rise in international oil and gas prices enabled the economy to achieve steady growth throughout the late 1990s and early years of the new millennium. In 1998 it grew by an impressive 5.1 percent, in 1999 3.2 percent, in 2000 2.4 percent, in 2001 2.2 percent, and in 2002 4.1 percent.[35] As well as creating much-needed new jobs, this upturn generated extra revenue for the government to spend on its counterinsurgency campaign. So, too, did the agreements concluded with the IMF, World Bank, and Paris and London Clubs. Indeed, this "financial windfall"[36] has proved pivotal, as both Zéroual and Bouteflika have used these extra monies to help pay for the expansion of the security forces and the self-defense militias, and to finance their counterinsurgency campaigns.

But they have not been the only ones to benefit from the liberalization of the economy. The opening up and deregulation of Algeria's markets has led to an explosion in illegal trading that has been ruthlessly exploited by the insurgents. As consumer goods have become harder to find in the shops, and the cost of those that can be found has kept rising, an increasing number of Algerians have turned to the black market or *trabendo*. Items purchased in this way are cheaper because no duty has been paid on them as they have been smuggled into the country. And it is by working in this parallel economy that many Algerians earn their livings. But by operating illegally, these smugglers and traders cannot easily ask the police for protection from the insurgents who extort money from them.

In an effort to reduce the size of the trabendo—and in the process decrease both the amount of money the government loses in unpaid taxes and the insurgents' income—Bouteflika has attempted to create more jobs in the mainstream economy. Yet his ability to do so, beyond helping the economy to grow, has remained limited. For a start, he is bound by the reality of Algeria's economic situation for which there is no miracle cure or magic wand. And he is further constrained by the agreements he and his predecessors entered into with the IMF, World Bank, and other foreign lenders. With few options left open to him, he launched an ambitious public works scheme called the Emergency Reconstruction Program (ERP) in 2001.

Scheduled to last three years and cost $6 billion, the government proposed setting the country's unemployed to work rebuilding and upgrading the country's infrastructure. And in so doing, it hoped to push economic growth up to 6 percent per annum for each of the years it lasted. Yet, from the start, it was plagued with problems. And as the disagreements over what to do first, which wilaya's needs were the greatest, and where the government was going to find the money to pay for it all rumbled on, the program stagnated.

The Nation-Building Process Under Abdelaziz Bouteflika

By the time Bouteflika took office in April 1999, the insurgency had passed its peak. Battered, divided, and forced to operate from remote mountain bases, the fighters of the GIA and GSPC continued to mount attacks but were unable to threaten the government as once they had. Weakened by constant infighting, they had left themselves vulnerable to infiltration and manipulation by DRS agents. And, as a result of their attacks in France and support for AQ, they had made some powerful enemies who now helped the government work toward their defeat. But more damaging was their ongoing failure to effectively resist the counterinsurgency campaigns waged against them. By a mixture of military, political, economic, and social means, successive governments and the security forces have been able to get the measure of them.

But despite the long odds against their victory, the GIA and GSPC have struggled on. And in so doing, by bombing, shooting, killing, and maiming, they have continued to threaten the security of the state and the safety of the civilian population. Yet that was not the sum of the instability that faced Bouteflika when he first took office. He was also confronted by an increasingly well organized and belligerent Berber movement, determined to win greater political and cultural rights for its community. In an effort to overcome these divisions, Bouteflika has done what all his predecessors have—embarked on a program of nation building.

Perhaps unsurprisingly, given the length of his political career and continued support for the policy of Arabization, Bouteflika has built his definition of the nation around the twin themes of Islam and Arabism. And equally predictably, in light of his past membership of governments that adopted similar approaches, he set about promoting this definition by controlling the discourse on national identity. As well as tightening his grip on the country's media, he has tried to dominate its political system and social space.

When Bouteflika took power, the media was already heavily censored and closely monitored. And the laws that existed were augmented by the climate of fear that the security forces and insurgents had created between them. Fully aware of what might happen to them or their families if they said the wrong thing, many journalists exercised extreme caution or simply left the country. But in 2001, Bouteflika tightened the screw on the media even further through his revision of the country's defamation legislation. By the time he had finished, it was a criminal offense to insult the president, members of the National Assembly, or military officers. The sentence for anyone convicted of such a crime was either up to twelve months in prison or a fine of between 50,000 and 250,000 dinars. Since its enactment, this law has been used to harass journalists and reporters, and a number have been convicted of breaking it.[37]

In June 2005, two reporters working for the French language newspaper *Le Soir d'Algérie* were convicted of insulting the president and jailed for six months each. So, too, was the paper's editor, Fouad Bu Ghanem, for allowing their stories to be printed and not exercising adequate control over his staff. And in a separate court case during the same month, three journalists working for the francophone newspaper *Liberty* were fined 250,000 dinars each after being convicted of defaming several army officers. The newspaper was also fined one million dinars for printing their articles.[38]

Four months later on 28 October 2005, members of the international nongovernmental organization Reporters Without Borders (Reporters Sans Frontières, RSF) gathered outside the Algerian embassy in Paris to mark the 500th day of Mohamed Benchicou's detention and call for his immediate release. Imprisoned on 14 June 2004, he had earned the lasting enmity of President Bouteflika during his time as editor of the Algerian daily *Le Matin*. In the run-up to the presidential election of April 2004, he and his newspaper openly opposed Bouteflika's candidacy. But, unfortunately for Benchicou, Bouteflika won. And within three months of his victory, Benchicou had been sentenced to thirty months in prison and *Le Matin* closed down.[39]

And more recently, RSF has expressed its alarm at the ongoing treatment of Noureddine Boukraa, a correspondent for the Arabic language newspaper *Ennahar*. He was placed under judicial control on 4 March 2008 by a court in Annaba after charges were brought against him by the region's chief of public security, Draï Messaoud. Boukraa was convicted of slandering Messaoud in an article he published on 12 November the previous year. In it, Boukraa accused Messaoud and other members of the Annaba police of taking bribes and harassing the opponents of certain powerful people in the region. Following the story's publication, Boukraa was repeatedly arrested and questioned by the police until he was finally convicted. Such incidents are common in Algeria and have been since the early 1990s. So much so that in the latest edition of its world press freedom index, RSF ranks Algeria 123rd out of 169 countries.[40]

In addition to intimidating individual journalists, the regime also used its financial influence over the Algerian print media to control what it said. All newspapers, magazines, and journals based in the country are obliged to print their publications on state-owned presses and pay the government a fee for doing so. On occasion, the government has refused to produce certain publications on the grounds that they have not yet paid for past work. But the process by which the government determines which newspapers and magazines it will punish in this way appears very arbitrary, as it refuses to print some publications even though they owe less money than others that it continues to produce.[41] This arrangement still arouses suspicion among many journalists. It also reinforces the frustration that many of them feel at having to use state-owned presses in the first instance.

Unfortunately for Bouteflika, asserting his control over the country's political system has not been so easy. From the moment he took office he has had to tread a difficult and, at times, dangerous path. The Islamist insurgents and Berberists have all attempted to derail his presidency and bend him to their separate wills. But surprisingly, some of the gravest challenges he has had to face have emanated from sources within the regime, most notably, the military's high command. Bouteflika knows better than anyone the immense political power wielded by the armed forces' commanding officers. It was they, after all, who forced Zéroual to resign early and helped him win the presidential election that followed. Yet as their treatment of Benjedid and Zéroual showed, they are quite prepared to withdraw their support at any given moment if they decide it is in their interests to do so.

The ruthlessness with which the high command has defended its political influence has marked Algeria deeply over the past two decades. In total disregard of the democratic process, General Nezzar and his coconspirators prevented the FIS from completing the victory that was rightfully theirs. In so doing, they outraged domestic and international opinion and helped drive the country into civil war. And since then, they have dispensed with presidents and prime ministers seemingly at will, regardless of how effectively they were carrying out their jobs, the extent to which the public approved of what they were doing, or the impact their removal might have on the security crisis.

From the very beginning, therefore, the primary purpose of the counterinsurgency campaign has been to safeguard the high command's political influence. Yet, ironically, it is precisely this determination, this absolute refusal to relinquish any authority that drove Zéroual to try to establish his own power base as he looked to free himself from his dependence on the military. His failure to do so not only sounded the death knell for his presidency, but damaged Algeria's limited and fragile democracy. Only when civilian leaders have total authority over the military will democracy be able to grow and thrive. The challenge for Bouteflika remains, how to succeed where Zéroual failed. Like him, Bouteflika needs to establish an independent power base, without alienating and antagonizing the high command while he does so, that is sufficiently robust to afford him greater freedom of action.

Yet the ongoing conflict benefits the military in more ways than one. As well as giving it opportunities to exterminate some of its opponents and insist on legal provisions that weaken others, the ongoing threat safeguards its access to the resources that keep it strong. So long as AQLIM issues threats and bombs Algiers, no government can afford to reduce the armed forces budget. Indeed, a deadly symbiosis has developed between the security forces and the insurgents whereby each helps justify the existence and actions of the other. And even if Bouteflika was inclined to reduce defense spending, in spite of the ongoing threat, he would find it difficult to do so in light of the military assistance provided by the international community. And that is to make no mention of the strenuous resistance the high command and officer corps would undoubtedly mount to any such cutbacks.

For the time being, Bouteflika must continue to tread his hazardous and lonely path. But even though the military still occupies its lofty position as the country's kingmaker, some progress has been made reinvigorating and strengthening democracy. Elections for the local, regional, and national assemblies continue to be held regularly. And in those elections Algerians now have a genuine choice between several well-established political parties representing a variety of interest groups. And the changes introduced by the 1996 constitution have given the National Assembly new legislative powers beyond those of simply rubber-stamping decisions made by the president. And perhaps most important of all, there is now an air of expectation that Algeria's political system should be democratic. No one, not even within the military's high command, is advocating a return to the authoritarianism of the Ben Bella, Boumedienne, and early Benjedid eras.

Yet such advances still constitute only cautious progress. Even though elections are held regularly, most of them are neither free nor fair. And while it is telling that the government feels duty bound to hold them at all, that sense of obligation has yet to prevent it from rigging the outcome. Competing political parties are allowed to exist and canvass for votes, but the odds continue to be stacked in favor of those that support the regime. And although the National Assembly more closely resembles a legislature than it has in the past, the president still wields formidable powers. Indeed, his appointment of one-third of the upper chamber's members and power of veto over all legislation passed by the Assembly give him a decisive edge. And even though there is now an expectation that Algeria's political system be democratic, few people believe it truly is.

Such a view was strengthened by the conduct and outcomes of the presidential election of April 2004 and the National Assembly elections of 2002 and 2007. In the days preceding and immediately following each of these elections, rival politicians, opposition groups, media outlets, and some international observers accused the regime of exerting undue influence over the electoral process. And one of the main ways it did so was through the judiciary. In the 2004 presidential election, Bouteflika's main rival was his former prime minister, Ali Benflis. As secretary-general of the FLN, a post he had held since 20 September 2001, Benflis could rightly expect to receive the party's nomination in the election. To prevent that from happening, Bouteflika had the courts prevent the FLN from meeting. And when it defied the ban and met on 3 October 2003, he arranged, on 30 December 2003, for the Court of Algiers to freeze its funds. Then on 22 January 2004, he encouraged his supporters within the party to hold their own congress to annul its endorsement of Benflis.

The regime's ability to shape and control the political system has been enhanced by its continued co-optation of moderate Islamic leaders and groups. Like Zéroual before him, Bouteflika readily engaged with prominent Islamic scholars like Mafoud Nahnah and Abdallah Djaballah and encouraged them and the parties they led to take part in the political process. By agreeing to do so, they helped legitimize that process and the rules and boundaries set down by the regime for participating in it. In this way, the regime has ensured that these individuals and parties have a vested interest in making the political system work, while being able to broadly influence their actions and behavior. The involvement of moderate Islamic organizations also reinforced the regime's claim to offer a more legitimate and convincing interpretation of Islam than the GIA, GSPC, and other insurgent groups.

Conclusions

As preparations for Algeria's half-centenary celebrations gather pace, its citizens are encouraged, somewhat inevitably, to reflect on their country's past. For older generations, the war of liberation remains the most hallowed of memories. More than any other, it is a source of immense pride, as Algerians, led by the National Liberation Front, wrenched themselves free from the shackles of colonial rule. And they have been encouraged to believe this by every government since independence. To them, the war was not only the means by which the French were driven out of Algeria, it was the crucible in which the nation was forged, finally made aware of its own existence. Some of the younger generations, too, revel in this history. For as long as they can remember, they have been told the same story, a version of events that remains under the strictest supervision of the country's political leaders. And while some of their peers might not care or are tired of being denied certain privileges because they did not participate in the war, they still largely accept its historical importance.

For the government, therefore, these festivities will provide some welcome relief from the recent doom and gloom and an opportunity to unite Algerians in remembrance of an event in which they can all take pride. And in the process it can admire its handiwork in helping maintain the memory of the war of liberation in its elevated position. Yet what the government cannot prevent are the comparisons ordinary Algerians continue to draw between the heady days of July 1962, when for a brief period anything seemed possible, and the subsequent course of the country's history. Such parallels only serve to emphasize the scale of Algeria's problems today. Ironically, therefore, the more the government urges the country to celebrate the war of liberation, the more attention it draws to its failings and the people's ongoing suffering.

Of course, Algerians have a great deal else, in addition to the war of liberation, of which to be proud. And the period from 1962 until the present day has not been one of constant sorrow. Boumedienne's presidency, in particular, is acknowledged by many as a golden age, a time of jobs and peace and stability before the army turned on the people. While the historical accuracy of such a view—which has also been promoted by successive governments since Boumedienne's death—might be questionable, that is hardly the point. What matters is that such memories (rose-tinted as they may be) also serve to highlight just how desperate the country's recent plight has been.

On 3 August 2008, a suicide bomber killed twenty-one people in a dawn attack on a police station in the historic Old Town of Tizi Ouzou. This incident, the latest in a series of bombings, is typical of the threat now confronting the Algerian government. Since its linkup with AQ, AQLIM has embarked on a new terror campaign, bringing death and destruction to the streets of the country's major towns and cities. Undoubtedly though, Droukdel's decision to follow this course of action has been shaped by his strategic situation. Since the late 1990s, the security forces have gained a decisive edge over his fighters. Unable now to seriously contemplate over-throwing the regime, he and his forces must wage war as best they can by asymmetric means.

But it has not always been this way. For a time in the mid-1990s, the insurgents held the advantage and drove the state to the very brink of col-lapse. During those dark years when the fighting was at its heaviest, thou-sands of soldiers, policemen, gendarmes, militants, civilians, and foreign nationals were killed. These fatalities helped drive the death toll ever higher so that today it almost certainly tops 120,000 people. And that is to make no mention of the thousands more who have been injured in one of the count-less attacks launched by either side or who have fled abroad or simply dis-appeared without a trace. In fact, according to virtually every indicator, the conflict in Algeria remains one of Africa's bloodiest and longest lasting.

Sadly for generations of Algerians, such internecine violence has been a tragic constant throughout their country's history. An early precursor to the Islamist insurgency of the 1990s was Moustapha Bouyali's armed revolt against the Benjedid regime. For several years throughout the early 1980s, he and his forces mounted a series of successful hit-and-run raids from their bases in the Atlas Mountains near Larbaa against the army units sent to apprehend them. Their objectives, in order of immediate importance, were to evade capture, harass the enemy, extend the uprising, spark a popular rebellion, overthrow the government, and establish an Islamic republic. In truth, they never got much beyond ambushing army units. But they did kill dozens of soldiers, force the army to pour thousands of troops into the area where they were operating in an effort to contain the rebellion, and under-mine the authority of the government in certain parts of the country.

Bouyali's revolt was the first time members of the Islamic movement attempted to achieve by force that which they had been unable to accom-plish by peaceful means—the transformation of Algeria into an Islamic republic. Yet their opposition to the government stretched all the way back to the colonial era. Represented since then by such groups as the AUMA, Al Qiyam, Dawa wa Tabligh, Takfir wa Hijra, the MNI, and later Rabitat al-Dawa, the FIS, the GIA, and the GSPC, the movement continues to reject the definition of the nation outlined and promoted by the country's political leaders. The AUMA came to oppose colonial rule on the basis that Algerians were not, nor should ever strive to be, French. But the definition of the nation, developed first by the Ben Bella and then the Boumedienne regimes, left its former members and supporters bitterly disappointed. To them, Algerians were Muslims above all else, not socialists. And the coun-try's political and legal systems and process should reflect that fact.

Arguably, it was this disillusionment that led to the creation of the later groups as the Islamic movement tried to bring about the changes it wanted. And it was its failure to do so that prompted Bouyali to take up arms, just as it was the failure of the FIS to do likewise—for reasons beyond its control—that sparked the insurgency of the 1990s. The FIS's attempts to win power, and the GIA's, AIS's, and GSPC's determination to seize it, emphasized the movement's dissatisfaction with how the Benjedid regime defined the nation, even after he removed the hated socialist dimension. In this way, profound disagreements over national identity have helped fuel much of the violence that has gripped Algeria over the past three decades.

Others, too, have rejected the definition of the nation developed by the country's postindependence leaders. The Berber community in particular feels very aggrieved at its continued exclusion from all such definitions. And this represents no mere oversight. Since 1962 successive governments have tried to make real their claims that Algerians are an Arab people by aggressively pursuing a program of Arabization. Its effect has been to steadily drive all languages other than Arabic from the public domain and, in the process, alienate and embitter the Berber minority.

And like the Islamic movement, Berbers have repeatedly, and sometimes violently, expressed their dissatisfaction with the official definition of the nation. The riots and demonstrations of the new millennium mirrored those of the so-called Berber Spring and, on both occasions, were organized by groups set up with the sole intention of securing the rights they felt their community deserved. The oldest and most important of these organizations is still the FFS, which was originally founded as a guerrilla group. For several months in 1963 and 1964, until the capture of its founder and leader Aït Ahmed, the FFS waged war on Ben Bella and his government. Since then, the Berberists have refrained from making any similar attempt to change government policy by force of arms. Yet that in no way means that they are happy with the status quo or signals any waning of their desire to have their community given the same recognition as the Arabs.

Just three years after the collapse of the FFS uprising, the government faced another armed rebellion, this time launched by the army's former chief of staff, Colonel Tahar Zbiri. In mid-December 1967, he led a small column of troops toward Algiers with the intention of arresting President Boumedienne once he got there. On the way, he hoped to gather support from other military commanders and ordinary people so that by the time he arrived at the capital the government would be unable to resist the mass movement that confronted it. Unfortunately for Zbiri, none of his former comrades would join him, and he was mostly shunned by the civilian population who were tired of the ongoing fighting. As a result, his troops were quite alone when they were finally intercepted by progovernment forces some fifty miles south of the capital. And after a short skirmish, they were decisively defeated. Zbiri fled to the Aurès where he continued to plot against Boumedienne.

Although never likely to succeed, Zbiri's revolt provided another painful reminder of Algeria's continued inability to drag itself out of violence. In the five short years since the country had won its independence, it had scarcely known any peace. For the first two months, it had been gripped by low-level civil war as the Tizi Ouzou and Tlemcen groups fought for control of the new state. And among the various rebellions and uprisings, Boumedienne, aided and abetted by Zbiri, had staged a successful coup d'état against Ben Bella. Alliances and friendships forged during the struggle against the French were ruthlessly abandoned in this frenzied quest for power. And all the while, the people longed for peace as they tried to rebuild their lives after the bloodshed and destruction of the war of liberation.

Algeria truly is a country born in violence. It was through violence that Algerians first gained their independence. And it was with violence that their new political leaders set about asserting and defending their authority. And just as violence invariably begets more violence, every head of state has had to see off an armed challenge. Most of the time—in fact on virtually every occasion—this opposition has been driven, at least in part, by dissatisfaction with the definition of the nation being promoted by the government of the day. And they in turn have responded by stepping up their nation-building efforts, often affirming and reaffirming the definition that is helping provoke the unrest.

The nation-building programs pursued by successive regimes, therefore, are both a cause and an effect of many of the outbreaks of violence that punctuate Algeria's postindependence history. Each of these programs has consisted of two broadly sequential phases. During the first, each regime has developed a definition of the nation, outlining its core characteristics. From 1962 to 1989, Ben Bella, Boumedienne, and Benjedid promoted definitions that emphasized the characteristics of Islam, Arabism, and socialism. And from 1989 until the present day, Benjedid, the HCE, Zéroual, and Bouteflika have all developed definitions that stress Islam and Arabism. Then, during the second, much longer phase, the regimes have set about promoting their definitions.

To do that, each regime has attempted to manipulate the public discourse on national identity by muzzling the media, dominating the political system, and occupying the social space. The only time when such control was not exercised was during the final years of Benjedid's presidency. For a brief period, the media was granted the freedom to investigate and report pretty much whatever it liked. And Algerians were allowed, for the first time ever, to set up their own political parties and vote in elections for any one of a number of competing candidates. Yet since the army's intervention, such liberties have been systematically abolished. Journalists and their editors are now subject to some of the most draconian laws found anywhere in the world. Not only does this legislation strongly encourage self-censorship, but it allows the authorities to bully, harass, and silence anyone who is critical of the government. And although elections are held regularly, power has been concentrated in the hands of the president, who continues to be chosen by the military's high command. Secure in its role as kingmaker for the foreseeable future, the army has the final say on who can hold power and participate in the political process.

What this all means is that the government is promoting a definition of the nation that is rejected and opposed by a significant number of Algerians, in a manner that both outrages and appalls many at home and abroad. In the past, this has been a recipe for discontent, unrest, violence, and armed opposition. It is difficult to see why it should not be so in the future. And it is in this way that Algeria's past catches up with it. Not only does history have the potential to repeat itself, but it also turns colonial rule into a contemporary and ongoing experience. For the definition of the nation developed by Algeria's postindependence leaders continues to be shaped by what happened to the country under the French. And perhaps more fundamentally, their very embrace of nationalism highlights their wholehearted acceptance of a framework of knowledge that the French used to legitimize their subjugation of Algeria.

From the earliest days of their colonization of Algeria, the French looked upon the local inhabitants as their inferiors. That they were so was made evident by their difference, by the fact they did not speak the same language, practice the same religion, observe the same customs, or generally behave like them. In addition to their religious beliefs, what really separated the locals from the French was their continued commitment to their tribes. The French had long since ceased to think of themselves as members of this or that tribe. And that was also true of the other civilized peoples of the world—the Germans, the Americans, and the English. Indeed, the French were citizens of a nation-state. Clearly, therefore, this was a superior unit of political, economic, social, and cultural organization and governance.

With Algerians' inferiority now firmly established, various arguments arose to justify and legitimize French occupation of their lands. One of these claimed that it was only right and proper that France assert itself over this lesser people. Just as it is natural for a predator to devour a creature that is weaker than itself, so it was natural for France to take that which the Algerians could not keep. Other arguments also called on France to conquer and administer this territory. But not because it was something that it could do, but rather that it was something it should do. As a civilized power, France had a moral duty to help lift the backward peoples of the world, including the Algerians, out of their savagery.

Such sentiments found their clearest expression in the concept of the

Mission Civilisatrice. In accordance with its strictures, and those of the doctrine of assimilation, the French set about trying to re-create Algerians in their own image. Integral to this complex and multifaceted process was the systematic destruction of the tribal units. In their place, the French built state structures and institutions similar to those that existed in France. From being one of the criteria against which Algerians were compared and found wanting, nationalism became the means by which the civilizing process was effected. And eventually, once the transformation process had been completed, it was to provide evidence of the mission's success.

The ideology of nationalism, therefore, the belief that the nation-state is the preeminent unit of sociopolitical organization and governance, was not only imported to Algeria by the French, but used by them to legitimize their occupation and rule of it. And even though the Mission Civilisatrice failed to cement the union between the two countries, Algerians' use of nationalism, its ideas and vocabulary, to express their grievances against colonial rule emphasized its enduring success. Indeed, French rule changed how Algerians think of themselves and each other by adding to the multiple identities that they each possess yet another, namely, that of the Algerian.

It has also shaped how the Algerian nation has been defined. The postindependence leaders' choice of Islam, Arabism, and socialism was profoundly influenced by the legacies of the Mission Civilisatrice, which limited the characteristics around which they could develop a national identity. What these leaders required were characteristics that were common to most Algerians, that distinguished them from the French, that stressed the ancient origins of the Algerian nation, and that granted them access to a glorious history and civilization of which they could be proud. Islam and Arabism clearly distinguished most Algerians from the colonizing French and offered a history and civilization that was as old as it was magnificent. Algeria's postindependence nation builders also required characteristics that outlined a vision of the future in which the unity and continued brilliance of the nation were beyond question. Socialism not only situated the fledging nation in a dynamic global movement, it was also antagonistic toward capitalism, which, the nation builders correctly concluded, had, in part, driven French colonization of Algeria.

Notes

1. The AIS was formally dissolved by the FIS leadership on 6 June 1999.
2. Its high point, in terms of numbers, came in 1995 when it consisted of 27,000 men. By 2002, it comprised just seven hundred.
3. Turnout for this election was 60 percent.
4. John Ruedy, *Modern Algeria: The Origins and Development of a Nation*, 2nd ed. (Bloomington: Indiana University Press, 2005), p. 277.

5. Matoub was kidnapped by GIA militants on 26 September 1994 and then released by them on 10 October 1994.

6. Ruedy, *Modern Algeria*, pp. 280 and 281.

7. Benflis became prime minister on 27 August 2000 following the resignation of his predecessor, Ahmed Benbitour. He remained in office until he was dismissed by Bouteflika in May 2003. He was replaced by Ahmed Ouyahia.

8. République Algérienne Démocratique et Populaire, *Amendement de Constitution du 8 avril 2002*, Article 3.

9. The FLN emerged as the strongest party, winning 35 percent of the vote and 199 seats in the National Assembly. Of the other major parties, the RND received 8 percent of the vote giving 47 seats, the MRN gained 9.5 percent of the vote and 43 seats, and the MSP 7 percent of the vote and 38 seats.

10. Indeed, *El Watan* described the result as "worthy of Kim Il Sung." Cited in BBC, "Algeria Press Aghast at Election Result," 10 April 2004, available at www.bbc.co.uk/2/hi/africa/3616461.stm (accessed 20 April 2006).

11. The election was contested by six candidates. Bouteflika's main challenger was his former prime minister, Ali Benflis. Standing for the FLN, Benflis received 6.4 percent of the vote. In third place, representing the MN, came Abdallah Djaballah, who won 5 percent of the vote. In fifth place was Louisa Hanoune, the first woman to stand in a presidential election. Representing the Workers Party (Parti des Travailleurs, PT), she received 1 percent of the vote. In last place came Fawzi Rabaine standing for the Ahd Party. He won 0.6 percent of the vote.

12. Cited in BBC, "Algeria Press Aghast at Election Result," 10 April 2004, available at www.bbc.co.uk/2/hi/africa/3616461.stm (accessed 20 April 2006).

13. Sahrawi also went by the name of Abou Ibrahim Mustafa. He replaced Hassan Hattab.

14. Martin Evans and John Phillips, *Algeria: Anger of the Dispossessed* (New Haven and London: Yale University Press, 2007), p. 287.

15. Hattab was killed in August 2003.

16. Evans and Phillips, *Algeria: Anger of the Dispossessed,* p. 287.

17. Cited in Arabic News, "Al-Salafeyah Movement in Algeria Claims Attack on Military Position in Mauritania," 7 June 2005, available at www.arabicnews.com/ansub/Daily/Day/050607/2005060717.html (accessed 20 April 2006).

18. Evans and Phillips, *Algeria: Anger of the Dispossessed*, p. 198.

19. Ibid., p. 255.

20. Ibid.

21. Cited in BBC, "US Miltiary Aid in Algeria," 10 December 2002, available at www.bbc.co.uk/1/hi/world/africa/2561163.stm (accessed 12 March 2009).

22. John Davis, "The Bush Model: US Special Forces, Africa, and the War on Terror," in *Africa and the War on Terrorism*, ed. John Davis (Aldershot, Hampshire: Ashgate, 2007), pp. 154 and 155.

23. The GSPC's attack on the Mauritanian army outpost on 4 June 2005 was a direct response to the country's involvement in the PSI.

24. Bruno Charbonneau, *France and the New Imperialism* (Aldershot, Hampshire: Ashgate, 2008), p. 78.

25. European Commission, "Euro-Mediterranean Code of Conduct on Countering Terrorism," 2005, p. 1, available at http://ec.europa.eu/external_relations/euromed/summit1105/terrorism_en.pdf (accessed 29 July 2008).

26. Ibid., p. 2.

27. European Commission, "Mediterranean Neighbourhood Countries: Commitment and Payments," 2007, p. 1, available at http://ec.europa.eu/external_relations/euromed/docs/meda_figures_en.pdf (accessed 29 July 2007).

28. Salah E. Zaimeche and Keith Sutton, "Persistent Strong Population Growth, Environmental Degradation, and Declining Food Self-Sufficiency in a Rentier Oil State: Algeria," *The Journal of North African Studies* 3, no. 1 (spring 1998): p. 65.

29. Ruedy, *Modern Algeria*, p. 274.

30. Ali Kouaouchi, "Population Transition, Youth Unemployment, Postponement of Marriage and Violence in Algeria," *The Journal of North African Studies* 9, no. 2 (summer 2004): p. 28.

31. Ibid.

32. As well as prime minister, Abdessalam also took on the post of minister of finance.

33. Sifi served as prime minister until 31 December 1995, when he was replaced by Ahmed Ouyahia.

34. Bradford Dillman, "The Political Economy of Structural Adjustment in Tunisia and Algeria," *The Journal of North African Studies* 3, no. 3 (autumn 1998): pp. 13 and 14.

35. Cited in Ruedy, *Modern Algeria*, p. 273.

36. Luis Martinez, *The Algerian Civil War* (London: Hurst & Company, 2000), p. 93.

37. In July 2006 Bouteflika used his presidential powers to pardon all journalists convicted of defaming him, the ANP, or the military. US Department of State, Background Note: Algeria, October 2007, p. 6, available at www.state.gov/r/pa/ei/bgn/8005.htm (accessed 7 December 2007).

38. Arabic News, "Three Algerian Journalists Sentenced to Prison," 16 June 2005, p. 1, available at www.arabicnews.com/ansub/Daily/Day/050615/2005061522.html (accessed 19 April 2006).

39. Arabic News, "Algerian Newspaper Editor Mohamed Benchicou's 500th Day in Prison," 28 October 2005, pp. 1–2, available at www.arabicnews.com/ansub/Daily/Day/051028/2005102826.html (accessed 19 April 2006).

40. Arabic News, "Journalist Who Wrote About Alleged Corruption Charged, Placed Under Judicial Control," 18 March 2008, p. 1, available at www.arabicnews.com/ansub/Daily/Day/080318/2008031822.html (accessed 1 April 2008).

41. Ruedy, *Modern Algeria,* p. 285.

Bibliography

Adamson, Kay. *Algeria: A Study in Competing Ideologies*. London and New York: Cassell, 1998.

Ageron, Charles-Robert. *Histoire de l'Algérie contemporaine (1830–1964)*. Paris: Presses Universitaires de France, 1963.

———. *La Guerre d'Algérie et les Algériens, 1954–1962*. Paris: Armand Colin, 1997.

———. *Modern Algeria*. Trenton, NJ: Africa World Press, 1991.

Aghrout, Ahmed, and Redha M. Bougherira, eds. *Algeria in Transition: Reforms and Development Prospects*. London and New York: RoutledgeCurzon, 2004.

Aldrich, Robert. *Greater France: A History of French Overseas Expansion*, London: Palgrave Macmillan, 1996.

Alexander, Martin S., and J. F. V. Keiger. *France and the Algerian War 1954–62: Strategy, Operations and Diplomacy*. London: Frank Cass, 2002.

Alexander, Martin S., J. F. V. Keiger, and Martin Evans. *The Algerian War and the French Army 1954–62: Experiences, Images and Testimonies*. Basingstoke, UK: Palgrave Macmillan, 2002.

Anderson, Benedict. *Imagined Communities*. London and New York: Verso, 1991.

Annuaire de l'Afrique du Nord 4 (1965).

Attinà, Fulrio. "The Barcelona Process, the Role of the European Union and the Lesson of the Western Mediterranean." *The Journal of North African Studies* 9, no. 2 (summer 2004): pp. 140–152.

Aussaresses, Paul. *The Battle of the Casbah. Terrorism and Counter-Terrorism in Algeria 1955–1957*. New York: Enigma, 2002.

Ayoade, John A. A. "States Without Citizens: An Emerging African Phenomenon." In *The Precarious Balance: State and Society in Africa*, edited by Donald Rothchild and Naomi Chazan, 100–118. Boulder and London: Westview Press, 1988.

Bennoune, Mahfoud. *The Making of Contemporary Algeria, 1830–1987*. Cambridge: Cambridge University Press, 1988.

Benrabah, Mohamed. *Langue et pouvoir en Algérie: Histoire d'un traumatisme linguistique*. Paris: Séguier, 1999.

Betts, Raymond F. *Assimilation and Association in French Colonial Theory 1890–1914*. New York and London: Columbia University Press, 1961.

Bouandel, Youcef, and Yahia H. Zoubir. "Algeria's Elections: Prelude to Democratisation." *Third World Quarterly* 19, no. 2: pp. 177–190.

Cavatorta, Francesco. "The Failed Liberalisation of Algeria and the International Context: A Legacy of Stable Authoritarianism." *The Journal of North African Studies* 7, no. 4 (winter 2002): pp. 23–43.

Chaliand, Gérard. *L'Algérie: Est-elle socialiste?* Paris: Maspéro, 1964.

Charbonneau, Bruno. *France and the New Imperialism*. Aldershot, UK: Ashgate, 2008.

Chatterjee, Partha. *Nationalist Thought and the Colonial World: A Derivative Discourse*. London: Zed Books, 1986.

Clegg, Ian. *Workers' Self-Management in Algeria*. London: Penguin Press, 1971.

CNRA. *Projet de programme pour la réalisation de la révolution démocratique populaire*, 1962.

Collot, Claude, and Jean-Robert Henry. *Le mouvement national Algerien: Texts 1912–1954*. Paris: L'Harmattan, 1978.

Conklin, Alice. *A Mission to Civilize: The Republican Idea of Empire in France and West Africa, 1895–1930*. Stanford: Stanford University Press.

Davidson, Basil. *The Black Man's Burden: Africa and the Curse of the Nation-State*. London: James Currey, 1992.

Davis, John, ed. *Africa and the War on Terrorism*. Aldershot, UK: Ashgate, 2007.

de Bernis, Gérard Destanne. "Industries industrialisantes et les options algériennes." *Revue Tiers-Monde* (July/September 1969): pp. 545–563.

de Prebois, Capitaine d'Etat-Major Francois LeBlanc. "Algerie," In *Du système de colonisation. Suivi par la France*, edited by M. A. T. Lachariere. Paris: Auguste Auffray.

Deschamps, Hubert. *Méthodes et doctrines coloniales de la France*. Paris: A. Colin, 1953.

Didier, Henri. *Le gouvernement militaire et la colonisation en Algérie*. Paris: E. Dentu, 1865.

Dillman, Bradford. "The Political Economy of Structural Adjustment in Tunisia and Algeria." *The Journal of North African Studies* 3, no. 3 (autumn 1998): pp. 1–24.

Entelis, John. *Algeria: The Revolution Institutionalized*. London and Sydney: Croom Helm, 1986.

———. "Islamist Politics and the Democratic Imperative: Comparative Lessons from the Algerian Experience." *The Journal of North African Studies* 9, no. 2 (summer 2004): pp. 202–215.

Eriksen, Thomas Hylland. "A Non-Ethnic State for Africa? A Life-World Approach to the Imagining of Communities." In *Ethnicity and Nationalism in Africa: Constructivist Reflections and Contemporary Politics*, edited by Paris Yeros, 45–65. Basingstoke, UK: MacMillan, 1999.

Evans, Martin, and John Phillips. *Algeria: Anger of the Dispossessed*. New Haven and London: Yale University Press, 2007.

Fanon, Frantz. *The Wretched of the Earth*. London: Penguin, 1963.

Fawtier, P. *L'autonomie algérienne et la république fédérale*. Paris: 1871.

Ferry, Jules. *Le gouvernement d'Algérie*. Paris: Colin, 1892.

Front de Libération Nationale. *Appel au people algérien* (1954).

———. *La Charte D'Alger* (1964).

———. *Réorganisation de l'UGTA: Projet analytique de développement du synidcalisme en Algérie* (1968).

Galula, David. *Pacification in Algeria 1956–1958*. Santa Monica, Calif.: RAND Corporation, 2006.

Geertz, Clifford. *The Interpretation of Cultures: Selected Essays*. London: Fontana, 1973.

Gellner, Ernest. *Nationalism*. London: Pheonix, 1997.
———. *Nations and Nationalism*. Oxford: Oxford University Press, 1983.
Goodman, Jane. "Reinterpreting the Berber Spring: From Rite of Reversal to Site of Convergence." *The Journal of North African Studies* 9, no. 3 (autumn 2004): pp. 60–82.
Hafez, Mohammed M.. "Armed Islamist Movements and Political Violence in Algeria." *The Middle East Journal* 54, no. 4: pp. 572–591.
Hanotaux, Gabriel. *L'înergie française*. Paris: Flammarion, 1902.
Harrison, Alexander. *Challenging de Gaulle, the OAS and the Counter-Revolution in Algeria 1954–1962*. St. Petersburg, Fla.: Hailer Publishing, 1989.
Hawthorn, Geoffrey. "Waiting for a Text?: Comparing Third World Politics." In *Rethinking Third World Politics*, edited by James Manor, 24–50. London and New York: Longman, 1991.
Henry, Clement M. "Algeria's Agonies: Oil Rent Effects in a Bunker State." *The Journal of North African Studies* 9, no. 2 (summer 2004): pp. 68–81.
Hobsbawm, E. J. *Nations and Nationalism Since 1780,* 2nd ed. Cambridge: Cambridge University Press, 1992.
Horne, Alistair. *A Savage War of Peace,* Rev. ed. New York: New York Review of Books, 2006.
Jackson, Henry. *The FLN in Algeria: Party Development in a Revolutionary Society*. London: Greenwood Press, 1977.
Joffé, George. "The Role of Violence Within the Algerian Economy." *The Journal of North African Studies* 7, no. 1 (spring 2002): pp. 29–52.
Kepel, Gilles. *Jihad: The Trial of Political Islam*. London and New York: I. B. Tauris, 2002.
Kettle, Michael. *De Gaulle and Algeria 1940–1960*. London: Quartet Books, 1993.
Kouaouchi, Ali. "Population Transitions, Youth Unemployment, Postponement of Marriage and Violence in Algeria." *The Journal of North African Studies* 9, no. 2 (summer 2004): pp. 28–45.
Lawless, Richard. "Algeria: The Contradictions of Rapid Industrialisation." In *North Africa: Contemporary Politics and Economic Development*, edited by Richard Lawless and Allan Findlay, 153–190. London: Croom Helm, 1984.
Layachi, Azzedine. "Political Liberalisation and the Islamist Movement in Algeria." *The Journal of North African Studies* 9, no. 2 (summer 2004): pp. 46–67.
———. "Reform and the Politics of Inclusion in the Maghrib." *The Journal of North African Studies* 5, no. 3 (autumn 2000): pp. 15–42.
Le Chef du Gouvernment, Président du Conseil des ministres. *Ordonnance no. 76–35 du 16 avril 1976 portant organisation de l'éducation et de la formation* (1976).
Le Président de la République. *Le Code de Famille* (1984).
Le Sueur, James. *Uncivil War: Intellectuals and Identity Politics During the Decolonization of Algeria*. London: University of Pennsylvania Press, 2001.
Lorcin, Patricia. *Imperial Identities: Stereotyping, Prejudice and Race in Colonial Algeria*. London: I. B. Tauris, 1999.
Maddy-Weitzman, Bruce. "Contested Identities: Berber, 'Berberism' and the State in North Africa." *The Journal of North African Studies* 6, no. 3 (autumn 2001): pp. 23–47.
Maddy-Weitzman, Bruce, and Daniel Zisenwine, eds. *The Maghrib in the New Century*. Gainesville: University Press of Florida, 2007.
Martin, Ivan. "Algeria's Political Economy (1999–2002): An Economic Solution to the Crisis?" *The Journal of North African Studies* 8, no. 2 (summer 2003): pp. 34–74.

Martinez, Luis. *The Algerian Civil War*. London: Hurst & Company, 2000.
———. "Why the Violence in Algeria?" *The Journal of North African Studies* 9, no.
2 (summer 2004): pp. 14–27.
McDougall, James. *History and the Culture of Nationalism in Algeria*. Cambridge:
Cambridge University Press, 2006.
Michaud, L. G. *Colonisation de l'ex-Regence d'Alger*. Paris.
Ministère d'Information et de la Culture. "Le choix industriel de l'Algérie." Dossier
Documentaire 16 (Novembre 1971).
Ottoway, David, and Marina Ottoway. *Algeria: The Politics of a Socialist
Revolution*. Berkeley and Los Angeles: University of California Press, 1970.
Parmentier, Mary Jane C. "Secularisation and Islamisation in Morocco and Algeria."
The Journal of North African Studies 4, no. 4 (winter 1999): pp. 27–50.
Pougin, A., ed. *Les Arabes et la colonisation en Algérie*. Paris: 1873.
Prochaska, David. *Making Algeria French: Colonialism in Bône, 1870–1920*.
Cambridge: Cambridge University Press, 1990.
Quandt, William. "Algeria's Transition to What?" *The Journal of North African
Studies* 9, no. 2 (summer 2004): pp. 82–92.
Raffinot, M., and P. Jacquement. *Le capitalisme d'îtat algérien*. Paris: Maspero,
1977.
Ranger, Terrence. "The Invention of Tradition in Colonial Africa." In *The Invention
of Tradition*, edited by Eric Hobsbawm and Terrence Ranger. Cambridge:
Cambridge University Press, 1983.
Renan, Ernest. *Qu'est que c'est une nation?* Conférence faite en Sorbonne le 11
mars 1882 (Paris: 1882).
République Algérienne Démocratique et Populaire. *Amendement de Constitution du
8 avril 2002* (2002).
———. *Constitution du 10 septembre 1963* (1963).
———. *Constitution du 27 juin 1976* (1976).
———. *Constitution du 23 février 1989* (1989).
———. *Constitution du 28 novembre 1996* (1996).
———. *Décrets de Mars*. March 1963.
Roberts, Hugh. *The Battlefield Algeria 1988–2002: Studies in a Broken Polity*.
London and New York: Verso, 2003.
Robiquet, Paul. *Discours et opinions de Jules Ferry*, Vol. V. Paris: Armand Colin,
1897.
Roy, Jules. *The War in Algeria*. New York: Grove Press, 1961.
Ruedy, John, ed. *Islamism and Secularism in North Africa*. New York: St Martin's
Press, 1996.
———. *Modern Algeria: The Origins and Development of a Nation*, 2nd ed.
Bloomington: Indiana University Press, 2005.
Ruf, Werner. "The Flight of Rent: The Rise and Fall of a National Economy." *The
Journal of North African Studies* 2, no. 1 (summer 1997): pp. 1–15.
Savarèse, Éric. *L'invention des Pieds-Noirs*. Paris: Séguier, 2002.
Silverstein, Paul A. "Martyrs and Patriots: Ethnic, National and Transnational
Dimensions of Kabyle Politics." *The Journal of North African Studies* 8, no. 1
(spring 2003): pp. 87–111.
Smith, Anthony D. *National Identity*. London: Penguin, 1991.
———. *Nationalism and Modernism*. London and New York: Routledge, 1998.
———. *State and Nation in the Third World: The Western State and African
Nationalism*. London: Wheatsheaf, 1983.
Stone, Martin. *The Agony of Algeria*. New York: Columbia University Press, 1997.

Stora, Benjamin. *Algeria 1830–2000: A Short History*. Ithaca and London: Cornell University Press, 2001.

———. "Algeria/Morocco: The Passions of the Past. Representations of the Nation that Unite and Divide." *The Journal of North African Studies* 8, no. 1 (spring 2003): pp. 14–34.

Tahi, Mohand Salah. "Algeria's Democratisation Process: A Frustrated Hope." *Third World Quarterly* 16, no. 2: pp. 197–220.

Tekhami, Amine. "Partisan Islamists in Algeria: A Case of—and for—Malleable Identities." *The Journal of North African Studies* 4, no. 1 (spring 1999): pp. 102–127.

Thénault, Sylvie. "L'Organisation judiciaire du FLN." In *La Guerre d'Algérie et les Algériens 1954–1962*, edited by Charles-Robert Ageron, 137–149. Paris: Armand Colin, 1997.

Thomas, Martin. *The French Empire Between the Wars*. Manchester, UK: Manchester University Press, 2005.

Trinquier, Roger. *Modern Warfare: A French View of Counterinsurgency*. Westport, Conn.: Praeger, 2006.

Verges, Miriam. "Genesis of Mobilisation: The Young Activists of Algeria's Islamic Salvation Front." In *Political Islam: Essays from Middle East Report*, edited by Joel Beinin and Joe Stork, 292–308, Berkeley: University of California Press, 1997.

Vignon, Louis. *Un programme de politique coloniale*. Paris: Plon-Nourrit, 1919.

Volpi, Frédéric. *Islam and Democracy: The Failure of Dialogue in Algeria*. London: Pluto Press, 2003.

Volpi, Frédéric, and Francesco Cavatorta, eds. *Democratization in the Muslim World: Changing Patterns of Authority and Power*. London: Routledge, 2007.

Willis, Michael. "Algeria's Other Islamists: Abdallah Djaballah and the Ennahda Movement." *The Journal of North African Studies* 3, no. 3 (autumn 1996): pp. 46–70.

———. *The Islamist Challenge in Algeria*. New York: New York University Press, 1996.

Zaimeche, Salah E., and Keith Sutton. "Persistent Strong Population Growth, Environmental Degradation, and Declining Food Self-Sufficiency in a Rentier Oil State: Algeria." *The Journal of North African Studies* 3, no. 1 (spring 1998): pp. 57–73.

Zartman, I. William. "Algeria at Forty: A Midlife Crisis." *The Journal of North African Studies* 9, no. 2 (summer 2004): pp. 216–222.

Index

Abane, Ramdane, 55, 61
Abbas, Ferhat, 41, 43, 49–50, 51, 80–81; proposal by, 52
Abderrahamane, Moulay, 26, 29
Abdessalam, Belaïd, 189
ABERC. *See* Berber Academy of Cultural Exchange and Research
Africa: colonization of, 22. *See also specific African countries*
Agriculture, 37; economy v., 116–117, 121–123; investment v., 122–123, 124; privatization for, 126–127; productivity in, 121–123. *See also* Autogestion
AGTA. *See* General Association of Algerian Workers
Ahmed, Hajj, 26, 30
AIS. *See* Islamic Salvation Army
Aït Ahmed, Hocine, 54, 74, 134, 198; against Ben Bella, 76–77; Berbers and, 99; capture of, 78; replacement by, 87
Algeria: conquest of, 25–31; divisions within, 59; against French migration, 95–96; history and, 104; incorporation of, 22; invasion of, 25–26; against Morocco, 77, 84–85; Soviet Union and, 106; US and, 106; World War II for, 48. *See also* French Algeria
Algerian Communist Party (PCA), 60
Algerian League for the Defence of Human Rights (LADDH), 100
Algerian Muslim Congress (CMA), 42–43

Algerian Nationalist Movement (MNA), 60
Algerianists, 132
Algerians, 7–8; identity for, 149, 198–201
Algiers Charter, 79, 92
ALN. *See* Armée de Libération Nationale
Alwan, Emad Abdelwahid Ahmad, 177, 184
AML. *See* Friends of the Manifesto and of Liberty
ANP: for Ben Bella, 86; for coup, 87; FFS and, 77–78; funding for, 90; *wilayas* against, 75–76; Zbiri and, 87–88. *See also* Boumedienne, Houari
APC. *See* Assemblées Popularies Communales
APN. *See* Assemblée Populaire Nationale
APW. *See* Assemblées Popularies des Wilayat
AQLIM. *See* Al-Qaida in the Land of the Islamic Maghreb
Arabic, 91, 94
Arabism, 4, 79; pan-Arabism for, 105–106
Arabization, 94–95, 133, 173, 198; Benjedid for, 102; Berbers v., 99–100; pan-Arabism for, 105–106
Armed Islamic Group (GIA), 175; deaths by, 147–148, 151–152, 154–158, 176–177; FIS v., 143–144; against foreigners, 148–149,

About the Book

JONATHAN HILL EXPLORES THE MULTIPLE causes of two decades of profound political change, social and economic upheaval, and bitter conflict in postindependence Algeria.

Hill focuses on the relationship between identity and sociopolitical stability as he examines the trajectory of Algerian nation building. How did French colonization and the war of liberation transform Algerian identities? How has the contestation of national identity contributed to the instability that emerged in the late 1980s? What part has the rise of Islamism and Berberism played? What has been the role of foreign actors? Addressing these questions, as well as the impact of the September 11 terrorist attacks, Hill argues that how the Algerian government defines the nation is inextricably linked to its ability now and in the future to maintain political and social stability.

J. N. C. Hill is lecturer in the Defense Studies Department at King's College London.